To June, Pat, Amanda, Casey, Marcia, and Daryle, for showing me how beautiful strong women can be.

And to Scott, for everything.

Fictions of Pleasure

EARLY MODERN FEMINISMS

Showcasing distinctly feminist ideological commitments and/or methodological approaches, and tracing literary and cultural expressions of feminist thought, Early Modern Feminisms seeks to publish innovative readings of women's lives and work, as well as of gendered experience, from the years 1500–1800. In addition to highlighting examinations of women's literature and history, this series aims to provide scholars an opportunity to emphasize new approaches to the study of gender and sexuality with respect to material culture, science, and art, as well as politics and race. Thus, monographs and edited collections that are interdisciplinary and/or transnational in nature are particularly welcome.

Series Titles

The Visionary Queen: Justice, Reform, and the Labyrinth in Marguerite de Navarre, by Theresa Brock

Eliza Fenwick: Early Modern Feminist, by Lissa Paul

The Circuit of Apollo: Eighteenth-Century Women's Tributes to Women, edited by Laura L. Runge and Jessica Cook

Fictions of Pleasure

THE PUTAIN MEMOIRS OF PREREVOLUTIONARY FRANCE

ALISTAIRE TALLENT

UNIVERSITY OF DELAWARE | UNIVERSITY OF DELAWARE PRESS

NEWARK

Library of Congress Cataloging-in-Publication Data

Names: Tallent, Alistaire, author.
Title: Fictions of pleasure : the putain memoirs of prerevolutionary France / Alistaire Tallent.
Description: Newark : University of Delaware Press, [2024] | Series: Early modern feminisms | Includes bibliographical references and index.
Identifiers: LCCN 2023018910 | ISBN 9781644533239 (paperback) | ISBN 9781644533246 (hardcover) | ISBN 9781644533253 (epub) | ISBN 9781644533260 (pdf)
Subjects: LCSH: Autobiographical fiction, French—History and criticism. | French fiction—18th century—History and criticism. | Prostitutes in literature. | Libertines in literature. | Women in literature.
Classification: LCC PQ637.A96 T35 2024 | DDC 843/.082—dc23/eng/20230508
LC record available at https://lccn.loc.gov/2023018910

A British Cataloging-in-Publication record for this book is available from the British Library.

∞ The paper used in this publication meets the requirements of the American National Standard for Information Sciences—Permanence of Paper for Printed Library Materials, ANSI Z39.48-1992.

udpress.udel.edu

Distributed worldwide by Rutgers University Press

Contents

Acknowledgments

I would like to thank Kathryn Norberg, Laura Rosenthal, Natania Meeker, and Mary MacAlpin, for their incredibly helpful insights, advice, and comments on an earlier draft of this manuscript. Thank you to Anne Hyde for bringing them together with the Colorado College Hulbert Center Manuscript Workshop in 2011. Thank you, too, to Jared Richman and Scott Purdy for your writerly advice and continuous encouragement.

Introduction

A gust of air replaced the gentle spring breeze wafting in from the open window as a young man burst into Claire Leris's bedroom. The genuine look of shock on her face reminded him of the dramatic flair she displayed on the Rouen stage. To be honest, he was himself a little surprised to be in her home, but the love letters and poems he had written had failed to impress her. He knew if he could just talk to her face-to-face, she would see the sincerity in his affection and desire for her. Then she would add him to her list of lovers. No, he had no delusions that he alone would be enough for her; he just wanted to be one of the privileged few with access to her charms.

But all thoughts of a gentle wooing evaporated at the sight of Claire's body, barely covered by her disheveled hair and her flimsy white nightgown as she lay across her bed, studying a script. Maddened with lust, the young man dashed to her bed and seized her in his arms. But the strong voice she had developed to project her lines on the stage carried her cries for help out the window and to the ears of an old neighbor and a servant. The two feeble defenders rushing to her aid armed with nothing more than a shovel and a broom should have been no match for a strong young man, but the would-be attacker quickly fled the house with his tail between his legs.

When her mother returned later that day, Clairon—as she preferred to be called—recounted the thwarted assault, a grin twitching at the corners of her mouth at the thought of her suitor's embarrassing lack of self-control and subsequent cowardice. Her mother, however, did not find the situation quite so funny and immediately went to the magistrate to press charges against Pierre Alexandre Gaillard de la Bataille. The local authorities found the failed attack too inconsequential to warrant anything more than a reprimand. But news of his ridiculous attempt at seduction and his pathetic response to Clairon's rejection traveled fast; Gaillard was soon the laughingstock of Rouen. The humiliated writer began planning his vengeance.

At least this is the backstory Clairon herself gives[1] for the origin of the lewd pseudo-memoir that appeared the next year entitled *Histoire de Mademoiselle Cronel, dite Frétillon, actrice de la Comédie de Rouen, écrite par elle-même* (1739). The obvious anagram of Clairon—alternately spelled Cleron—in Mademoiselle Cronel, and of course the mention of Rouen, left little doubt who the supposed memoirist was. Her nickname Frétillon comes from the verb "frétiller," meaning to quiver or wriggle, and signals the uncontrollable sexual desires the narrator reveals. An obscene slander, the text portrays Cronel as physically unattractive and with little talent. The burgeoning acting career she describes is only possible because her lack of morals allows her to sexually manipulate important men. A series of embarrassing anecdotes reveal her shamelessly voracious sexual appetite, which she does little to control, flitting wherever and to whomever her desires lead. In this way, Gaillard de la Bataille had indeed exacted his revenge.

In her real memoirs composed sixty years later, Clairon refers to the *Histoire de Mademoiselle Cronel* as "that disgusting slander of me that everyone in Europe read."[2] In the end, however, the book was more of a boon to her career than a hindrance. Such publicity was invaluable, on a level to rival any modern-day celebutante's leaked sex tape. Furthermore, most people recognized the pseudo-memoir for what it was—a fiction composed by an enemy of Clairon's. Still, the hint of scandal was there, and when she returned to Paris to join the Opéra, she reportedly threatened to slap any of her colleagues who dared call her "Frétillon."

Despite—or perhaps because of—the scandal, in 1743 Clairon debuted at the Comédie française in the title role of Jean Racine's *Phèdre* to widespread acclaim. She went on to become one of the most celebrated actors of the eighteenth-century French stage, admired by David Garrick and muse to Voltaire. After her retirement in 1766, she worked to reform the laws discriminating against performers.[3] It is doubtful that, at the time she wrote her memoirs in the late 1790s, many readers remembered the scandal of the *Histoire de Mademoiselle Cronel*. But Clairon had clearly not forgotten.

The *Histoire de Mademoiselle Cronel* also had a lasting impact on the French literary landscape. After another edition of the 1739 version was published in 1740, a sequel appeared in 1741, added on to another reprint of the first. Apparently, this edition was a success, as both parts were reprinted the next year. The following year, the third part of Frétillon's story came out, but with a fascinating narrative twist. In its preface the narrator amazingly claims that the second part of her story was completely false. This third part, then, takes up Cronel's story where the first part left off. That same year a fourth part appeared, continuing the story from part 3. In addition to this flurry of publications in 1739–1743 (during which time the real Mademoiselle Clairon's career at the Comédie française blossomed), the eighteenth century then saw seven more editions of the *Histoire de mademoiselle Cronel* published. The novel appeared in 1750, 1752, 1758, 1762, 1772, 1780, 1782, and there is one edition without a date. Gaillard's act of vengeance proved to have a greater reach than he could have anticipated.

Even more significantly, the *Histoire de Mademoiselle Cronel* appears to have inspired a series of imitators. In parts 2–4, Mademoiselle Cronel abandons the bumbling pursuit of her basest desires and becomes a clever, successful, and satisfied heroine and businesswoman, balancing affairs of the heart with more lucrative relationships. This kind of saucy and sassy heroine reappeared in a dozen similar pseudo-memoirs, forming the microgenre I call the prostitute, or *putain*, memoir. These texts were produced in more than 120 editions altogether, from 1739 to 1801, and in each a sexually promiscuous and confident woman recounts her adventures and escapades, her independent lifestyle, and her professional skill in selling her sexual favors. While most of these memoir novels from eighteenth-century France have faded into obscurity, re-examining them today provides a useful glimpse into the popular imagination of the time, including what readers found amusing.

Fictions of Pleasure, then, is an introduction to this subgenre of the French libertine novel, focusing on four such memoir novels that represent not only the microgenre, but also a site of resistance to ancien-régime power structures. With fictional female narrators who proudly declare themselves sex workers (often reclaiming the insulting French term *putain*) and offer titillating tales of their sexual adventures, the putain memoirs at first glance seem to hold little intellectual value. Certainly, almost all have a lighthearted tone and mostly happy conclusions. But seen as a whole, these novels represent something larger than a fun read: they are a literary and popular expression of dissatisfaction and revolt against wealthy and aristocratic powerholders in the fifty years leading to the French Revolution of 1789. What sets these novels apart from the more traditional voices of opposition to the ancien régime is the alternative fantasy of an egalitarian society they propose. Rather than contrasting the moral depravity of the aristocracy with images of a virtuous bourgeois family, centered around modest and domestic mothers and obedient daughters (as in the writings of Jean-Jacques Rousseau and others), these narratives celebrate independent women in control of their own sexuality, decision making, and destiny. As the narrators recount with glee their many sexual escapades maneuvering through public and private spaces as easily as they traverse the boundaries of social class, the stories they tell emerge as more than just obscure erotica to stimulate and amuse; they illustrate an appealing imaginary alternative to accepted social mores through images of powerful women who stand in a marginalized but no less successful zone of personal power.

My purpose in this book is twofold. First, I intend to establish the putain memoir as a genre with several unifying characteristics within a specific literary context. Second, I offer a close reading of four representative novels to reveal their discourse opposing the ancien régime in order to shed new light on the libertine literary tradition and on conceptions of gender in prerevolutionary France. The alternative discourse of the putain memoirs stands in sharp contrast to the voices of criticism most scholars of eighteenth-century France have explored. The fantasy of Rousseau's idyllic republic, in which strong men come together in the public sphere to make laws while chaste and modest women stay home to care for the children—which was at the heart of prerevolutionary calls for reform—holds no appeal for the putain narrators. Their critique of eighteenth-century society does not focus on its immorality, but instead on the unequal distribution of its pleasures.

Such complaints were not necessarily the concerns of real sex workers of the time, however. There is currently no evidence that any of the putain memoirs were written by actual courtesans. None of the novels received the royal seal, so all were published anonymously. For some of the novels, authorship remains a mystery; for others, literary scholars have been able to trace the author back to a specific person. Since every identified author is a man, it is safe to assume that most, if not all, putain memoirs are fiction.

Despite each novel's unique voice and the specific adventures described within, a paradigmatic storyline emerges among them. Most of these novels start with a preface, but in a departure from the common practice in other novels of their time, these preceding remarks are rarely written in the voice of a male editor or publisher. Instead, it is usually the putain herself who openly and often proudly admits to being an author as well as a sex worker. The memoir usually begins with some reference to the heroine's parents, who either are absent (dead or preoccupied with other matters) or have led her down the path of vice through instruction or example. The heroine recognizes that her sexual curiosity developed at an early age—around thirteen in most cases—and gives a detailed account of her first sexual experience. She willingly and eagerly enters the mercenary sex trade as soon as she learns that she can make money by following her natural desires.

All of the putains achieve, even if only for a brief period of time, the status of *fille entretenue*, the mistress of a wealthy man, an *entreteneur.* In addition, each narrator's adventures contain some combination of the following elements: a stay in a brothel, a bout of venereal disease (usually easily cured), a stay in a prison, a visit to a convent, excursions in public dressed as a man, trips to the opera or theater (either as a performer or a spectator), and an unhappy experience with love. A long series of lovers and adventures follows until one of four endings occurs. Sometimes the putain ends her memoir in the midst of her success and promises to continue her activities and to write a continuation of her memoir soon. The putain memoirs *Histoire de Mademoiselle Cronel*, *La Belle Allemande*, *Vénus en rut*, *Confessions d'une jeune fille*, and *Juliette* end in this way. Other times, the putain recognizes at the end of her tale that her charms are fading, but nevertheless regrets nothing. Such is the ending of *Psaphion* and *La Cauchoise*. Some putains find a happy way to retire from prostitution. The narrators of *La Fille de joie*, *Margot la ravaudeuse*, and *Histoire de Mademoiselle Brion* describe this ending. Finally, some unfortunate putains are forced out of prostitution through arrest or death. *La Tourière des carmélites*, *Mademoiselle Javotte*, and the *Mémoires de Suzon* have this tragic end. Whatever their endings, all the putain memoirs are pseudo-autobiographies, all follow a chronological narration, and the narrator always conveys joy and pride in the telling of her story.

In addition to their similar plots, these memoirs also share another important feature: the narrator is not only a female libertine, but also, as we have seen, an admitted sex worker. Whether or not they explicitly call themselves "putains," as the narrator of *La Cauchoise* (1784) does on the first page of her memoir, the heroines of these novels always recognize and acknowledge the exchange of sex for money as a part of their libertine pursuit of pleasure. Only one of the fictional putains has personal wealth; all the others embrace their profession out of financial need as much as personal preference.

When *La Cauchoise*'s La Dumonci proclaims, "I am a putain; I declare it openly" ("Je suis putain, je le déclare ingénument"), she is reappropriating an otherwise pejorative term.[4] The *Dictionnaire de l'Académie française* from 1762 (fourth edition) defines "putain" as "an insulting term to describe a girl or woman engaged in prostitution" ("terme d'injure qui se dit d'une fille ou d'une femme prostituée").[5] Then, as if the negative connotation of the word were not clear enough, the definition concludes with the brief but clear sentence, "It is a dishonorable term" ("C'est un terme malhonnête").[6] But for the fictional women who took up the title of putain, such dishonor exists only in the minds of hypocritical and prejudiced prudes. The putains take pride in their ability to make a living selling their bodies.

The frankness of the heroines regarding their profession is something their name should reflect. The only English word most dictionaries provide as a translation for *putain* is "whore," but that word fails to convey the professional pride these women display, their disregard for the judgment of others, and the subtle seductions they conduct. Yet a term like "courtesan" implies more refinement than any of them achieves. These characters are a unique product of eighteenth-century France, and as such deserve a French title. For this reason, I have elected to highlight their uniqueness by calling them putains, sometimes alternating the French term with its imprecise translation "prostitute" or with the more widely accepted term "sex worker." The fact that in modern French the word *putain* is a ubiquitous and vulgar curse word makes the term all the more appropriate for these characters narrating subversive stories and breaking the rules of language and etiquette.

I have identified thirteen putain memoir novels, in my research relying heavily on the *Bibliographie du genre romanesque, 1750–1800* by Angus Martin, Vivienne Mylne, and Richard Frautschi, who in turn based most of their assertions on the nineteenth-century catalogs of Antoine Alexandre Barbier, Jules Gay, and other bibliographers.[7] I include an appendix of all of these novels, which provides descriptions and publication histories of each text. The four putain memoirs selected for closer analysis here—*La Belle Allemande*, *Margot la ravaudeuse*, *La Cauchoise*, and *Histoire de Juliette*—offer a broad representation of the genre. They span almost the entire chronological spectrum of the genre's development, with initial printings from 1745 to 1797; they show varied levels of explicitness—from the polite euphemisms of *La Belle Allemande* to the blunt vulgarity of *La Cauchoise* and the hideous violence of the Marquis de Sade's *Juliette*—and they are an appropriate mix of better-known novels (*Margot la ravaudeuse* and *Juliette*) and heretofore less recognized titles (*La Belle Allemande* and *La Cauchoise*). Further, each of the four novels presents particularly well the characteristics found in most, if not all thirteen of the putain memoirs.

One novel will be the focus of each chapter from chapter 3 to chapter 6. While the order of the chapters here allows these novels to emerge in chronological order, this structure does not imply an evolution in the genre. Even though some progression occurs—for example, from a more euphemistic tone to a blunter one—the order of these four chapters is intended to reveal, first, the fact that salient criticisms and subversions of the patriarchal social order appear in the novels, and then the more specific ways these critiques play out.

Before turning to the novels, however, I place the putain memoir genre into its literary and historical contexts. Chapter 1 traces the origins and development of the French prostitute narrative as part of a larger tradition of erotic writing, materialist philosophy, and the libertine novel. By both sorting through the conflicting generic definitions previous scholars have proposed for similar texts and comparing the putain memoirs to other examples of libertine and erotic literature from France, Italy, and Britain, I establish the genre's place within the larger libertine discourses of early modern and Enlightenment Europe.

Chapter 2 continues situating the novels, this time within the historical context of the demimonde of eighteenth-century Paris, comparing the narratives of the fictional heroines with historical evidence concerning real sex workers of the time. The similarities between fact and fiction demonstrate the celebrity of the real mistresses who existed in that milieu and how they captured the popular imagination, while the differences reflect the fact that the fictional heroines presented merely a fantasy of materialist, libertine principles brought to life, without the biological consequences of a sexually promiscuous lifestyle. The putain narrators are able to avoid many of the harsh realities facing real sex workers and *filles entretenues* in the Parisian demimonde of the eighteenth century and lead relatively charmed lives. The putains rarely face pregnancy, exploitation, or violence, and their bouts of venereal disease are usually quickly cured. Their good fortune points to the utopian fantasy these works depict—a world where hard work and talent lead to success, and cleverness and strategic alliances allow women to undermine the privileges of the powerful with impunity.

Chapter 3 begins the presentation and analyses of the books with *La Belle Allemande, ou Les Galanteries de Thérèse* (1745), which demonstrates well how the prostitute memoirs critique and subvert the power structures of the ancien régime, including the undeserved privileges that wealthy and aristocratic older men enjoyed. The narrative depicts the unconventional choices and attitudes that lead to the narrator's celebrity, financial success, and personal satisfaction. Not only does Thérèse call into question the rigid social barriers of the patriarchal order in ancien-régime society with her lifestyle and her status as a putain, but she also, like her putain sisters, makes pointed criticisms of the powerful men she meets, rejects marriage and filial obedience, encourages a redistribution of wealth and pleasure based on personal merit, and provides amusing anecdotes proving the power of her sexuality. Thérèse exemplifies how putain memoir novels reveal the tensions and frustrations that lay beneath the surface in prerevolutionary France, proving that these stories are not just spicy erotic fantasies but contain serious political subversions. Similarly, the monarchy and its hierarchical society were not undermined solely by intellectual *philosophes* proposing radical ideas in salons and the *Encyclopédie*; popular fiction also played an important role in this effort.

Chapter 4 focuses on *Margot la ravaudeuse* (1753), which best demonstrates how putain heroines avoid confinement to the private, domestic sphere and manipulate both private and public spaces for their own benefit. Margot, a dancer at the opera, perfects her ability to leap from public to private spaces on and off the stage. The uses of public and private space in the putain texts—from the heroines' boudoirs to the theater—problematize the work of Jürgen Habermas on the emergence of the authentic public sphere in the eighteenth century.[8] With the support of feminist critiques of Habermas, I show how these heroines are uniquely able to ignore the gendered division of space, and in so doing create a pleasurable public sphere—a space with different goals than Habermas's bourgeois public sphere, and accessible to more people. With a rational focus on profit and a wary disdain for sentimental love, putains like Margot demonstrate how clever and disciplined women can achieve independent success and personal satisfaction that far exceed the purported domestic bliss of nurturing wives and mothers.

In chapter 5, the story of *La Cauchoise* reveals a key element of the putains' successful escape from the traditional marriage plot, seeking out and relying upon a system of female friendships. The complex relationships the narrators share with the women in their lives offer mutual support, mentorship, and sexual pleasure at the exclusion of men. They form a kind of social network that resembles the *fraternité* of the Revolution, with individuals not related by blood joining together for mutual benefit and the common good. This network exposes again the professionalism of the narrators, who demonstrate pride in their successful careers, financial acumen, an awareness of their own commodification, and a surprisingly unsentimental attitude toward romantic love.

Finally, chapter 6 focuses directly on a topic at the core of all the subversions present in the previous chapters: the putains' rejection of motherhood. Despite Sade's extreme and gruesome perversion of the themes of the putain memoirs, his *Histoire de Juliette* (1797) nevertheless provides useful insights into the importance of motherhood as a theme and how rejecting it became the putains' greatest transgression in the revolutionary period. The fact that Sade chose the putain memoir form to present his greatest female libertine proves the popularity of the genre. Just as his Justine can be seen as a perversion of the tragic heroines of sentimental novels like Samuel Richardson's *Pamela; or Virtue Rewarded* (1740) and Rousseau's *Julie, ou La Nouvelle Héloïse* (1761), Juliette reveals the prostitute heroine to be another convention that Sade and his readers clearly recognized. Furthermore, Juliette's repeated rejections of motherhood, culminating in the murder of her own daughter, bring to light the power dynamics at play when a woman chooses not to utilize her power to create life. Turning to the significant scholarship on the portrayal of mothers as "privileged victims" enjoying excessively cruel tortures in Sade's fiction, I assert that the putains recognize the incompatibility of reproductive power with real political and financial power and consistently choose the latter.

Fictions of Pleasure ends with a discussion of the end of the French putain memoir novel and proposes explanations for the lack of this kind of fiction after 1800. When Sade carried the tropes of the genre to an uncomfortable extreme in *Histoire de Juliette*, the subversive putains were cast in a different, more dangerous light. At the same time, the vastly transformed political landscape in France after 1789 rendered moot many of the prostitute memoirs' critiques of their society. Ultimately, theirs was a genre that lost its edginess. Emblematic of the nineteenth-century fictional prostitute, Marguerite Gautier from Alexandre Dumas fils's *La Dame aux camélias* (1848) is a victimized courtesan with a heart of gold. Her example highlights the significant departure from the playfully subversive putains and represents well the remarkable attitudinal shift in France after the Revolution. Sexually active and even aggressive women who eschewed marriage and critiqued French society from the revealing vantage point of its margins no longer inspired authors or sold books. Thus, we see the putain memoir as a product of its time and, in that way, as a useful and previously overlooked lens for exploring discourses of resistance and conceptions of women from that period.

My analysis of these texts draws heavily on Lynn Hunt's groundbreaking work, *The Family Romance of the French Revolution* (1992). Her reinterpretation of the French Revolution as a rebellion of sons banding together to slay their fathers, and then coming to terms with their own violence, captures well the political unconscious before and after the beheading of King Louis XVI. I build on her claim that this political unconscious "was structured by narratives of family relations" by exploring the ways the putain memoirs rejected traditional family structures and sought out new organizing principles for society.[9] Hunt astutely recognizes the growing desire among the French to replace their political parents with a different kind of family, as well as the extraordinary creative effort necessary "to imagine a polity unhinged from patriarchal authority."[10] The putain memoirs, I argue, were a form of imaginative exercise, playing out the possibilities of a world without the gender and class boundaries critical to the patriarchal society of the ancien régime.

I am also indebted to the work of Kathryn Norberg, whose chapter "The Libertine Whore: Prostitution in French Pornography from Margot to Juliette" in *The Invention of Pornography* (1993) proposes grouping prostitute narratives from eighteenth-century France as a body of work with insights to reveal.[11] I share her belief that discourses about sex workers, fictional or otherwise, expose a great deal about a society's "new attitudes towards old political hierarchies," as well as how that society views women and female sexuality.[12] While my definition of the genre differs a bit from hers, and I prefer the French word *putain* to the term "whore," I take as a point of departure for all my analyses her assertion that "the libertine prostitute doesn't adhere to the new notion of womanhood. She is not modest, dependent, loving or maternal; she does not believe in romantic love and refuses to remain within the private, family sphere. Rather she is a public woman who, like Margot, is independent both financially and morally, intelligent, rational and responsible."[13]

Like Norberg, I often employ contrasting examples to reveal salient features in the putains. Whereas Norberg situates the happy and unapologetic "whore" against the unfortunate "virtuous courtesan" forced by circumstances into sex work, I cast a wider net, juxtaposing the putain with the modest and domestic heroines of sentimental literature. In eighteenth-century France, the best-known and most influential example of this kind of feminine virtue was the title character of Rousseau's best-selling *Julie, ou La Nouvelle Héloïse*. *Julie* was a smash hit, and a large body of research has explored the novel's impact on popular beliefs about the ideal marriage, family, and especially woman.[14] Without rehearsing here the vast scholarship on the topic of Rousseau and women, I assert that Rousseau's Julie represents a larger discursive practice (attributable in no small part to Rousseau himself) lauding women who deny their own physical and emotional desires—as Julie does by abandoning her relationship with Saint-Preux; who submit to their father's will—as Julie does by marrying Wolmar; and who situate their entire identity within their roles as mothers—as Julie does by sacrificing her own life for her child. By the Revolution, the notion of a peaceful and virtuous nuclear family predicated on the submission of women as daughters, wives, and mothers was a well-established and influential imaginary alternative to the ancien régime. This "domestic utopia" played out alongside the libertine fantasy I identify in the putain memoirs and formed the dominant discourse of reform against which the subversiveness of the putain memoirs stands in stark relief.[15]

When the leaders of the French Revolution proclaimed their ideals as *liberté*, *égalité*, and *fraternité*, they were perhaps unaware that they were echoing three of the guiding principles of the putain memoirs. The narrators of those novels demand the "liberté" to pursue their desires uninhibited by religious rules or social expectations. Further, the putains manage to create for themselves the freedom to determine their own lives, escaping the personal and financial control of a father or husband, selecting their sexual partners to obtain their own pleasure or profit, and moving about in public and private spaces. Through their escapades and manipulations, the putain narrators achieve an "égalité" to male libertines in their equal access to pleasure and satisfaction. Finally, they see themselves as a part of a collective of like-minded individuals, helping and supporting each other in their struggles against tyranny: a "fraternité" of putains.

If a group of titillating fictional memoirs with admittedly oversexed and often manipulative heroines seems an unlikely source for such lofty revolutionary goals, the novels' role as vehicles for protofeminist critiques is even more surprising. And yet the putain memoirs are proof that, as the patriarchal social order of the ancien régime crumbled into another version of the patriarchal social order in the revolutionary era, not all eighteenth-century minds saw that evolution as ideal or desirable. Some authors found the voices of female sex workers, observers doubly marginalized by French society, as the best means to articulate their frustrations. Some readers reveled in watching women disobey and discredit sexist double standards. The pleasurable fictions these writers and their readers sought out are stories that weave together scenes of sexual stimulation, subversive discourses, and tender examples of sisterhood to create a libertine utopia. Even though the egalitarian paradise the putain narrators inhabited never came to pass in reality, its existence on the page and in the eighteenth-century collective imagination is undeniable.

1

Subversive Stories

Literary Contexts and Categories

In the middle of her narrative, *La Cauchoise*'s La Dumonci describes a lavish *partie de plaisir* she attends at the country estate of a friend's debauched *entreteneur.* There she discovers the owner's impressive library of libertine literature. Astonishingly, she remembers every title in that libidinous book collection of nearly fifty titles and kindly lists them for the reader. These texts—including "L'Ode à Priape," "La Foutromanie," *Le Portier des chartreux, Thérèse philosophe, La Fille de joie, L'École des filles, Les Bijoux indiscrets, Vénus dans le cloître,* and *La Putain errante,* among many others—provide a catalog of popular libertine and erotic texts from the late eighteenth century, giving us a glimpse of the libertine literary tradition to which the putain memoirs contributed.[1]

La Dumonci's bibliography reflects the wide variations among the many texts of seventeenth- and eighteenth-century libertine fiction. In these narratives, the libertine's pursuit of freedom from restrictive authorities and prudish cultural mores, particularly from the Church, takes many forms. Often, but not always, these expressions manifest in sexually explicit narratives, punctuated with long philosophical passages justifying lubricity through materialist explanations of human anatomy and nature. Some anticipate modern pornography in their graphic content, while others employ euphemisms and convey a cautionary message, warning against succumbing to the very passions they describe.

Categorizing these disparate texts into neatly defined genres has proven to a be a vexing task for literary scholars. In addition to the variety of forms, themes, and tones in this corpus, there exists little scholarly agreement on the terminology to designate these nuances, with terms like "libertine," "erotic," "materialist," "lewd," "obscene," and "pornographic" often taking on different connotations depending on the text under examination and the qualities being highlighted. Teasing a genre like the putain memoirs out of such a complicated literary landscape might seem impossible. However, the scholarly ambivalence around definitions and descriptions of libertine, erotic, philosophical, and pornographic texts is the perfect context for the stories the putain narrators tell and the narrative structures they employ to tell them. The strength of the putain memoir genre is its ability to enact multiple discourses while simultaneously undermining the purported divisions they appear to reinforce. More specifically, these novels subvert the notion that lines can be drawn between that which is proper and that which is prurient. By blending the erotic and the philosophical, the critical and the pornographic, these texts enact a structural and narrative subversion, reflecting the social and political subversions of their narrators. In the same way the putains reject the false binaries of respectable versus lascivious and passionate versus rational, their memoirs reject equally limiting generic definitions. The putain memoirs, then, provide a useful point of entry for exploring the entire genre of French libertine literature.

The ability to accommodate a variety of characteristics from the rich and complex libertine tradition is one of the specific qualities that make the putain memoir novels an identifiable genre. This chapter examines three other common features among all the putain memoirs: the first-person narration by a female prostitute, the acknowledged self-commodification of the prostitute for her own financial gain, and the materialist philosophical justifications for the narrators' libertine choices. After describing those commonalities and comparing their deployment in the putain memoirs with their use in similar preceding and contemporaneous texts, we will turn to the more contested signifiers of the genre: the terms "pornographic," "libertine," and "erotic." Even a cursory glance at the some of the vast scholarship on defining and refining these generic descriptors reveals a cacophony that resembles the tangled affairs and intrigues of the prostitute narrators themselves. These novels are stories about women who refuse to fit into the narrow categories devised for them. The putains are not mere ruined maidens, nor are they lascivious temptresses, calculating manipulators, or clever libertines. Rather, they are all at once. It is precisely that ambivalence that allows these texts to pose such pointed critiques, and that enables the subgenre to expose so clearly the inherent contradictions and conflicts in the broader libertine genre.

What makes a putain memoir a putain memoir is, of course, the first-person narration by a woman engaging in sex work. The salacious combination of a female narrator and the subject of prostitution has long been a staple of erotic, obscene, and titillating fiction, dating back to antiquity in Lucian's *Dialogues of the Courtesans* from the second century.[2] In that collection of fifteen dialogues, prostitutes discuss concerns such as pregnancy, the jealousy of clients and other prostitutes, and the challenges of maintaining delicate relations with wealthy, long-term customers—topics that, with the exception of pregnancies, feature prominently in eighteenth-century prostitute narratives as well. During the Middle Ages, prostitutes were common in the bawdy French *fabliaux*, the short, comic narratives that conveyed satirical critiques of the Church and the nobility. In fact, *Richeut* (1159), which is generally considered the first fabliau, is the story of a prostitute and unsurprisingly anticipates many of the themes of the putain memoirs that followed, including the narrator's clever ruses to dupe her customers and her refusal to discriminate among her lovers according to their class.

By the sixteenth century, the trope of the didactic whore dialogue was well established as a means of critiquing hypocrisy and titillating readers. Pietro Aretino, the leading figure in early modern erotic literature, expanded this conceit into a tradition henceforth inseparable from his name. This Italian, whose works are considered to be, in Lynn Hunt's words, the "prototype of seventeenth-century pornographic prose," is best known for his 1534 *Ragionamenti*, a series of dialogues between two sex workers: a seasoned veteran, Nanna, and a newcomer.[3] In the first dialogue, Nanna discusses with her friend which option she should choose for her daughter: the life of a wife, a nun, or a prostitute. Nanna explains how she has experienced all three states and recounts her adventures, first in a licentious and dangerous convent, then married to a cuckold (whom she kills when he begins beating her after catching her in bed with another man), and finally as a prostitute. After hearing these tales, her friend advises her to set her daughter up as a prostitute, since the nun betrays her vows and the wife betrays her husband, but the whore at least is honest. In Aretino's 1536 *Dialogo*, another sex worker, again named Nanna, gives her daughter advice on how to be most successful as she enters the same profession.[4] Aretino also famously wrote a series of lascivious sonnets, the *Sonetti lussuriosi* (1524), to accompany a set of sixteen engravings of various sexual positions. Not only were Aretino's writings translated into French and widely circulated in the seventeenth and eighteenth centuries, but his name also became associated with the images illustrating his sonnets, so that the engravings alone were often called "Aretino's postures."

Aretino is also erroneously associated with another Italian work of the time, *Dialogo di Maddalena e Giulia*, also known as *La Puttana errante*, particularly in the many eighteenth-century French versions of the prostitute dialogues, often under the general title *La Putain errante*.[5] *La Retorica delle putane* (1643), the work of another Italian, Ferrante Pallavicino, is also frequently misattributed in eighteenth-century bibliographies, as it too tells the tale of the indoctrination of a young girl into prostitution, this time through a series of fifteen lessons.[6]

Building off this subversive and ironic narrative trope of wise sex workers dispensing sage advice to eager ingenues, seventeenth-century authors of lewd texts extended the structure to include didactic conversations between any two female libertines, whatever their professions (if any). For example, in the scandalous *L'École des filles, ou La Philosophie des dames* (1655), Suzanne and her cousin Fanchon discuss the pleasures of sex and the many ways to achieve them, with Suzanne encouraging Fanchon to put aside her modesty and give her virginity to her young suitor.[7] Later, Fanchon returns to update her cousin on her newfound pleasure and to seek advice on preventing pregnancy.

The other major sexually explicit French work of the seventeenth century, *L'Académie des dames, ou Le Meursius français* (1680), yet again turns to the educational dialogue and takes place again between two cousins. The original Latin version from 1659 or 1660 claimed to be a translation of the writings of a Spanish poet, Luisa Sigea, and *L'Académie des dames* was a further translation from the Latin into French. The "académie" here refers to the lessons Tullia gives to Ottavia on the secrets of the marriage bed and how to achieve sexual satisfaction. Although the women of *L'École des filles* and *L'Académie des dames* are not prostitutes, they—like their Latin and Italian counterparts—provide a female voice to describe sexual organs, positions, and activities.

The putain memoirs of eighteenth-century France, however, return to Lucian's and Aretino's practice of presenting erotic content through the voice of not just any female libertine but a prostitute. Dropping the dialogue form in favor of a memoir, these novels are subtler in their didactic purpose and present a longer narrative. The titillation and subversion of a woman speaking about sex remain, but now in the form of a kind of bildungsroman autobiography, popularized in works like Pierre Marivaux's *La Vie de Marianne* (1731–1742), for example. In fact, first-person narration, as either a memoir or an epistolary novel, dominated prose fiction through most of the eighteenth century, whether libertine or otherwise. There are multiple reasons for the growth of these forms, not the least of which is the quest for verisimilitude. Georges May and other literary scholars have explained that the need for the appearance of truth in eighteenth-century texts made memoir and epistolary novels more convincing and marketable than fiction recounted by an omniscient third-person narrator.[8] At a time when the status of prose fiction was questioned because it was unfounded in history and had no corresponding genre from antiquity, a plausible preface explaining how these "true" memoirs or letters were found gave such fictional work an air of legitimacy. Writers of memoir novels also followed the models of several true confessional memoirs from the seventeenth century that were reprinted between 1715 and 1730, including those of Henriette d'Angleterre.[9]

Furthermore, the memoir novel, as the first-person narration of the intimate details of one person's life published and circulated among many paying readers, blends aspects of the intimate and the open, of the private and the public, in much the same way prostitutes do. As in other libertine texts, including *Thérèse philosophe* (1748), the putain memoir's form creates a feeling of intimate access to a beautiful woman's sex life. But in the case of the putain memoirs, the added parallel between the narrative structure and the heroines' activities heightens the effect. In short, a memoir novel offers intimate details to anyone who can purchase the book or pamphlet, just as a sex worker offers intimate acts to anyone who can pay for their services.[10]

In addition, the putain memoir is structured so that the female is deliberately telling her life story to an audience, be it her readers, one particular reader, or a listener. Her story is always told in chronological order from childhood to the present moment. In contrast, earlier examples of titillating female narrators lacked this methodical chronological structure. The whore dialogues of the Italian Renaissance, as well as their seventeenth-century French imitators like *L'École des filles*, do not seek to tell a complete life story. Instead, the woman's speech is primarily meant to instruct and to excite, rather than to describe herself.

The memoir of a female libertine is the preferred narrative form of several eighteenth-century erotic works, such as *Thérèse philosophe* and *Félicia, ou Mes fredaines* (1775). The narrators of these works, despite their unrepentant enjoyment of sexual pleasures and nontraditional relationships, seem unaware of the transactional nature of their relationships with their corrupters/lovers. While the philosophical Thérèse and Félicia ultimately embrace a libertine lifestyle, engage in sexual relations outside marriage, and benefit from the financial support of their male partners, they never think of themselves as courtesans, or even kept mistresses.[11] Such a lack of self-awareness robs these heroines of the agency and professionalism that define the putains. The putain recognizes that while exploring sexuality is a part of obeying natural law, passion and pleasure do not always accompany the sexual act. While the heroines of the putain memoirs are all lubricious, have taken up prostitution out of genuine enjoyment of sex, and find real pleasure much of the time, they are pragmatic enough to recognize that their financial security means sometimes having to simulate their desire or enjoyment. Such dissimulation is part of the trade of a putain but would undoubtedly undermine other female libertines' claims of simple obedience to nature. The narrators of the putain memoirs, however, are acutely aware of their own material needs and how transforming the sexual desire they arouse in wealthy men into a source of income can allow them to meet those needs while maintaining their independence. In striking contrast to other libertine heroines, the putain narrators openly admit to their work as prostitutes and present their stories with a mix of sexual titillation and financial acumen.

In her book *Infamous Commerce* (2006), Laura Rosenthal explores the topic of the early modern sex worker's interest in and knowledge about financial matters.[12] Her sources include around thirty prostitute narratives from eighteenth-century England, including prostitute biographies, "actress biographies, crime stories, scandal narratives, and novels."[13] With such a wide-ranging variety of genres, it is not surprising that the stories she examines range in tone from euphemistic suggestion to explicit language, and in purpose from cautionary tales against the slippery slope for a girl who strays from virtue to protofeminist calls for equality as a means of protecting women from this profession of last resort. Rosenthal divides these texts into two categories: libertine and reformist narratives, with both groups nonetheless depicting "the economic meaning of the transaction of prostitution . . . even to the point that prostitutes begin to embody the kind of commercial identity that can empower or threaten the individual through self-control, self-sacrifice, and self-division in marketplace exchanges."[14] In other words, the growing sense of professionalism in depictions of prostitutes that began to emerge (a professionalism the French putains also display), transforming them from the oversexed pleasure seekers of the seventeenth century to practical, rational sex workers focused on profit in the eighteenth, reflected the rise of larger social anxieties of the time around the emergence of capitalism and the commodification of human labor.[15]

In a similar way, the French putain memoirs emphasize the financial needs of their heroines and the profitability of selling their bodies. What is difficult to find in the putain memoirs, however, is the kind of anxiety Rosenthal describes over the commodification of the sex worker's labor into capital that can be exchanged for consumer goods. In France, the eighteenth-century prostitute seems to represent a less ambivalent optimism in the burgeoning capitalist marketplace. These women carefully explain their need for an income and the salient, rational argument for transforming the desire they inspire into demand they can exploit to enrich themselves. Their self-commodification—turning their bodies into objects that can be bought and sold—is not a tragic last resort, but an expression of liberating self-control. Also valuable are their contributions to the economy as consumers of clothing, jewelry, and furniture, as well as their support of the commodified labor of other people such as tutors and hairdressers. Their expenditures are not shallow, conspicuous displays of wealth solely for superficial pleasures, but reinvestments in themselves; wearing expensive clothes and jewels, maintaining a carriage and horses, and making other displays of wealth advertised their desirability, attracting future *entreteneurs* and ensuring future income.[16] In both their decision to demand payment from the men they sleep with and their deliberate consumption of luxury goods as a form of marketing, the putains turn otherwise self-indulgent pleasures into rational business practices.

When the putains professionalize their libertine activities, they ensure their own participation, and indeed agency, in the commodification of their bodies and their skills. Their commerce permits them a great deal of upward social mobility, as well as an ability to "navigate public and private versions of identity" with the same ease that Rosenthal identifies in many of the British libertine narratives.[17] The best-known and most influential example of the professional prostitute's successful social ascent is in John Cleland's *Memoirs of a Woman of Pleasure* (1748), more commonly known as *Fanny Hill.* Fanny unabashedly embraces her occupation as a prostitute, enjoying both the sexual experiences and the wealth they bring. Like many of her French counterparts, she recounts her escapades with a zeal that belies her expressions of embarrassment in the preface.[18] Furthermore, her fictional tale resembles many of the French putains' in that she enjoys all the benefits of a libertine lifestyle without facing its negative consequences, as Rosenthal remarks: "She never contracts venereal disease; she never walks the streets (except for fun); she never has a client who refuses to pay her; rioters never attack her house; Mrs. Cole's bawdy house provides an affectionate, all-female family; her first keeper turns out to be decent and attractive; she finds a never-ending supply of work; and she ends up married, rich, virtuous, and in love."[19]

While none of the French putain narrators enjoys quite as many fortunate circumstances as Fanny, they all describe achieving a remarkable level of professional success and personal satisfaction. In both the English and the French prostitute narratives of the eighteenth century, we find women creating for themselves an identity based not on birth but on a deliberate manipulation of appearances and an adherence to a larger profession. This professional identity distinguishes the putain from the mere libertine, while it also establishes the putain memoirs as a distinct microgenre.

While the putains' unabashed avowal of their prostitution sets these narrators apart from other libertines, the one thing their memoirs have in common with almost all eighteenth-century erotic literature is a materialist justification for the protagonist's choices. Like all eighteenth-century libertines, the putains view sexual acts not as the sinful self-indulgence of a weak soul, but as the logical result of the laws of nature. This interpretation of sexual desire is based on a mechanistic view of the universe as composed of bodies in motion, an idea popularized in the seventeenth century with the revival of atomism and scientific developments like Isaac Newton's laws of motion.[20] According to these newly popularized ideas, human bodies are no different from other forms of matter: subject to the same gravitational attraction of other bodies through invisible forces. By the eighteenth century, a renewed interest in Epicurean philosophy meant that many Enlightenment thinkers no longer saw pleasure as a temptation by the devil, but as a worthy goal for a satisfying life. Writers like Jean-Baptiste Boyer d'Argens (generally accepted as the author of *Thérèse philosophe*), Julien Offray de La Mettrie, and the Marquis de Sade are now well known for their articulations of this materialist philosophy, but the lesser-known authors of putain memoirs also put those principles to work in their stories.[21]

Libertine novels played an important role in conveying the moral lessons of what Catherine Cusset terms the "ethics of pleasure." Drawing on materialist philosophy, eighteenth-century authors demonstrated how a belief "that the aim of human life was to seek pleasure and avoid displeasure" could be put into practice.[22] But the voluptuous scenes of pleasure-seeking in these novels are often interrupted by long philosophical passages explaining the rationale for embracing sexual pleasure and the foolish hypocrisy of denying one's natural instincts. Natania Meeker calls these discourses "materialist dicta," and she illustrates how in *Thérèse philosophe* they "emphasize the force of the passions, the naturalness of desire, and the link between happiness and pleasurable sensation."[23] Even though the philosophical Thérèse is not a putain, the same kinds of dicta appear in the prostitute narratives as well.

Once seeking sexual gratification is no longer viewed as superficial self-indulgence, the materialist libertine like the putain narrator can accept and follow the dictates of her natural desires. As Margaret C. Jacob explains, materialism also served as a means of articulating desire. The writers of libertine—or what she terms pornographic—fiction in the eighteenth century depicted bodies as reduced to their moving particles, allowing for an almost scientific objectivity, as "nature is abstractly mechanized and bodies in motion are made wholly sufficient, encapsulated by the experimental gaze of the natural philosophers."[24] Jacob further reminds us that the pornographer and the materialist philosopher shared the same task of challenging a traditional hierarchy founded on religious dogma and social etiquette, further blurring the distinction between libertine and erotic.[25]

The putain memoirs depict characters who find personal satisfaction and happiness through the wholehearted acceptance of their own sexual needs. Their narrators put into practice materialist philosophy when they reject prudish prejudices and obey nature's dictate to copulate. The materialism of the putains, however, is carefully selected. While they recognize that sexual desire is nature's way of ensuring the continuation of the human species, the heroines themselves rarely reproduce. In fact, with all the sexual activity to be found in the memoirs, these fictional putains are remarkably infertile. The realistic, probable outcome of pursuing pleasure is conveniently absent in the putain memoirs. Certainly, some of the putains do find themselves arrested upon occasion, and bouts of venereal disease are common, if easily cured. Nevertheless, the materialist philosophy of the putain memoirs plays out in a libertine utopia with few negative consequences.

Identifying the common features among the putain memoirs and how they overlap with other libertine texts is a straightforward endeavor. Determining which eighteenth-century texts qualify as libertine is more challenging. A number of qualifiers have accompanied books like the *Histoire de Dom Bougre, Portier des Chartreux* (1741), *Thérèse philosophe*, and the writings of the Marquis de Sade since their publication—adjectives including among others, "erotic," "philosophical," "licentious," "libertine," and "pornographic." Certainly, the authors themselves would never have called their fictional memoirs "pornographiques"; instead, the terms *érotique*, *libertin*, and *galant* denoted sexually explicit writing in eighteenth-century France.[26] The adjective "pornographic" is perhaps the most contested term, because of its modern connotations and the fact that applying it to pre-nineteenth-century texts is technically anachronistic.

In the strictest etymological sense, the putain memoirs are pornography in that they are writings (-graphy) about prostitutes (porno-). But pornography as a category of creative product did not exist until the nineteenth century, and the word itself did not appear until 1769 in Nicolas Edme Rétif de la Bretonne's half treatise–half novella, *Le Pornographe, ou Les Idées d'un honnête homme sur un projet de règlement pour les prostituées propre à prévenir le malheur qu'occasionne le publicisme des femmes avec des notes justicatives*. In this ambitious title, Rétif refers directly to the etymology of "pornographer," meaning one who writes about prostitutes. There is no stimulating erotic content in Rétif's proposal; rather, it is a systematic plan to organize strictly controlled municipal brothels to serve the sexual needs of unmarried men and thus protect the virtue of chaste women.

Amy Wyngaard contests, however, such a dismissal of Rétif's *Le Pornographe* as "at once seminal and irrelevant" to the development of the pornographic novel.[27] In *Bad Books: Rétif de la Bretonne, Sexuality, and Pornography* (2012), she presents a reading of the novella—and in particular the frame narrative surrounding the proposal—that demonstrates its critical position, along with Rétif's *L'Anti-Justine* (1798), in the emergence of pornography as a form of writing that focuses on sex as a means for pleasure instead of as a means of political and social critique. Her analysis interestingly situates Rétif's two texts as antithetical responses to the works of the Marquis de Sade, *La Philosophie dans le boudoir* (1795) and *Justine* (1791). At the same time, she posits both authors as pivotal sources of the kinds of narrative changes that allowed the modern pornographic novels to emerge from the vaguely erotic, salacious, and often politically motivated genre we find up until the 1790s.

Even without the anachronism, the putain memoirs still fall short of our modern understanding of pornography. According to Lynn Hunt's introduction to *The Invention of Pornography*, a pornographic text is one with explicit descriptions of sexual organs for the *primary* purpose of arousing sexual feelings in the reader or viewer (my emphasis).[28] But very few of the putain memoirs ever even describe the sexual organs at play; more often the shock of these racy novels comes from the explicit mention of words like *vit* (cock), *con* (cunt), and *foutre* (fuck). Like many obscene novels in prerevolutionary France, they contain long philosophical passages that offer a materialist justification for sexual promiscuity and for sex outside of marriage in addition to the depictions of sexual activities. The presence of these arguments alone is enough to show that sexual arousal is not necessarily the primary aim of these novels.[29]

Furthermore, as Robert Darnton's significant body of research on the illegal book trade reveals, booksellers and publishers grouped sexually explicit texts with works containing political and religious criticisms (without salacious content) into a single category called "philosophiques."[30] *Livres philosophiques* were those books that "could get them in trouble, books that had to be handled with care."[31] Darnton further explains, "We consider *Du Contrat social* political theory and *Histoire de dom B . . .* pornography, perhaps even as something too crude to be treated as literature, but the bookmen of the eighteenth century lumped them together as 'philosophical books.' If we try to look at their material in their way, the seemingly self-evident distinction between pornography and philosophy begins to break down."[32] Thus, neither the term nor the concept of pornography was in existence at the time of the putain memoirs.

With or without the term "pornographic," scholars recognize a clear shift in the tone and intention of salacious fiction by the end of the century. Like Lynn Hunt, Amy Wyngaard situates this change in the 1790s when early modern pornography, "a politically and socially motivated form," loses its political subversions and philosophical pretensions to "focus on sexual pleasure as an end in itself."[33] Hunt connects this shift to the French Revolution, when "pornography began to separate from politics, perhaps because of the very success of the pornographic attack on the ancien régime in France."[34] In this case, the putain memoirs are emblematic of early modern pornography.

This transition is perhaps best found in the work of the Marquis de Sade, whose works combine long philosophical discourses undermining religious and legal authorities with graphic scenes of sexual deviancy and violence. Indeed, Sade is the author cited specifically in the *Dictionnaire critique, littéraire et bibliographique des principaux livres condamnés au feu, supprimés ou censurés* (1806) as exemplary of "pornography" in its first French usage as a category of books censored for moral rather than religious or political reasons.[35] And certainly, the violence and objectification of people in Sade's depictions of sexual scenes prefigure the definition employed by opponents of modern pornography like Catharine MacKinnon and Andrea Dworkin. Dworkin's denunciation of pornography for how its presentation of women "dehumanized as sexual objects . . . who enjoy pain or humiliation; . . . as sexual objects tied up or cut up or mutilated or bruised or physically hurt; or . . . in scenarios of degradation, injury, torture, shown as filthy or inferior, bleeding, bruised, or hurt in a context that makes these conditions sexual" contains echoes of Sade's themes and accumulative writing style.[36]

Clearly, our modern understanding of pornography owes a great deal to the writings of Sade. Still, even though he is the author of a putain memoir, the objectification of women, their humiliation and their torture, are nowhere to be found in other putain memoirs, and for this reason "pornographic" is a qualifier that potentially evokes more harm than can be found in the novels we explore here.

The presence of philosophical passages that are sometimes interwoven into scenes of sexual seduction and intercourse in texts like the putain memoirs creates disagreement about the appropriateness of the label "libertine" as well. Many anthologies of libertine novels and critical studies of the libertine fiction of the seventeenth and eighteenth centuries begin their explanation of what constitutes libertine writing with the etymology of the word "libertine." The term was used in ancient Rome to designate free citizens born from a freed slave. Later it came to represent any freed slave.[37] Within the literary context, elements such as calls for sexual liberation, critiques of society's mores and its prejudices, and an explanation of sexuality as part of a materialist philosophy reflect the tradition generally considered libertine. But the definition of the libertine novel is the subject of much scholarly debate. Almost any writing of the seventeenth and eighteenth centuries that is critical of religious, social, or moral restrictions can be and has been considered libertine, from the proto–science fiction of Savinien de Cyrano de Bergerac to the brutal pornography of Sade. Drawing on René Pintard's work on seventeenth-century libertine intellectuals,[38] Joan DeJean defines libertinism as "the defense of liberty and liberation against any form of restraint" and "dedicated to the glorification of freedom in all possible forms."[39] Raymond Trousson prefers a similarly broad definition when he explains that "libertinism, in whatever form, maintains something transgressive."[40] Such a vague modifier becomes the only (albeit awkward) unifier when trying to discover what links, in Trousson's words, "the erudite Epicureanism of a Gassendi, the radical skepticism of a La Mothe Le Vayer, the playful raunchiness of La Fontaine's *Contes* or the fantasies of Cyrano, with the eighteenth-century writers preaching the primacy of nature and the pleasures of the senses, from Crébillon to Casanova, from Laclos to Sade."[41]

In *The Autonomy of Pleasure* (2016), James Steintrager begins his discussion of libertinage as a system of thought with an examination of the term "libertine," and his exploration highlights the elusiveness of the word, as well as its complicated interplay with the pornographic:

> But what exactly did libertine mean? True, we frequently find an emphasis on sensual and more precisely on sexual pleasure. [However,] not all libertinage even included this element—there are degrees, various configurations, different formations that respond to changes in governing and social organization, to historical events, to the rise of new media technologies, and to developments intrinsic to libertinage itself. It might be better not to try to define libertinage once and for all. . . . Notwithstanding, we are soon returned to those family resemblances—obscenity, lewdness, and most especially, explicit descriptions of sexual intercourse—that mark what we understand to be the pornographic today.[42]

Recognizing the inherent challenges of uniting such disparate texts, Steintrager almost seems ready to abandon the task, turning instead to the concept of the pornographic as a point of reference.

Fortunately, he quickly returns to the definition of libertine, dividing libertine literature into three subgenres, which emerge in roughly chronological order. First are the "gently ironic novels of seduction and amorous education" that proliferated during the Regency, with works like Claude-Prosper Jolyot de Crébillon fils's *Les Égarements du cœur et de l'esprit* (1734) and Charles Pinot Duclos's *Les Confessions du comte de* *** (1741).[43] The second subgenre, "licentious libertine fiction," begins in 1740s with *Histoire de dom Bougre, portier des Chartreux* and *Thérèse philosophe*. Texts in this category "reveal a deep association with *philosophie* as a historically circumscribed movement and group identity" and "encouraged thinking beyond the limits of legally, socially, politically, and even metaphysically acceptable."[44] The third of Steintrager's subgenres of libertine literature constitutes the radical phase of libertinage in works such as "La Foutromanie" (1775) by Gabriel Sénac de Meilhan and Andréa Nerciat's *Les Aphrodites* (1793). Authors in this subgenre "made every effort to blend license with liberty and obliterate the distinction as an ideological nicety worthy of sardonic suspicion and skeptical critique."[45] A broader view of putain memoirs certainly reflects such a progression through the century. Not surprisingly, given that the putain memoirs' publication dates coincide with Steintrager's second and third categories, his descriptions of licentious libertinage and the radical phase reflect the content and style of the putain memoirs.

Steintrager's subcategories of the libertine are specific and avoid the other generically ambiguous term, "erotic." Previously many scholars identified the libertine text as one without erotic content, advocating for personal freedoms without delving into details about the actions such freedoms allow. Implying that sexually explicit material corrupts the libertine message, Peter Nagy for one argues in *Libertinage et révolution* (1975) that the author of libertine writing has nobler intentions than in erotic writing. For Nagy, libertine literature, while still "using erotic themes and an erotic form, goes beyond them in the goal of the writer and in the meaning of the work in a philosophical and artistic direction."[46] Joan DeJean's early work on the libertine writers of seventeenth-century France displays a similar interpretation as she makes a clear distinction between the sexually explicit literature of that time and what she considers a more rationalist, truly libertine text. In *Libertine Strategies* (1981) she focuses on texts such as Charles Sorel's *Francion* (1623), Théophile de Viau's *Fragments* (1623), and Cyrano de

Bergerac's *L'Autre monde* (1657), but excludes the two major erotic texts from the seventeenth century, *L'École des filles* and *L'Académie des dames*. DeJean clarifies that these sexually explicit novels exist outside her definition of libertine texts, not because of their descriptions of sexual organs and acts, but because they contain nothing more than sexual titillation.[47] Therein DeJean reaffirms the divide that reduces erotic writing to nothing more than sexual stimulation.

Similarly, Jean M. Goulemot distinguishes libertine from erotic writing in his study *Forbidden Texts* (1991) when he claims that the libertine story involves seduction as a means of expressing philosophical ideas, often in the form of rational and materialist explanations of sexuality and human desire.[48] On the other hand, an erotic story contains no resistance on the part of the victim to the efforts and entreaties of her seducer. Without the need to persuade, then, erotic texts contain primarily descriptive tableaux to excite readers rather than articulations of libertine philosophy. In Goulemot's assessment, the structure of the erotic novels is merely a succession of episodes with "nothing that links the episodes together except the desire and the pleasure which recur in the form of a leitmotif." Indeed, he clarifies, "it is either the partner, the place, or the positions that change."[49]

Henri Coulet is even more specific in his categorization. He maintains that libertinage finds a "decent language" to discuss love, and that "as soon as the problem of style is pushed aside, and the writer calls things by their name, the work is no longer libertine."[50] Thus, for Coulet, no sexually explicit text, with or without rational philosophy, would be considered libertine. For instance, Coulet catalogs the Marquis de Sade not as a "libertine" but instead as a philosophical writer—recalling the broad term used in the eighteenth-century clandestine book trade.[51]

Such a clear-cut distinction is obviously problematic, especially in the context of eighteenth-century texts. An either-or attitude toward explicit depictions of sexual acts versus direct articulations of libertine philosophy falls apart in the face of novels like *Thérèse philosophe*. Indeed, many critics of eighteenth-century French literature acknowledge the various nuances in libertine writing without distinguishing between libertine and erotic. Michel Delon, for one, recognizes the great variety within libertine literature, calling it a "category that encompasses pornographic writing as well as moralizing representations of seduction, descriptions of sexuality that are explicit as well as those that are implied."[52] Patrick Wald Lasowski accommodates the diversity of libertine novels with a multiplicity of subgenres: "worldly gallantry (Crébillon,) the cynicism of girls (Fougeret de Monbron), and obscenity (Gervaise de Latouche)."[53] Again, the need for a catch-all word like *philosophique* for the variety of texts becomes apparent.

One possible reason for the more ambivalent terminology in the eighteenth century is the fact that the century saw a larger body of sexually explicit and subversive works than ever before. New editions of the Italian classics as well as seventeenth-century erotic works reappeared alongside new stories of sexual liberty and clever seductions among the aristocracy.[54] The eighteenth-century libertine novel began to flourish in the 1730s.[55] The elegant style and careful use of innuendo—particularly in the works of Crébillon and Laclos—place them squarely within even Henri Coulet's definition of libertine as using "decent language." But what unites the fancy prose of a novel like *Les Égarements du cœur et de l'esprit* and the frank descriptions of works such as *Le Portier des chartreux* remains difficult to pin down.

Similarly, the many different criteria for delineating between libertine and erotic writing make placing the putain memoirs in one or the other category impossible. Some putain memoir novels may appear to have the lofty intentions that Nagy requires. Some contain philosophical passages that resemble the rationalism of Bergerac and Viau. The heroines of some novels simulate resistance to their seducers, whereas others encounter resistance from potential lovers and must resort to the seductive language Goulemot uses to identify a libertine text. Many putain narrators revel in their unpretentious language, but some of the earlier novels are quite euphemistic, with exactly the elevated style Coulet seeks. And yet there are always descriptions of sexual tableaux. Thus, the putain memoirs are a fluid genre of both the erotic and the libertine traditions.

We can understand exactly how the putain memoirs blend the libertine and erotic traditions if we associate the term "libertine" with freedom and "erotic" with sexual arousal. Thus, libertine works include those that call for greater personal freedom and criticize those people and prejudices that seek to limit an individual's freedom—whether the text discusses sexuality or not. La Mettrie's *L'Homme machine* would then be libertine, as would *Thérèse philosophe*. An erotic text, however, would be one that seeks to arouse its readers sexually—with or without philosophical justifications—through either veiled innuendo or blunt descriptions. *Thérèse philosophe* would consequently be both libertine and erotic.

The putain memoirs of prerevolutionary France similarly blend aspects of libertine and erotic writing and thereby occupy a powerful place in the French literary tradition. By expressing their resistance to social and religious conventions through erotic writing and sexual themes, they blend the erotic tradition of sexualized female discourse with the libertine desire for personal freedom. The putains critique the hypocrisy of religious zealots who claim to exemplify moral purity and self-control but are as dominated by their sexual desires as the sinners they condemn. They specifically decry the moral prejudices that try to turn their sex drives into cause for shame. Finally, as the following chapters will demonstrate, the heroines of the putain memoirs transgress the barriers that constrained polite society, frustrated materialist philosophers, and limited women's choices in life. In doing so, they prove that such boundaries are not only permeable but also arbitrary and artificial. In the same way, the heterogeneous collection of the putain memoirs, with objectively identifiable characteristics uniting them, explode efforts to limit and constrain the category "libertine." With their simultaneous variety and underlying commonalities, the putain memoirs are more than just a microgenre of the libertine novel; they are a microcosm of the genre. Exploring these novels then becomes a useful point of entry into the study of eighteenth-century libertine literature.

The time of the putain memoirs' composition and publication, their subversive themes, and their sexual content place them at the crossroads of what are often seen as two distinct literary movements: the libertine tradition and the development of erotic writing into modern pornography. While the level of sexual explicitness varies with each text, these novels are clearly part of the French libertine tradition. Nevertheless, the heroines of the putain memoirs are independent in a very remarkable way. They are free to pursue their sexual desires, free to criticize those who would stop them, and free to defend their choices with arguments from materialist philosophy. They offer a unique kind of libertinage in which the drives that nature inspires rarely have negative consequences, and in which women suffer no more than men. Such fantasies of pleasure without consequences of course depict an impossible utopia, but one that is no more unrealistic than the superhuman sexual feats of Dom Bougre, or for that matter, the fatal broken hearts in sentimental novels. Above all, the libertine utopias of the putain memoirs are fantasies of freedom—freedom from moral or social restraints and freedom from serious disease and pregnancy. This hopeful vision of liberty makes the putain memoirs libertine, and these texts thus constitute an important part of the libertine tradition.

2

Fact versus Fiction

Parisian Prostitutes Meet Libertine Fantasies

Some of the most entertaining moments in the putain memoirs occur when the narrators undermine the verisimilitude the memoir form is meant to create. For instance, within the first few pages of the 1755 edition of *La Belle Allemande*, the narrator Thérèse mentions two real-life celebrities—the ballerina and *fille entretenue* La Camargo and the famous actress Mademoiselle Clairon, supposedly the inspiration behind the first putain memoir—as her colleagues. She argues that if La Camargo can count cardinals among her ancestors, shouldn't she in a similar way claim an illustrious origin? ("Camargo compte des Cardinaux parmi ses aïeux, ne pourrais-je pas, si je voulais, jouir du même privilège?"). On the same page she also refers to herself as "Frétillon's rival in the career of honor" ("rivale de Frétillon dans la carrière d'honneur").[1] Within those same pages Thérèse also calls herself an author, a writer, and the heroine of a novel. She recognizes at the start of her memoir that she will now face the "dangers and inconveniences that come with being a professional author" ("les dangers et les inconvénients attachés à la profession d'auteur").[2] She then promises to offer the whole truth in her memoir because "the first quality of a writer must be a love of truth" ("la première qualité d'un écrivain doit être l'amour de la vérité").[3] In her reference to Frétillon she explains that she is now excited to join her rival in the "inseparable glory of being the heroine of a novel" ("la gloire inséparable de la qualité d'héroïne de roman").[4]

Reinforcing this slippage between author, narrator, putain, and main character, Thérèse makes a deliberate mistake toward the end of her preface. In an effort to justify the apparently vain inclusion of an engraving of her image in this latest edition, Thérèse reminds readers that publishers and even booksellers often include their own portraits in the works they sell. She then quotes a line from Virgil's *Eclogues*: "Quid Domini facient, audent cum talia fures?" ("What would the masters do when their servants dare such things?") Then, as if suddenly remembering that as an uneducated prostitute she cannot possibly have read Virgil, she immediately exclaims: "Oops! Sorry, I forgot that I don't know Latin. The desire to justify myself must be creating supernatural powers inside me." ("Ha! Pardon! J'ai pensé oublier que j'ignorais le latin. L'envie de me justifier opère peut-être en moi des mouvements surnaturels.")[5] She then explains that she fears another "little extravagance might slip out" ("de laisser encore échapper quelque nouvelle extravagance").[6]

In this anecdote the real-life author, who unlike Thérèse does know Latin, makes an appearance. The reader is not allowed to drift off into the world of the putains, pretending to believe it all to be true. Instead, the reader becomes complicit in the fiction about to unfold and will have to accept the details meant to establish verisimilitude (like references to real members of the Parisian demimonde) while simultaneously ignoring the evidence to the contrary.

In this chapter I will compare this world of the putains with the actual milieu they pretend to occupy. This tracing of the lines between fact and fiction serves two purposes. First, we begin to recognize the aspects of these narratives that were fictional fantasies. What exactly did the authors and their readers want their libertine utopia to entail? Then, the details that do correspond to the historical evidence concerning courtesans and other sex workers in eighteenth-century France provide information about the authors and their familiarity with the kinds of women they describe.

In the end we must, like the reader catching Thérèse accidentally using Latin, keep in mind that the putain narratives are works of fiction, libertine fantasies of empowered, sexually independent women without any responsibility to accurately depict the cultural and biological realities of their actions. Even though many aspects of these characters' lives and careers correspond to what we know about real eighteenth-century sex workers, their stories serve us best, not as snapshots of the lived experiences of eighteenth-century French courtesans, but as glimpses of a part of the collective imagination of the time. They show us how some people—in fact, a great number of people, judging from the number of reprintings necessitated by demand for the books—envisioned a libertine utopia as an alternative to the misogyny and paternalism of ancien-régime France.

Information about the lives of real eighteenth-century sex workers and the attitudes and assumptions of Parisian readers of the putain memoir novels contributes to our understanding of the putain memoirs' appeal and purpose. Readers would naturally compare the heroines of these stories to what they knew or thought they knew about real *femmes galantes* to determine which characteristics were genuine, which were exaggerated, and which were invented. In other words, what a Parisian might have found outrageous is what made the novels remarkable; what would have seemed believable is what made them powerful.

The sources of what we know about the real sex workers of eighteenth-century Paris are primarily the records of the police and institutions that regulated the illicit trade. In 1667 Louis XIV created the position of lieutenant général de police de la ville, prévôté et vicomté de Paris in order to consolidate the many competing agencies responsible for keeping order in the capital as well as to more efficiently keep an eye on the activities of elite men in the capital. Agents and officers under the lieutenant general submitted this intelligence in the form of special reports. By the middle of the eighteenth century a separate department within the police dedicated to *femmes galantes* was responsible for gathering information on the elite courtesans of Paris and their equally important clients. These efforts stemmed more from a desire to keep an eye on the men in question than to stop or inhibit this form of prostitution. Most often, madams provided the inspectors with information in a tacit exchange for their tolerance of the illegal activities of their protégées working as elite mistresses.

At the same time, other sex workers, those who had to work in brothels and acquire nonexclusive customers by walking the streets, were more frequently arrested, and our information about them comes from records of police interviews at the time of their arrest. Interestingly, the majority of the police documents about both classes of sex workers, the tolerated and the incarcerated, contained narratives of varying lengths of the woman's origins, her entrance into the trade, and often even details about her appearance, residences, and "specialties."[7] Even though the police records on Parisian prostitutes from the 1750s to the 1770s often read like putain memoirs—with detailed information about the young women's lives, economic origins, and earliest sexual experiences—the similarities between the putains of the novels and the sex workers of eighteenth-century France remain for the most part superficial.

The reports of police inspectors and the penitentiary records of la Salpêtrière prison and the hospice des vénériens (prison hospitals for venereal disease) provide useful—if sporadic—data concerning the types of women working in the sex trade from 1747 through the French Revolution. The work of contemporary journalists such as Louis-Sébastien Mercier's *Tableau de Paris* (1782), as well as the memoirs of Jean François Barbier, Giacamo Casanova, Alexandre comte de Tilly, and Jean-François Marmontel, provide further information and a sense of the cultural attitudes and contexts of the time.[8] All of these sources inform the rich and detailed studies of Erica-Marie Benabou, Nina Kushner, and Clyde Plumauzille.[9] Although their works focus on different times and facets of eighteenth-century prostitution, these three scholars have made valuable contributions to our understanding of the world in which the fictional putains appeared.

In her posthumously published *La Prostitution et la police des mœurs* (1987), Benabou relies primarily on the police records for 2,069 women arrested in Paris for prostitution in the years 1765, 1766, and 1770 to present an image of the lifestyle of sex workers in eighteenth-century France.[10] It is difficult to tell exactly how representative these snapshots are, given that estimates of the number of prostitutes in late eighteenth-century Paris vary greatly (from eighteen thousand to sixty thousand, depending on the source) for a number of reasons, including contradictory records and inconsistent definitions of "prostitute." Nevertheless, among these women she uncovers many demographic similarities to the putain narrators. For instance, only a third of the sex workers in the police records reported having been born in Paris or its suburbs. Most, like the fictional putains Thérèse and La Dumonci, came from other cities, villages, or the countryside.[11] Also, the putains are—like 87 percent of the cases in Benabou's police records—unmarried. But the motivation behind this independence is a key difference. While the unmarried heroines of the putain memoirs explicitly proclaim their refusal to marry as a way to maintain their own professional and financial independence, Benabou proposes that it was simply that the economic hardships at the time meant that few women—sex workers or not—could afford to marry in their early twenties. Perhaps for this reason, the average Parisian prostitute arrested in the second half of the century was between 22 and 26 years old—considerably older than the fictional putain at the height of her success. The real women prostituting themselves were still saving up for dowries into their mid-twenties, while the putains never express that goal; marriage was not their ambition. Furthermore, many of the memoirs end before the narrator reaches her mid- to late twenties.

In addition, real sex workers appear to have faced a more precarious and fluid financial status than the fictional putains. Benabou describes many degrees of prostitution, beginning at the bottom of their professional ladder with the poorest and dirtiest streetwalkers, "the prostitutes of back alleys and vague territories nicknamed *barboteuses* because they lived in the mud (*la boue*)" ("les prostituées des rues écartées et des terrains vagues baptisées 'barboteuses' car elles vivent dans la boue et dans la fange").[12] Then there were *raccrocheuses*, hookers, who lived in badly furnished rooms and were often the targets of police action. A slightly better quality of life was to be had by the *boucaneuses* living in a brothel but still roaming the city to solicit their own customers. Other categories in this lower zone of prostitution were the often-diseased women following regiments of soldiers and turning tricks for very little money in or near the barracks, the serving girls making extra money in the back rooms of taverns, and the daughters still living with their parents but earning a little extra money from neighborhood boys.[13]

Socially and financially above these women is the category of the *fille entretenue*, who chose her benefactor from the many wealthy men attracted to her, and who, because of the desire she inspired, held a certain power over her *entreteneur*.[14] The *filles entretenues* were usually young dancers or singers in the opera. In fact, being a singer or dancer in the opera (like being an actress) was usually reason enough for one to assume that a female performer was someone's mistress, no matter her personal behavior.[15] The *entreteneur* was her official sponsor and as such generally provided her with an apartment, food, and clothing in exchange for her favors. Being *entretenue* was usually a great accomplishment in the mercenary sex business.[16]

While achieving the status of a kept mistress was the pinnacle of an eighteenth-century sex worker's career, it rarely provided a definitive happy ending. The work and the status of women in the sex trade could vary greatly from one moment to another and change quickly. Mercier dramatizes this precariousness of a courtesan's popularity in his *Tableau de Paris*, explaining how "the fashion that raised her up comes along to change. An insignificant rival that she didn't notice, that she disdained, appears in her ranks, sparkles, eclipses her and makes everyone desert her salon. The superb courtesan, despite still having her beauty, finds herself the next year alone with immense debts. All the lovers have fled, and when her affairs are liquidated, she'll hardly have enough left to buy her shoes and her rouge." ("Mais la mode qui l'éleva, vient à changer. Une petite rivale qu'elle n'apercevait pas, qu'elle dédaignait, se met insolemment sur les rangs, brille, l'éclipse, et fait déserter son salon. La courtisane superbe, quoique ayant encore la beauté, se trouve l'année suivante seule, avec des dettes immenses. Tous les amants se sont enfuis; et quand ses affaires seront liquidées, à peine aura-t-elle de quoi payer sa chaussure et sa rouge.")[17] In the world of the putain memoirs, however, the ups and downs of their business rarely result in the kind of tragic descent from grandeur to oblivion that Mercier describes.

In fact, the fictional sex workers of the novels explored here conveniently escape many of the harsh realities Benabou depicts. Even though they sometimes work in brothels, they all acquire the coveted status of *fille entretenue*, usually with a long succession of wealthy sponsors. While they do often advertise their availability by taking long strolls through the Palais Royal and the gardens of Paris, these promenades are a long way from the open solicitation in the streets or in military camps of a *barboteuse* or *raccrocheuse*. Instead, the fictional putains live for the most part a life of luxury, with plenty of fortuitous turns of luck whenever they find themselves in a jam. Most putain narrators work independently, fleeing the control of madams or pimps the better to take charge of their labor as well as their bodies. They usually enjoy the luxury of choosing when, where, and with whom they have sex, and they refuse to grant a monopoly of their sexual favors to any one lover or sponsor. The female independence and sexual agency they exhibit openly defied the eighteenth-century social order and indeed exceeded the possibilities afforded to real prostitutes.

In *Prostitution et révolution* (2016), Clyde Plumauzille focuses on the sex trade during 1789–1804, a period after the zenith of the putain memoir's popularity, but her information nevertheless provides insight into which aspects of Parisian prostitution remained relevant through the end of the century. Her methodology is similar to Benabou's, drawing data from the intake records of women incarcerated for prostitution and venereal disease. In the same way, most of the women in her study were streetwalkers and not the more elite *filles entretenues*. The majority of the women in the records she consults were born outside of Paris, although the average age was slightly younger at the end of the century. Almost all Parisian sex workers during the Revolution were unmarried, and both Benabou and Plumauzille view this status as a temporary independence on their long but inexorable path toward marriage. According to these historians, then, the fictional putain's disdain for marriage and determination to remain independent represents a mindset that real sex workers likely would not or could not have adopted.

One of the most fascinating details about late eighteenth-century prostitutes Plumauzille reveals is their declared profession at the time of arrest. Like their predecessors, the majority of these women gave some kind of work in the textile industry (seamstress, laundress, or clothing repairer, for example), just as in earlier records. But after 1789 we find a small percentage of inmates doing something quite shocking: openly naming prostitution as their profession. Such a bold declaration, an unabashed admission, directly mirrors the key element of a putain memoir—a recognition that her sexual relationships are for money and an expression of professional self-awareness.

Plumauzille, however, sees these declarations as not quite the deliberate act of defiance of putain narrators and instead an attempt to normalize their work. Indeed, many of these women followed their declarations with a clarification that they would rather work in this way than steal. In these statements, the sex workers transformed the illicit sex they were accused of from immoral debauchery into an honest way to earn a living; in Plumauzille's words, they were "asserting their prostitution as a kind of economic means of subsistence" ("faisant valoir leur prostitution comme un mode de subsistance d'ordre économique").[18] Their open affirmations as prostitutes, devoid of any remorse, neutralize the moral stigma of prostitution; these women have nothing shameful to hide. In addition, they reveal how these women refuse to express remorse over their form of employment, and their desire "to distinguish their activities as prostitutes from other criminal activity and reinscribe it into an unfair and constraining economic system" ("se refusent à exprimer un quelconque remords [et] révèlent en outre la volonté de ces femmes de distinguer leur pratique prostitutionnelle du reste de la criminalité, et de la réinscrire dans une logique économique injuste et contraignante)."[19]

The image of eighteenth-century prostitution we find through the research of Benabou and Plumauzille is one of women in difficult situations turning to sex work out of economic necessity. The freedom to articulate their choice of illegal (and morally disdained) behavior as a professional decision to avoid truly criminal behavior was perhaps a product of the French Revolution itself and the less restrictive laws and attitudes of its early years. The information both historians present nevertheless suggests that these women chose their path reluctantly, often with no other possible alternative, and always in hopes of a respectable marriage as the happy ending toward which they are working. But given the circumstances in which these data were collected—answers to police questions upon arrest—are we to believe that these women were truly forced to have sex for money and that they sincerely hoped to marry once this unpleasant period of their lives was over?

There are clearly many reasons to believe the sincerity of this narrative. Certainly, streetwalking and turning tricks for little money were dangerous and often painful and humiliating ways to survive, and the women seized by the police were undoubtedly the profession's most vulnerable. The safety and serenity of a committed relationship with one man would certainly have appealed to them in that moment. Still, as women accused of and about to be punished for deviating from the prescribed path of feminine behavior, and standing before authority figures, it was undeniably useful to express remorse for such a digression and to reaffirm their adherence to that system. The demographic information they provide in these interviews hints at their unspoken pleas of defense, seeming to imply: "Of course I want to do what society expects, to have only legally sanctioned sex with one man who in turn protects me financially, but circumstances beyond my control prevented me. Yes, of course, I will become that monogamous wife as soon as I can." It is doubtful that an accused prostitute would look at a police official and proclaim a love of the independence she enjoys outside of marriage and her intentions to make as much money as she can from randy men.

But in the putain memoir novels, that is exactly what the heroines articulate. Even though they resemble the women of these police files in some ways—namely, in their provincial origins and their experiences with various forms of prostitution—they manifest a very different attitude than we find in those documents. The fictional putains take great pleasure and joy in their work. Whatever financial need they may feel at different times in their lives, they never turn to mercenary sex as a last alternative. Instead, they view themselves, as some revolutionary prostitutes did, as professionals engaging in a career like any other. They also emphasize the respectability of what they do, praising their own work ethic and carefully honed skills. Perhaps most importantly, the putain narrators never present themselves as victims of circumstance. They have proudly and cleverly managed to rise above the economic situation of their birth to achieve wealth and success. The libertine utopia of the novels allows women to enjoy and celebrate prostitution in a way no real sex worker would have. But it also allows for an imagined possibility of a world where the work of a prostitute is not something to be lamented and pitied, where selling her body is a form of empowerment and not degradation, and where women can escape male control through their sexuality with positive outcomes.

The closest real eighteenth-century sex workers came to the level of success, fame, and wealth the fictional putains enjoy were as *filles entretenues*, the elite prostitutes that Nina Kushner examines in *Erotic Exchanges* (2013). In this detailed study, Kushner recreates and astutely analyzes the social milieu, the Parisian demimonde, in which socially and financially privileged men paid large sums of money for relatively long-term and officially exclusive sexual relationships with women. The ways and reasons some women entered this sexual marketplace, and the people and contracts that arranged and defined their relationships, in many ways resemble the scenarios depicted in the putain memoirs.

Kushner's primary sources—case studies from the police reports of inspectors and their spies, as well as letters from madams to the police from

1747 to 1771—are in fact narratives about these kept women, and her study thus more aptly depicts the demimonde in which these women lived and worked than do Benabou's or Plumauzille's statistical analyses. Because each of the fictional putains achieved this elite status and few of them faced the dire circumstances of arrest and imprisonment of a common streetwalker for very long, *Erotic Exchanges* serves as an especially useful historical study to compare real-life eighteenth-century prostitution with the fictional accounts.

Kushner argues clearly and forcefully that the *filles entretenues* should be seen as professionals engaged in a kind of work that granted them a degree of agency and at least a "potential for financial success" at a time when alternate life paths—including the normative "marriage plot"—offered women little freedom of choice and even less control of their own sexuality.[20] The putain memoir novels present exactly this kind of professionalism, with narrators declaring their status as prostitutes and showing pride in their career choice, while also describing their skills and business savvy as crucial requirements for the job.

Another aspect of the fictional putains' professionalism is the contractual nature of their relationships. The putain and her *entreteneur* are never just two lovers who find each other, the one giving her body as a token of her love, the other generously supporting her to show his affection. These are business transactions, with explicit terms and often even written receipts. The real kept mistresses of the eighteenth-century demimonde dealt in the same kinds of contracts. Although their contracts with patrons were not written or legally enforceable, the agreements were nonetheless an essential feature of this sexual market. These verbal contracts spelled out explicitly how much financial support a patron would provide his mistress in exchange for her services, reminding all that these were still transactions of prostitution.

In addition to the professionalization of prostitution, the astonishingly formulaic narratives in the police reports recounting how these women came to be a part of the demimonde resemble in some cases the putains' stories. Two of the four categories of backstories Kushner identifies can be found in the fictional memoirs. Some women appear to have left some other form of employment to become a kept woman out of a desire to pursue, according to the police inspectors, their libidinous impulses. In the novels, Margot for one leaves her work as a clothing repairer, or *ravaudeuse*, to pursue the more lucrative, and perhaps more pleasurable, work as a prostitute. A much more common path in the memoir novels is through the girl's own parents who initiate and sometimes sell their daughters into prostitution, a practice that is also described in the inspectors' narratives. While the central question for Kushner here is about the ownership of the young woman's sexuality, in the putain narratives there is little concern about the girls' agency. Always the daughter is thrilled to be able to satisfy her urges at last, and she has no qualms about her mother (and it is always a mother brokering these deals) benefiting financially from the sale of her virginity and subsequent relationships. Once the fictional putain matures, however, she begins to chafe under the parental control and either severs her relationship with her mother completely, as Thérèse from *La Belle Allemande* does, or explicitly reverses the power dynamic and forces her mother into the subservient and dependent role in their household, as happens in *Margot la ravaudeuse* and in the first putain narrative, *Histoire de Mademoiselle Cronel.*

On the other hand, the other two categories of origin stories in the police files reflect more the sentimental novels of a virtuous girl's fall into a life of vice. The inspectors describe how some women found themselves in Paris with their virtue intact but without family connections or support. With few options, these girls quickly, but presumably reluctantly, entered the sex trade. Similarly, women of a second type naively chose to sacrifice their sexual honor—i.e., virginity—to a persuasive seducer, only to find themselves abandoned and similarly lacking in options.

These narratives of descent are not part of the putain narratives, but they do create a strong and salient critique of the marriage plot of the eighteenth century, mirroring the putains' vehement rejection of this expectation that a young woman maintain her sexual honor while employed for nearly a decade to earn her dowry. Kushner demonstrates how the examples of the young women in the police reports expose the inflexibility in this normative script, the same inflexibility prostitute narrators decry in their memoirs. For the putains, such a goal—monogamous marriage after years of chastity—simply holds no appeal. They mock the idea of true love and view marriage as an unattractive situation placing them once again under the control of a man. For the real working-class women, the marriage plot ignored the multiple vulnerabilities they faced, particularly in the urban setting of Paris.

The people in the lives of both fictional and real *filles entretenues* were also similar. Kushner looks closely at Paris's elite madams, not as working or former prostitutes themselves, but as women who brokered patron-mistress relationships and, in so doing, developed and maintained connections with clients and providers. Kushner explains, "Madams were the hubs of overlapping networks of buyers and sellers of elite sexuality."[21] These networks were not only representative of the sociability of the demimonde; they also demonstrate the support systems that women in the sex trade created, presumably in the absence of any legitimate financial or social support from the legal system or ancient-régime patriarchy. The webs of relationships in the real Parisian demimonde included male clients, but the putain memoirs emphasize the connections among the women living and working in precarious positions on the margins of society. As will be explored in chapter 5, these networks are an essential aspect of how these characters survive and thrive, as well as part of the novels' subversion of the prerevolutionary social order. Kushner posits that without the madams as intermediaries, the demimonde's networks would have come unglued. Similarly, without the networks of madams, mistresses, and their female friends, the putains might have faced some of the same vulnerabilities as real eighteenth-century sex workers did.

Both the fictional putains and their real-world counterparts enjoy another important relationship: liaisons with *greluchons*, the boyfriends who enjoyed their sexual favors without having to pay. In both contexts, these relationships reveal even more ways in which these women were able to exercise a greater level of agency in their lives. Sometimes these men were not only exempt from paying but also financially supported by the women in exchange for sex—a direct inversion of the usual gender dynamics of elite prostitution. Kushner's observation that the mistresses occupied a unique position in which they could also be patrons (with all the power and emotional and financial vulnerabilities that position implied) applies equally well to the fictional putains.

Unfortunately, *Erotic Exchanges* does not provide much information concerning the private daily lives of the demimonde's kept women. Clearly, the police records have little to say about the interests and opinions of kept women. For instance, what did they do when they weren't working? Did they have hobbies? Did they ever express opinions about their clients or other women? Did they form meaningful friendships with each other or with other women (or men)? These are the kinds of questions the police reports do not answer. The putain memoirs, on the other hand, relish in providing these details. Of course, the accuracy of the activities and amusing anecdotes we find in the novels is doubtful. Chances are slim that the authors knew of real examples of women capable of humiliating wealthy and influential men with the kind of impunity the putain narrators enjoy. Although the novels reflect many aspects of what we now know about the *femmes galantes* they purported to reveal, the unlikely events they recount help us see those details as halfhearted attempts at verisimilitude offered with a wink and a nod.

And who would have enjoyed the exaggerated sexuality and clever subversions in the putain memoirs? Who would have appreciated the kernels of truth mixed with fictional characters and adventures? As Robert Darnton explains in *Forbidden Best-Sellers of Prerevolutionary France* (1995), it is difficult to determine exactly who sold, purchased, and read illegal texts produced on the clandestine presses and circulated with relative secrecy.[22] Some publishers kept sporadic records of what they sold and to whom, but given the illegality of these novels, many transactions certainly went undocumented. Furthermore, novels could be lent to friends and read aloud to an audience in taverns and inns. Consequently, recorded sales of a text do not necessarily reflect the only people reading it.

In eighteenth-century France the difference between an officially sanctioned book and a banned text involved several degrees of illegality. Legal books received increasingly restricted permission from the king, ranging from the *privilège* to a simple *tolérance*. Other works were unequivocally forbidden. Not surprisingly, all the putain memoirs fell into this category and were printed outside France and smuggled across the border to booksellers. Enterprises like the Société typographique de Neuchâtel would receive orders from individual bookstores asking for illegal books to be mixed in with their legitimate orders, and because books were usually shipped unbound, the illegal ones were often hidden within the pages of a legal work. But there are few records of who purchased the books from the booksellers. The catalogs of the libraries of some well-known and wealthy book collectors are somewhat informative, but it is hard to say what members of the general public were buying and reading these novels.

From the details contained in the novels, however, we can surmise certain qualities about the intended reader of the putain memoirs. These narrators appeal in many ways to heterosexual male fantasies of female sexuality, and thus appear to target male readers. The putains are women with large sexual appetites who generally prefer having sex with men and describe ecstatic pleasures from penetrative sex. On the other hand, they just as often depict disappointing, dissatisfying, and even disturbing encounters with old, unattractive, and licentious male clients. Further, several putains express in sincere and cogent philosophical digressions their frustration with the unfair advantages men enjoy to the detriment of women. Thus, the perspective of these novels cannot be seen as purely masculinist or feminist, and it would appear that many male and female readers would have enjoyed the stories.

Given the realistic aspects of the novels, such as the plausible introduction to prostitution through a parent, the networks of mutual assistance, and the relationships with *greluchons*, the target audience presumably would also include members of the Parisian demimonde, who would be familiar with those details. Still, because most *entreteneurs*, especially the more powerful and well-connected ones, are the butts of jokes and the victims of pranks and exploitation by the putains, one imagines the ideal reader existing just on the margins of this society. Certainly, the status of an outsider, familiar with an exclusive group but not quite able to enjoy all the benefits, coincides with what we know about the authors of the novels. They too appeared to exist on the edges of the Enlightenment's literary circles and the tight-knit communities of salon culture. The examples of the probable authors of two of the novels examined here are representative.

The author of *La Belle Allemande, ou Les Galanteries de Thérèse*, Antoine Bret, was born in Dijon in 1717; like many of the putains, he arrived in Paris from the provinces as an adult. Even at first glance, it is clear that Bret was familiar with the circles of the Republic of Letters. He was perhaps best known for his 1773 edition of Molière's plays, *Œuvres de Molière, Avec des remarques grammaticales, des avertissements et des observations sur chaque pièce*, which was republished seven more times by the end of the century. His authority on this subject was most likely due to his prolific work in the theater, composing at least seventeen plays, mostly comedies, many performed by the Comédie française. His theatrical works were collected in five different anthologies.[23] Bret also wrote two essays of literary criticism, *Essai de contes moraux et dramatiques* (1765) and *Essai d'une poétique à la mode* (1770). Furthermore, his work as a royal censor, determining which manuscripts would receive the royal seal to permit their publication, implies a trust from the authorities and a professional legitimacy.

But the praise he received at the time of his death hints subtly at a lack of respect for his literary work. The *Almanach littéraire, ou Étrennes d'Apollon pour l'année 1793* eulogized him a year after his demise as "an enlightened man, a good citizen, a modest writer, a good and faithful friend. He had a pure, virtuous, and sensitive soul. His heart was unchanging. He was never tortured by envy nor tempted by satire." ("Un homme éclairé, un bon citoyen, un auteur modeste, un bon et fidèle ami. Son âme était pure, vertueuse et sensible. Son cœur ne se démentit pas un instant. Jamais l'envie ne le tourmenta, jamais la satire ne lui plut.")[24] This praise seems to have stemmed more from his engagement in and support for the Revolution than from any genuine admiration for his writing; he receives nine compliments about his character and only one mention of him as a ("modest") writer.

Despite the number of collections of his theatrical works, his plays, mostly comedies, are not well known today, and it is not clear who collected his plays into the numerous anthologies: admirers, friends, or himself. Whether his works of theater were successes or not, his work in erotic fiction certainly placed him in a less than favorable light. In addition to *La Belle Allemande*, and his two Grecian courtesan memoirs, *Cythéride, Histoire galante, traduite du grec* (1743) and *Lycoris, ou La Courtisane grecque* (1746), he also composed another libertine novel, *Le B*** [bidet], histoire bavarde* (1748), which saw three more editions in the following six years.[25] Subsequently, he enjoyed a similar success with his 1751 *Mémoires sur la vie de Mademoiselle de Lenclos* (first published in Amsterdam), which was reprinted seven times. This text, despite its title, is not a memoir novel like *La Belle Allemande*, but a biography with third-person narration based on Bret's research. Lenclos was an admired *salonnière*, but she was nevertheless better known as a courtesan who enjoyed several relationships with important aristocrats including the cousin of Louis XIV, known as Le Grand Condé, and François, duc de la Rochefoucauld. Bret's choice of such a subject, and his seemingly ill-fitting categorization of this work as a memoir, point to his probable interest in and experience with prostitute narratives.

The image of Antoine Bret that emerges from these few facts is of a nice but mediocre dramatist, working as a sort of literary government functionary and writing racy stories on the side. Another historical footnote further cements his place among—but not really accepted by—the literary elite of the salons. In the 1967 edition of Françoise de Graffigny's *Lettres d'une Péruvienne* (1747), editor Gianni Nicoletti asserts that Antoine Bret was not only supposedly Graffigny's last great (and probably chaste) love but also the author of the historical introduction added to her novel for its 1752 edition.[26] Nicoletti offers no evidence to support this claim, and other scholars who subscribe to this theory cite only Nicoletti as their source. Even if Bret was the author of this important addition, the fact that no one gave him credit at the time, or since, is a good indication of his secondary status among the elite.

Even though Antoine Bret is generally recognized as the author of the anonymously published *La Belle Allemande*, some sources cite another writer: Claude Villaret.[27] Villaret was born in 1715 in Paris, where he is said to have dissipated his youth instead of studying to be a lawyer as his family intended. He began writing libertine and satirical texts, including a pamphlet targeting a number of well-known writers and actors entitled *Prédictions générales et particulières pour l'année 1741* and most famously a satire of Samuel Richardson's *Pamela* called *L'Antipaméla, ou Mémoires de M. D**** (1742). The authors targeted in the *Prédictions générales* included Voltaire, Marivaux, and Prévost. The entry on Villaret for the *Biographie* *universelle ancienne et moderne* expresses doubt that this pamphlet or any of the other "mediocre productions" attributed to Villaret in his early career were indeed his work. In the case of the *Prédictions*, the biographer is even suspicious of Villaret's name appearing on copies of the pamphlet, using the ambiguous phrase, "His name was written on some copies." ("On a écrit son nom sur des exemplaires.")[28]

After leaving Paris in 1748 because of financial problems, Villaret fell in love with an actress and joined the theater, performing under the name Dorval to some success in the provinces, and became the director of an acting troupe in Liège in 1756. In 1759 he left the theater and returned to Paris, where he wrote *Considérations sur l'art du théâtre*, a response to Rousseau's *Lettre à M. d'Alembert sur les spectacles* (1758), as well as a compilation of quotes called *L'Esprit de Monsieur de Voltaire*. Villaret seems to have left his youthful rebelliousness behind as he matured. Some friends helped him attain a post at the *Chambre des comptes* where he was tasked with reorganizing the archives, which had been partially destroyed by a fire in 1738. From this work he developed into a serious historian, continuing the work of Paul François Velly on the *Histoire de France depuis l'établissement de la monarchie jusqu'au règne de Louis XIV.* Unfortunately, by 1766 Villaret was suffering from severe urinary retention, and wounded himself one day while inserting a catheter. This wound became infected, and he died three days later.

Both Bret and Villaret would have been just under thirty years old when *La Belle Allemande* was first published, and both men appear to have begun their literary careers with libertine works before moving on to more serious endeavors. Furthermore, Bret and Villaret actually knew each other in Paris. They collaborated on a one-act comedy written in verse, *Le Quartier d'hiver*, presented at the Théâtre-Français in 1743. It stands to reason, then, that *La Belle Allemande* may very well have been another joint effort by Villaret and Bret. At the very least, it is quite possible that the true author may have shared an early manuscript or at least discussed the project with his colleague. Whatever their relationship, both potential authors would have been familiar enough with the demimonde to be able to produce a text that would appeal to its readers.

The putain author about whom we know the most is *Margot la ravaudeuse*'s Fougeret de Monbron.[29] An irascible misanthrope born in 1706, Louis Charles Fougeret de Monbron was the second son of an affluent provincial tax collector in the region around Péronne. A member of the nouveau riche, thanks to his father's position and successful speculation in the *système de Law*, Fougeret had the means to join the exclusive *gardes du corps du roi* (the household cavalry of the king), and later purchased the position *valet de chambre ordinaire du roi*, which he sold at a profit just a few years later. This financial acumen, plus his share of an inheritance from his father, gave him the means to travel and write for the rest of his life, without concern for the success of his work.

Fougeret's first publication, *Discours sur la volupté* (1740), hints at his interest in libertine writing, and his next reveals his access to more respectable literary circles. His *Le Canapé couleur de feu* (1741) employs the same conceit as Crébillon fils's *Le Sopha, conte moral* (1742): an enchanted sofa recounts the amorous encounters it has witnessed and the secrets it has learned.[30] Even though Fougeret's *Le Canapé* appeared before *Le Sopha*, it was generally believed that Fougeret had plagiarized an early manuscript of Crébillon's story and not the other way around.

After a six-week stay in England, Fougeret was apparently proficient enough in English to translate into French *La Chronique des rois d'Angleterre*,[31] published in England in 1743. This translation was also highly criticized, this time for Fougeret's decision to abandon the serious tone appropriate for history, instead choosing a "burlesque" style.[32] Fougeret's next translation, *Histoire de l'expédition de l'amiral Byng dans la Sicile en 1718, 1719 et 1720* (1744), was more acceptable, sufficiently serious to earn the privilège from the royal censors. That same year Fougeret's penchant for biting satire becomes evident. Louis XV's miraculous recovery from a near-death illness the year before inspired a spate of odes celebrating the king and his health. The next year the cantankerous but always incisive Fougeret highlighted the sycophantic monotony of these hollow tributes in two satirical odes, "Ode dans le goût des autres" and "Discours prononcé au Roi par un paysan de Chaillot."[33]

Fougeret's gift for satire was only beginning to blossom, however. In 1745 Fougeret took on none other than Voltaire with a parody of his epic poem *La Henriade* entitled *La Henriade travestie*. In fact, when Madame de Graffigny became aware of the manuscript for Fougeret's parody, she asked a mutual friend, the Abbé Pérau, to convince the satirist to include a preface praising Voltaire to demonstrate that there was no ill will. Graffigny hoped an apologetic preface "where Voltaire will be made to understand that he is not the object of critique" would soften the blow ("où on lui fera sentir que ce n'est point lui que l'on critique").[34] A friend of Graffigny's, François-Antoine Devaux, wrote to her expressing a similar concern, wondering what his *idole* would think of the satire: "My God, what will my poor idol say? Will he be able to find enough walls to bang his head on?" ("Mon Dieu, que dira mon pauvre Idole? Trouvera-t-il assez de murs pour se cogner la tête?").[35]

Fougeret, of course, refused to undertake any form of appeasement or apology, but Voltaire evidently had a good sense of humor about the "homage." While Voltaire's immediate reaction to Fougeret's satire is unclear, Élie-Cathérine Fréron reports in *l'Année littéraire* in 1756 that Voltaire laughed while reading the parody. ("[Voltaire] lui-même avait ri en lisant cette parodie.")[36] On the other hand, Madame de Graffigny recalls how an angry Voltaire responded to a reminder that even Virgil had been satirized with the dry comment that in Virgil's place he would not have been offended, but that he was not sure how Virgil would have reacted in his. ("On a dit à Voltaire, qui se fâchait, que l'on avait travesti Virgile. Il a répondu que, s'il était à sa place, il n'en aurait pas fait plus de bruit, mais qu'il ignorait ce que Virgile aurait pensé s'il était à la sienne.")[37] Nevertheless, she reports that when the prestigious author ran into his impersonator on the steps of the Comédie shortly after the publication of *La Henriade travestie*, the two greeted each other politely. ("Ils ont fait connaissance avec beaucoup de politesse.")[38] These anecdotes of literary gossip provide a glimpse of Fougeret de Monbron's relationship with and attitudes toward the literary elite. The author of *Le Canapé couleur de feu* and *La Henriade travestie* was clearly familiar with important and famous figures but lacked the kind of deference to leaders that would have earned him true acceptance within their circles.

Fougeret spent the next few years traveling and chronicling his voyages in a manuscript that he would later publish as *Le Cosmopolite, ou le Citoyen du Monde* (1750). It was also during these years (1745–1748) that he composed *Margot la ravaudeuse* and encountered John Cleland's *Memoirs of a Woman of Pleasure*. His abridged translation of the novel, entitled *La Fille de joie, Ouvrage quintessencié de l'anglais*, was published in 1751, two years after the original English text, and is one of the most widely read putain memoirs of the century.

The last decade of Fougeret de Monbron's life saw more traveling, two new major works, and a brief stay in the Bastille prison. In 1757 he published *Le Préservatif contre l'anglomanie*, denouncing the English culture he had once admired, and this work was quite successful at that particular moment, the start of the Seven Years War against England. But lest anyone think Fougeret was overcome with patriotic zeal, his *La Capitale des Gaules, ou La Nouvelle Babylone* took aim at Paris just two years later. When Fougeret de Monbron died in 1760, he left his entire fortune of over 8,000 livres and all his possessions (including his manuscripts and papers) to his illiterate servant Marie-Françoise Duval—minus 10 livres to each of his family members. His contemporaries and scholars view this final act of defiance against society's expectations as a fitting reflection of Fougeret's attitudes and philosophy in life.

Clearly, then, Fougeret de Monbron had access to the respectable literary society that included Crébillon fils and the friends of Madame de Graffigny, but through his own choices or because of personality conflicts he remained outside of those circles. Like Bret and Villaret, his personal life was one in which he would have certainly encountered many *femmes galantes*, both the kind who worked in brothels and more elite courtesans. In fact, Fougeret recounts conversations with many prostitutes in his memoirs, *Le Cosmopolite*. Certainly, the writer's firsthand knowledge of the demimonde and its women supplied the credible elements in his putain memoir.

Whatever we may speculate about authorial intent, and whatever realistic attributes we find in the putains, their narratives remain philosophical articulations unconstrained by realistic outcomes. They are utopian visions that do not fully think through the implications of the materialist philosophy they employ. Like the simulated pleasures the putains enact to flatter their customers, these stories are designed to elicit a reaction. They play with illusions and dissimulations to make pointed critiques. The putain memoirs are fictions of pleasure: the pleasure the narrators find in telling their stories, the pleasure the readers find in the details of their sex lives, and the pleasure the authors found in cleverly mocking the social hierarchies and institutions that limited their potential.

3

La Belle Allemande, or The Empire of Beauty

Despite the many details in the putain memoirs that accurately depict the demimonde of eighteenth-century Paris, these texts are almost certainly all works of fiction. From the deliberate disruption of verisimilitude in instances such as Thérèse's admission that she forgot she does not know Latin after quoting Virgil, to the general implausibility of the narrators' endless escapades and the fortuitous turns of events that resolve them, the putain memoirs contain countless reminders that they are indeed fiction.

These stories cannot, however, be dismissed as mere entertainment. Between the titillating scenes and hyperbolic exclamations lie biting social critiques of the ineffective nobility and the unjust distribution of wealth and power in ancien-régime France. In this chapter I will explore how one of the putain narrators, *La Belle Allemande*'s Thérèse, reveals these weaknesses in her society by exploiting them for her benefit. While her indictment of patriarchal power is common in all the putain memoirs, Thérèse is exceptional in her lengthy and explicit reflections on how she usurps that power and the ways she uses it. No other putain narrator directly questions the value of family lineage, ridicules wealthy and noble men, and comments on her own sexual power over the men she seduces in quite the way Thérèse does. Furthermore, it could be argued that, as one of the earliest putain memoirs, this novel helped establish the genre as a vehicle for expressing political discontent up to the Revolution.

La Belle Allemande's indictments of eighteenth-century injustices are so successful and memorable because of the novel's uniquely irreverent tone and deliberately hyperbolic humor. Thérèse's vanity is ever on display, despite halfhearted objections to the contrary. In fact, it is the almost self-deprecating quality of her descriptions of her adventures and people's reactions to her that lends credibility to all her assertions. If the narrator is in on the joke of how silly and vain she is, we can trust her to see through the superficial subterfuges of other people as well. Nowhere is this narrative style, and its strategic use to highlight power dynamics, on better display than in the scene where Thérèse first attends the opera. With effusive glee that barely masks her shrewd analysis, Thérèse describes the sensation she causes as she steps into the auditorium to take her seat:

> As soon as I was seated, I became the object of the attention of all the professional onlookers. . . . I was not immune to the sweetness of seeing myself the object of such tender curiosity. . . . I was too attentive to the various movements I was causing to pay attention to the show. Several lords came to my loge to compliment me and to proposition me. One could understandably become vain from less. I had gained everyone's approval without having to beg for it. I felt like I was in the middle of a harem of men destined for my pleasure, where I had all the power of a sultan to toss my handkerchief at the lucky man who appealed to me. I found this experience so much to my liking that I decided to continue, since all the brilliant society of the opera were sighing for me. I made some of them happy.
>
> (Dès que je fus placée, je devins le but de tous les lorgneurs de profession. . . . J'étais sensible à la douceur de me voir l'objet d'une tendre curiosité. . . . J'étais trop attentive aux mouvements que j'excitais pour m'occuper du spectacle. Plusieurs seigneurs vinrent me complimenter dans ma loge et me faire des propositions. On pourrait sans injustice être vaine à moins. J'avais enlevé presque tous les suffrages de l'assemblée, sans les avoir mendiés. Je me figurais d'être dans un sérail d'hommes destinés à mes plaisirs, où je pouvais commander en sultane et jeter le mouchoir à celui qui aurait le bonheur de me rendre sensible. Je me trouvai si bien de cet essai, que je continuai; tout le monde brillant de l'opéra soupira pour moi. Je fis des heureux.)[1]

In summing up this experience she says, "I had the glory of seeing at my feet illustrious heads that didn't blush at forgetting their grandeur in my presence. I understood better than ever before that there is nothing in the world above a pretty woman, and that the empire of beauty knows no bounds." ("J'eus la gloire de voir à mes pieds des têtes illustres, qui ne rougirent pas d'oublier leurs grandeurs en ma présence. Je compris mieux que je n'avais fait jusqu'alors qu'il n'y a rien dans le monde au-dessus d'une jolie femme et que l'empire de la beauté ne connaît point de bornes.")[2]

These last two sentences express both the source and the means of the putains' subversions of ancien-régime patriarchy: the empire of beauty. In this passage we find a vertical hierarchy as in eighteenth-century France, but with the order inverted: a woman occupies the top with nothing above her, and the men who usually enjoy prestige and *grandeur* place their heads at her feet, bowing before her. With the corporeal imagery of feet and heads as a reminder that the putain's power comes from her body, we see the men under her spell reduced to purely physical beings at the mercy of their sexual desires. They lose all ability to think rationally; their minds cannot even remember their illustrious and grand positions. Interestingly, these men cannot even control whether they blush or not, a trick the putains often use to feign modesty and manipulate men. Finally, we note that the power Thérèse holds is an empire, not a kingdom. Her authority is like that of a Caesar (or later, Napoleon): the product of victories and popular appeal, and not through a passive inheritance of a divine-right monarchy. This passage begins with her glory and ends with her boundless empire, both of which are her deserved rewards in the libertine utopia of the putain memoirs.[3]

In this chapter I will explore how Thérèse, representative of all the putain narrators, performs this coup d'état. She harnesses what she calls "beauty"—her ability to arouse desire and give pleasure—into a source of power, replacing the unjust and ineffective source of power in ancien-régime society: noble birth. Throughout her story Thérèse undermines the value of the family, a concept at the very foundation of the aristocracy's privileges and, indeed, patriarchy. The powerful nobleman and the authoritarian parent have done nothing to deserve the power they exert over others, and in the world of the putain memoirs, an unearned power is an illegitimate one. On the other hand, the putains and the attractive young men they desire deserve to enjoy power, both because of how they achieve it—by generating pleasure for themselves and others—and in how they use it—to reverse certain inequities and redistribute wealth. In Thérèse's lighthearted and often tongue-in-cheek memoir, we find seriously subversive passages espousing the virtues to be found in all social classes. In her relationships and escapades, we encounter fathers, aristocrats, and wealthy (but miserly) non-nobles who prove to be metaphorically and often literally impotent.

The empire Thérèse describes and the benefits she enjoys through her career are in direct conflict with the political and social order of her time. Even though in the eighteenth century the term "patriarchy" would not have been understood in the sense of a male-dominated society, the modern definitions of the term aptly describe ancien-régime France.[4] Patriarchy indicates a society in which men enjoy disproportionate political, economic, religious, and familial power and authority. In early modern France, the patriarchal system relied upon three principles to justify and perpetuate this male domination. Firstly, power and privilege were benefits passed down within families from generation to generation. Therefore, one's birth and ancestry were vitally important. Secondly, crucial to ensuring filial obedience in all its forms was a tacit and universal belief that paternal figures—father, husbands, aristocrats, and ultimately the king—somehow deserved their power. Presumably, God chose the patriarchs of eighteenth-century France, by allowing them to be born the right sex, to the right family, at the right time, and they maintained their authority through a general trust in their strong leadership and wise decisions. Finally, strict social barriers between members of different classes were necessary to reinforce this hierarchy. Certainly, by the time of the putain memoir novels in the mid-1700s, those boundaries had already begun to blur considerably. The proliferation of the nobility of the robe and the growing wealth of many non-noble families through banking and commerce had created tensions that would only increase as the century progressed. Nevertheless, as the spring and summer of 1789 would reveal, the medieval social structure of three distinct estates—the clergy, the nobility, and everyone else—remained steadfast.

The putain memoirs attack these foundations in multiple ways. Most obviously, the narrators explicitly state that birth and ancestry have no importance. They demonstrate this disdain through their words and actions, defying parental authority, eschewing the paths of marriage and motherhood, ridiculing nobles and fathers, assisting powerless younger men, and engaging in intimate contact with members of all classes equally. The result is an image of French patriarchy as illegitimate and crumbling from its own incompetence. In its place emerges a meritocracy where a person of any sex or class can develop the necessary skills to earn legitimate power and prosperity. The putains' independence and sexual autonomy are not a threat to this fictional world, but instead aspects of a freedom that leads to the greater public good.

The success of a putain like Thérèse, however, is not immediate. Thérèse recounts her education in prostitution and sexual manipulation starting with the lessons of her mother. Thérèse is born with striking beauty and a libidinous nature, both qualities she considers herself fortunate to have inherited from her mother. When Thérèse begins to mature, her mother realizes how lucrative her looks can be for the family, and she begins to find customers. From her birthplace near the German border, Thérèse and her family move to Paris, where her physical attributes can be best appreciated and where she is less likely to run out of fresh clients. In Paris, Thérèse works in various brothels between engagements with *entreteneurs* who consistently demand her fidelity. Monogamy proves difficult for the lusty Thérèse, who gains and loses numerous clients until she falls in love with a handsome young neighbor midway through her narrative.

Once Thérèse falls in love, she refuses to serve the customers her mother finds for her. Her lover helps her hide from her furious mother in a convent for a while, and she only returns to work when her lover breaks off the relationship to protect his reputation. After this episode, Thérèse becomes a true professional, determined to never again be swayed by emotion. She recounts her further adventures, including the *entreteneur* who insists that she wear a chastity belt, a wild orgy, and her resulting brief and benign encounter with syphilis. Through well-managed infidelities, Thérèse consistently outsmarts the wealthy and powerful men who believe themselves to be in control of the situation and of her body. She is unrepentant and enjoys her lifestyle immensely, ending the novel with a "satisfaction that [she] will not even try to describe" ("une satisfaction que je n'entreprendrai point de décrire").[5]

Thérèse's story depicts success and fulfillment from a lifestyle that rejects all the prescribed behaviors for a woman of her age and social class, a lifestyle completely at odds with the patriarchal society of early modern France. She insists, like many of the other putain narrators, that her achievements are the result her own talents, wit, and skills, and not from any inherited privileges. In fact, the narrators of the putain memoirs often explicitly disparage the importance of family lineage. Heredity and genealogy, which determined social class in the ancien régime and were crucial criteria for marriage, hold no value for the putains. Most of them begin their memoirs with a refusal to give a listing of their ancestors. Likewise, Thérèse asserts that her family history is of no importance:

> It's completely up to me to give myself an illustrious origin. . . . The clergy, the nobility of the robe, the nobility of the sword, don't they each have as much claim to polish up the obscurity of my heritage (or of anyone else's)? But I wouldn't think of imposing on them. Although I am ambitious and vain, the object of my vanity is nothing as fragile as the advantages of a mysterious birth. A beautiful woman has neither ancestors nor descendants; she herself composes her whole family. Her charms make her noble. A few well-organized intrigues, infidelities conducted with skill, rapid and tumultuous passions, a perpetual series of pleasures, a brilliant fortune, twenty lovers ruined for her: those are her titles, and I don't want any others.
>
> (Il ne tiendrait qu'à moi de me donner une origine illustre. . . . Le clergé, la robe et l'épée ne m'offrent-ils pas aussi bien qu'aux autres de quoi vernir l'obscurité de ma race? Mais je ne prétends pas en imposer. Ambitieuse, et vaine, ma vanité n'a pas pour objet quelque chose d'aussi fragile que les

avantages d'une naissance chimérique. Une jolie femme n'a ni aïeux, ni descendants: elle compose elle seule toute sa famille; ses charmes font sa noblesse: des intrigues bien ménagées, quelques infidélités conduites avec art, des passions rapides et tumultueuses, une suite perpétuelle de plaisirs, une fortune brillante, vingt amants ruinés pour elle, voilà ses titres, je n'en veux pas d'autre.)[6]

What begins as an amusing reference to her mother's promiscuity at the time of her conception becomes an assertion of individual self-worth. Usually one's lineage depends on a father recognizing his offspring, but this putain takes that power for herself. As an author, she can give herself any origin she wishes. She composes her own family in two senses: she alone is the whole content of her family tree, and as a writer she composes her family by choosing to include whomever she wants.

In addition, the advantages of such titles are fragile when compared to a courtesan's charms and her skillful management of lucrative affairs. As she lists the "beautiful woman's" titles, she begins with what the putain does—managing intrigues and carefully conducting her infidelities—and ends with the benefits she enjoys: passion, pleasure, fortune, and ruined lovers (who bolster her reputation). In the eyes of the putain and in the world of these novels, the prostitute's titles are stronger than those of the nobility because she has earned them.[7]

By deliberately refusing to comment on her ancestry and heritage, the putain devalues a crucial part of social hierarchy in eighteenth-century France. Members of the nobility justified their privileges by knowing and asserting who their ancestors were. By rendering pedigree meaningless, Thérèse shows that unlike the aristocrats, the putain's success is based on personal merit (beauty), hard work (careful manipulation of male desire into financial support), and luck (but not the luck of a noble birth).

In addition to dismissing the significance of their ancestors, the narrators of the putain memoirs lead independent lives, rebelling against parental authority and refusing to give up their autonomy for a husband. After years under the tutelage of her mother/procuress, Thérèse savors the liberation she feels when her mother moves back to the provinces. She explains: "I found myself free, and I could follow my inclinations without being constrained. I was beginning to get tired of the dependence in which I had been living up until then, and I thought it was high time I left wardship and became my own guardian." ("Je me trouvais libre, and je pouvais suivre mes inclinations sans être contrainte. Je commençais à me lasser de la dépendance dans laquelle j'avais vécu jusqu'alors, et je trouvais enfin qu'il était temps de sortir de tutelle, and de me gouverner par moi-même.")[8] Her phrasing in this passage is key. While Thérèse first suggests that her mother chose to leave Paris, and she simply opted to stay in the capital, she quickly reframes this change in residences as an act of self-emancipation. She is dissatisfied with having to obey and chooses to leave the situation where she was given orders. In fact, in the original French she decides to "govern herself." This moment thus represents more than a coming of age: Thérèse is seizing the power to govern from the parental, and thus patriarchal, source of authority. Her wresting this control from the patriarchal order is proven a legitimate seizure by the fact that she makes better use of it. Thérèse uses her sexuality, not to unite families or to continue a family line through reproduction, but to undermine social boundaries and work toward the greater good.

Before Thérèse's mother becomes an onerous authority figure, she is a wise and useful mentor, teaching her daughter the secrets of seduction and the tricks of the trade. The kind of mothering she models bears no resemblance to the ideal of a nurturing mother instilling virtue in her children like so many other literary heroines. That kind of maternal influence is generally absent in libertine novels, where we find proxy mothers like Madame C . . . in *Thérèse philosophe*, Madame de Merteuil in *Les Liaisons dangereuses* (1782), and Madame de Saint-Ange in Sade's *Philosophie dans le boudoir*. The biological mother initiating her daughter into a libertine lifestyle, as Thérèse's does, is a deeper indictment of the supposed natural virtue of maternal care, and a unique feature of many of the putain memoirs.

Unlike Madame de Volanges in *Les Liaisons dangereuses* and Eugénie's mother in Sade's *Philosophie dans le boudoir*—that is, mothers who simply fail to preserve their daughters' virtue—the putains' mothers often help them enter the sphere of libertinage and start them on the path that will bring their daughters satisfaction and sex.[9] Even the putains who do not have mothers actively instructing them and finding clients for them can credit their mothers for their path to prostitution, even if it was an unwitting influence. Sometimes the putain's mother is absent, having died young or being too occupied with other concerns to pay much attention to her daughter.[10] Like many young women in libertine novels, the putains are also good at finding mentors and other "pseudo-mothers" to instruct them in the ways of the demimonde and prostitution.[11] In the world of the putain memoirs these madams, neighbors, and other female friends who connect the inexperienced putains with interested clients are more fairy godmother than wicked corruptors.

On the other hand, motherhood itself holds no appeal for the putains, even those with the example of a savvy and pleasure-seeking maternal figure. As we will explore in chapter 6, very few of the putains ever become pregnant—a surprising detail, considering their vast number of sexual encounters with men. Of the thirteen prostitute heroines of the genre, only three ever have children, and none of those mothers devotes any attention to her child.

The fact that the putains are not mothers directly opposes a vision of womanhood that held increasing popular appeal throughout the century. The heroine of Rousseau's *La Nouvelle Héloïse* becomes an exemplary wife and mother, and even sacrifices her own life to save her child. Similarly, in his educational treatise *Émile, ou De l'éducation* (1762), Rousseau describes Sophie, meant to be the ideal mate for Émile; Sophie receives an education that will best prepare her for her natural destiny as a wife and mother. Before Rousseau, there was the powerful literary example of the strong mother Madame de Chartres in *La Princesse de Clèves* (1678), who successfully instilled a love of virtue in her daughter. And the well-known letters of the real Madame de Sévigné to her daughter are a testament to maternal concern and affection. After Rousseau, readers encountered the cautionary tale of *Les Liaisons dangereuses*'s Madame de Volanges, who allowed her daughter to befriend Madame de Merteuil with disastrous consequences. In this case, the critical importance of a mother's role is underlined in the tragic failure of Madame de Volanges.

The valorization and praise of motherhood is sometimes seen as granting women an elevated status as the eighteenth century progressed.[12] As mothers who can instill a love of virtue in their children, women escape the misogynist stereotype of dangerous and immoral temptresses, doomed since Eve to lead men into wickedness and sin. Instead, the image of the nurturing mother as the source of virtue grants the women the power not only to save the souls of their own children but to ensure the smooth functioning of society as a whole.

On the other hand, the emphasis on women as mothers also isolated them in the domestic sphere to perform maternal duties rather than enjoy direct participation in the economy or in the political developments of the period. We will look in chapter 4 at how the putains resist that isolation and facilitate their own direct participation in the economy. In the meantime, it is enough to recognize that the putain memoirs were written during a period when motherhood was increasingly becoming seen as not only a noble occupation for women but their sole function.

When the putain narrators reject marriage and motherhood, they are removing themselves from the patriarchal matrix. Without the guidance and control of a father, then a husband, they should, according to the thought, have become lost, marginalized, and without resources, victims of their own sexuality. But instead these women thrive on their own. They are better managers of their lives than any potential husband would have been, and certainly better than their own bumbling fathers.

Thérèse for one does not know who her biological father was; her mother could only narrow the possibilities down to seven men, and both father figures in Thérèse's life are inept and unhelpful. Her mother's husband at the time of Thérèse's birth is a baker in his seventies who is repeatedly cuckolded, from his wedding day on, but good-naturedly "adopts" all of his wife's children by other men. After a few years, Thérèse's mother leaves this man she calls her "stupid husband" and moves from Colmar to Metz. There she meets another man and begins a "second marriage," deliberately mocking the institution and sacrament, since her legal husband was still living back in Colmar. Thérèse's new stepfather is equally ridiculous, a language teacher whose "French was as bad as his German," and he figures in the story only once, when he gets into a fight with their neighbors and the family must move, forcing Thérèse to end a lucrative relationship with a wealthy financier.

Not only are the patriarchs of the putains' families incompetent, the social and economic powerholders in France at large are even more so. In the world of the putain memoirs, wealthy older men such as aging nobles, avaricious financiers, and disdained fathers enjoy undeserved, illegitimate privileges that the putains happily usurp. The putains' critiques of these men, like their subversions, are, not surprisingly, always sexual in nature, painting the men as impotent in both senses of the word. Unlike other criticisms of the monarchs and the nobles, which express outrage at the sexual debauchery of the aristocracy, the problem with the nobles in these novels is not what they are doing, but instead how they are doing it. Having a lot of sex is not a fault in the world of the putain memoirs; being a dissatisfying lover, however, is unforgivable. Over and over the putains meet extraordinarily rich and titled men with atrocious appearances and sexual dysfunctions. Such men who cannot inspire the putains' desire do not receive their respect or trust.

The debauched nobleman rendered impotent from years of self-indulgence is a recurring theme in the putain memoirs, and the heroines never try to hide from their readers their scorn for these men. One of Thérèse's first encounters with such a man is at Madame G***'s brothel, where she attempts to satisfy a *grand homme*, or nobleman, and describes his unresponsive body, calling it a "skeleton I was given to revive [from] an extremely deep sleep" ("le squelette qu'on m'avait donné à ranimer avait le sommeil extrêmement dur").[13] Her descriptions of men like this customer abound with images of death and frigidity from overuse and exhaustion, in stark contrast to other men's flames of passion. With this man she notices that "a deathly cold seemed to have taken over his soul, and [she] despaired of being able to melt this ice" ("un froid mortel semblait avoir entrepris son âme, et je désespérais de réussir à fondre la glace").[14] In an even more graphic description, Thérèse refers to the wealthy marquis de R . . . as an "octogenarian Adonis whose soul remembers being voluptuous." Thérèse describes at length his pathetic frustrations with his inability to find satisfaction: "Reduced to having to be content with the prestige of a contemplative love, his heart searched unceasingly for the way to ignite his burnt-out desires. In his vanity he believed himself still visited by occasional sparks of sensuality, but these weak sparkles were always immediately snuffed out by the chill of a worn-out imagination." ("Réduit à se contenter des prestiges d'un amour contemplatif, son cœur cherche sans cesse à ranimer des désirs éteints. Vainement il se croit encore visité de quelques étincelles de sensualité, ces faibles bluettes sont tout à coup amorties par le froid d'une imagination épuisée.")[15]

Of course, the metaphor of fire and flames representing love and passion is not new to the putain memoirs. Yet in this passage the classic image goes beyond a clever euphemism for sexual dysfunction to articulate a larger indictment about the ineffective and unproductive nobility. Of course, this older man cannot inspire flames of passion in either himself or Thérèse, but passion is not the only function of fire and heat. Fire provides light in the dark, protects us from the cold, and cooks food to nourish our bodies. This elderly marquis can provide none of those important functions—for himself or for others. He contains only weak sparkles, reminiscent of fireworks that may look as beautiful as his fancy, expensive clothes but quickly fade out, leaving nothing behind. Furthermore, fire is a powerful element that should be somewhat feared. A raging conflagration can destroy homes and lives. But an aging aristocrat does not merit Thérèse's attention or respect. He can neither harm nor help anyone. The contrast between a cold, impotent older man and a hot, virile young lover does not simply highlight the former's lack of sexual prowess but is a larger indictment of the ineffectual and useless aristocracy.

Thérèse has no awe for the wealth, titles, and power of these men. The geriatric marquis de R . . . merely inspires pity in her, which only serves to bore her quickly.[16] Later Thérèse expresses her disgust with another aged aristocrat, the extraordinarily wealthy Monsieur de R., who has just broken off with his most recent mistress and is looking for a new one.[17] Although Thérèse is predisposed to dislike this man—her mother has forced her to leave the man she loves to try to become de R.'s new mistress—her visceral reaction to his appearance goes beyond resentment: "One can imagine that I did not have a particularly charming image of Monsieur de R., but I soon realized that my imagination was considerably better than the reality. I hated him without knowing him; I was horrified after seeing him. What an abominable face: dark and wild-eyed, with a pallid and sallow complexion, truly the appearance of a reprobate! We all make allowances for ugly people, but it's just not permitted to have such a face! Oh, that hideous man!" ("On peut croire que je ne me faisais pas une image charmante de de R., mais j'avoue que mon imagination avait été bien au-dessous de la réalité: je le haïssais sans le connaître, j'en eus horreur après l'avoir vu. Quelle abominable figure, des yeux sombres et farouches, le regard égaré, le teint pâle et livide, une vraie physionomie de réprouvé; on passe la laideur, mais il n'est pas permis de porter de ces visages-là. Ah le vilain homme!")[18] This is how Thérèse describes one of the wealthiest and most distinguished men in Paris.

These descriptions of repulsive men are always immediately followed or preceded by a satisfying experience with an attractive younger man.[19] The man with the sleeping skeleton is followed by a boisterous young musketeer "full of fire" ("un mousquetaire bruyant et plein de feu") whose passion "made up for the annoyance [she] had to bear in the preceding adventure" ("dédommagea de l'ennui que j'avais essuyé dans l'aventure précédente") with that "paralytic."[20] A chevalier relieves Thérèse during her relationship with the octogenarian Adonis, and quickly takes his place when she cannot stand the boredom anymore. This lover is immediately followed by a handsome young neighbor with "features . . . perfect for touching the heart" and "eyes full of fire," who then introduces her to three of his equally attractive friends.[21]

The putains, then, don't hate men; they despise men with undeserved power. Even if in this fictional libertine world merit comes from sexual attractiveness and prowess, the underlying critique is salient. An older, less capable generation holds power over the younger, abler generation, which is poised to lead with more strength and success. Furthermore, the putain narrators do more than simply point out the disparity; they are actively engaged in transferring the benefits of power to the deserving while also modeling the kind of legitimate power that merit and skill can generate.

As sex workers these narrators use their sexual availability to men of all classes to get access to the wealth and luxuries that would otherwise be out of reach. Without the privileges of a noble birth or a strategic marriage, the putains like Thérèse nevertheless enjoy the finer things of the well-to-do and gain access to the people, places, and accessories of those classes. Their *entreteneurs* provide them with seats at the opera, furnished apartments, gifts of clothing and jewels, and a lifestyle full of drinking chocolate and champagne and wearing emeralds and ermine.

When the young putain decides to embark on a career of prostitution, she knowingly enters a profession that bestows social mobility. In the novels, as in real life, the financial success and popularity of a sex worker could vary greatly from one moment to the next. A woman could both be a *fille entretenue* and still go out in the streets from time to time to pick up extra money. A woman might find herself one day walking the streets and become *entretenue* the next, only to wind up back in a brothel a short time later.[22] Thérèse, like all the putains, is unperturbed by these fluctuations, and quickly regains the status of kept mistress after each setback.

Nevertheless, the general trajectory in the putain memoirs is the rise of a woman from a lower class and impoverished family to wealth, fame, and status thanks to her sexual liaisons with nobler and wealthier men. Almost all of the putains are born either to peasant families in the country or to Parisian working-class parents. Thérèse is the granddaughter of a wigmaker, and her mother's husband at the time of her birth is a village baker. But by the time she is a teenager, she is sleeping with some of the most powerful men in the city of Metz. Once she establishes herself in Paris, she can include a chevalier, a couple of marquis, and a "Baltic lord" among her lovers.

One might expect that the social status of the putains' sexual partners would reflect a similar rise, that each lover or client is of a higher rank than the last. In fact, however, the putains have sex with men of all degrees of wealth and social class throughout their careers. Most of the time their lucrative arrangements with wealthy *entreteneurs* are, understandably, far from physically satisfying. The putains, then, never hesitate to find gratification (and sometimes extra money) in the arms of others. Most putains maintain one or more *greluchons* who, as Thérèse explains, serve a vital function in the lives of the putain:

> Even though a secondary lover is deprived of the honors of antecedence, he is not to be pitied. Since he owes his happiness to nothing more than our choice, and this choice is made freely, he is only all the more sincerely loved. A woman's heart loves independence. To please someone who has

> the right to our graces is not a favor; it is a debt that we repay, and it is not at all pleasant to pay one's debts, as I know from daily experience. It is easier to give than to give back. It's that our soul is proud, and its vanity is flattered by being generous.
>
> (Un amant en second, quoique privé des honneurs de la préséance, n'en est pas plus à plaindre. Comme il n'a obligation de son bonheur qu'à notre choix, et que ce choix se trouve libre, il n'en est que plus sincèrement aimé. Le cœur des femmes aime l'indépendance; rendre heureux quelqu'un qui a droit de prétendre à nos grâces, ce n'est plus un bienfait, c'est une dette qu'on acquitte; il n'est point du tout amusant de payer ses dettes, je m'en rapporte à l'expérience journalière; on donne plus volontiers qu'on ne rend; c'est que notre âme est fière, et que sa vanité se trouve flattée d'être généreuse.)[23]

In this explanation we find the major attraction, besides sexual, that these young men hold for the putains. Because the putains are not paid for the favors they grant, they owe their *greluchons* nothing. Instead, these relationships grant the putains a kind of power that is different from what they hold over their paying customers. In both cases they provide men "happiness," but with the *greluchons* this gift puts the men in a position of owing a debt to the putain—even if it will only be paid in gratitude. Furthermore, the relationship represents her sexual autonomy: it is a "choice" that is "freely" made involving her "independence." The secondary lovers permit the putain to be more than professionals accommodating the tastes of the men who select them as mistresses. Despite those unpleasant engagements, these narrators do enjoy a sexual freedom that allows them to interact with any man they choose.

In *The Invention of Pornography* Lynn Hunt demonstrates how the pornographic pamphlets of the French Revolution promoted a kind of democratized sexuality, with one citing a prostitute offering lower prices to patriots.[24] While many putains espouse similar promises of equal access to all men (who can pay), the adventures they recount with *entreteneurs* and *greluchons* are at once more generous and more despotic than the revolutionary-era prostitute offering a special rate. The putain has sex with her *greluchon* boyfriends free of charge, making herself available to any man, even one who could not afford even her discounted prices. But unlike the prostitute accepting all clients who call themselves patriots, the putain selects her privileged lover. She still espouses a capitalist pricing scheme based on supply and demand, but she simultaneously subverts that system by giving away her precious commodity from time to time. The putain takes control of this commodification of her body and her sexual labor and thereby asserts her power over the men who desire her. She holds the power to be capricious and tyrannical.

Nevertheless, there is a certain equality among the putain's paying customers. For instance, at any given moment the putain will be sleeping with men from a variety of social classes. A lackey, a count, and a bishop can all be good lovers. Thérèse, for one, seems to reject any distinctions among the three *états* of ancien-régime society, because she sleeps with members of the aristocracy, clergymen, and any other men who strike her fancy. She first learns the lesson that men of all classes have something to offer from her mother:

> My mother possesses the spirit of her trade as a woman of the world. She must be familiar with the morals of the century, having done business with the robe, the sword, and finance. She neglected nothing in her instruction. She didn't even mind lowering herself to the vilest of classes in order to add new discoveries to her enlightenment; artisans, valets, everything was subjected to her attentive examination. Despite occupying the lowest ranks of society, these vile mortals are no less worthy of attention and are that much more useful to us because their crude and base vices are openly on display without distracting our eyes with the phony exterior that covers the same thing in more polite circles.
>
> (Ma mère possède l'esprit de son métier autant que femme du monde. Elle doit connaitre les mœurs du siècle, ayant commercé toute sa vie avec la robe, l'épée et la finance; elle n'a rien négligé pour s'instruire, elle n'a pas même dédaigné de descendre jusqu'aux états les plus vils, afin de pouvoir ajouter de nouvelles découvertes à ses lumières: artisans, valets, tout a passé à son examen. Ces vils mortels, pour occuper les derniers rangs de la société, n'en sont pas pour cela des objets moins dignes d'attention; d'autant plus propres à nous instruire, que chez eux les vices grossiers et tous nus s'y montrent à découvert et sans que les yeux puissent être fascinés par ces dehors imposteurs qui couvrent souvent le même fonds dans un monde plus poli.)[25]

Once again Thérèse uses the dismissive synecdoche of "the robe" and "the sword" to reference the noble elite of the ancien régime, implying that these privileged men have no inherent qualities to warrant their advantages. They are only distinguishable by the accessories they hold. They have the same "crude and base vices" as those in the "vilest" classes. In fact, common men who lack the insincere exterior of polite manners are superior to aristocrats because their crudeness is more honest.

The lexicon of instruction that pervades this passage is another important aspect of the putain memoirs. Here Thérèse explains that sexual encounters with men from different professions and classes provide the putain with a useful education, one that is all the more instructive for its variety. The exposure to these different kinds of men brings her more than just money and physical pleasure; it is a way to learn about the world, the better to do her job and improve her life. Through the example of her mother, Thérèse learns not only to be wary of appearances, but also that men of all stations can bring "new discoveries."[26]

During her time working in Paris at Madame G***'s brothel, Thérèse finds this lesson reinforced by her proprietress, who teaches her to welcome any customer, whatever his social class. Madame G***'s establishment famously serves anyone: "People of all colors and from all classes; mercenaries, clerks, soldiers, magistrates, merchants, abbots, citizens, foreigners, all were admitted." ("Gens de toutes couleurs et de tous états; partisans, commis, guerriers, magistrats, commerçants, abbés, citoyens, étrangers, tous étaient admis.")[27] In fact, on her first day at the brothel Thérèse satisfies an aging *grand homme* and a vigorous young *mousquetaire*. With their liberality, Thérèse, her mother, Madame G***, and the other putains reinforce a preference for the pursuit of pleasure and money to the superficial distinctions of birth and class. Blessed with beauty and skills of manipulation that attract men of all classes, the fictional putains have the opportunity to equalize all the estates in their descriptions of lovers and even to express a preference for commoners that negates the supposed virtues of the aristocracy.

The source of the putain's power is a kind of allure that often seems like a kind of magic spell, as seen in Thérèse's first appearance at *les spectacles*. Like an enchantress, Thérèse easily convinces her clients to give her money and gifts. In addition, the putains themselves control when and with whom they have sex. Thérèse, for one, is keenly aware of the power she holds over an interested marquis, who despite his attractive appearance would be a bad client because he is known to neglect his mistresses financially: "In vain the young and attractive marquis de *** (for he had informed me of his name) tried to win me over with that fortunate gift for pleasing that nature had given him. In vain, prostrate at my feet, he added the most tender proclamations to the most brilliant promises. Despite all his sighing and painful complaining about the obstacle I was placing before his happiness, I was inexorable." ("En vain le marquis de*** [car il m'avait instruite de son nom], jeune, aimable, employait pour me vaincre, cet heureux don de plaire qu'il avait reçu de la nature; en vain prosterné à mes pieds, il joignait aux plus tendres protestations les plus brillantes promesses: il eut beau soupirer, se plaindre douloureusement, se désespérer de l'obstacle cruel que j'opposais à son bonheur, je fus inexorable.")[28] The prudent Thérèse is no slave to her desires and refuses to give in to this cheapskate. Her restraint brings her the pleasure of knowing that she can deny this man his satisfaction. In this case we find a putain who not only has the gift of arousing a passionate desire in an attractive aristocrat, but also has the power of self-control when needed.[29]

Perhaps the most exaggerated examples of the putain's power are Thérèse's show-stopping appearances at the theater. As we saw in her first visit to the opera, Thérèse exerts more than an influential power over the crowd; they are completely under her control. Similarly, during her next trip to the theater, Thérèse causes such a stir that she feels compelled to intervene like a benevolent dictator. With hyperbolic fervor, Thérèse describes how the audience showers her with waves of applause and admiration:

> The magnificence of my appearance confused the usher, who assuming by my dress that I should be seated with distinction put us in the first loge. For an instant I had the fleeting thought of rejecting this honor, but my pride won out. I was flattered to see myself presented to the public with some sort of dignity. It was certainly a coup d'état! In occupying this place, I would win it for all the women like me. It was therefore in the best interest of my profession that I take possession of this honor. . . . Over a hundred opera glasses pointed my way revealed to me the curiosity of the spectators. . . .
>
> The onlookers had no difficulty finding out who I was. My name running from mouth to mouth told them everything. A confused murmur began to rise, followed by universal applause. This clapping was not exactly to my taste; it always in some way obliges the actor to whom it's directed. . . .
>
> My modesty began to find this unanimous concert a bit alarming. For a while I pretended not to know that I was the object. The orchestra level—too full of good will and noticing the effect that my modesty was having on me—absolutely refused to see my glory be the victim of my restraint. . . . They crowded around my loge, my name ringing from the rafters. The more insistent ones climbed on the shoulders of the others to get a better look at me. I saw them coming from across the hall, carried along like a triumphant leader, breaking through the crowd, coming up to whisper a few impromptu sweet nothings to me, and melting away immediately to make room for the others. The actors on stage could not regain the

audience; it was general mayhem, and only I could stop it. It was not fair that my glory should take precedence over the general interest of public pleasure. I pulled myself away despite their efforts to keep me with even more furious applause.

(La magnificence de mon ajustement abusa l'ouvreuse de loges qui, jugeant à mes habits que je méritais d'être placée avec distinction, nous installa dans la première des loges. Une réflexion, qui passa rapidement, me fit douter si j'accepterais cet honneur; mais l'amour-propre me décida. Je me trouvai flattée de pouvoir présenter publiquement avec quelque sorte de dignité. C'était d'ailleurs un coup d'état: en occupant cette place, j'acquérais le même droit à toutes mes semblables. L'intérêt du corps voulait donc que j'en prisse possession. . . . Plus de cent lorgnettes braquées contre ma figure me mirent au fait de la curiosité des spectateurs. . . .

Les regardants n'eurent pas beaucoup de peine à savoir qui j'étais; mon nom courant de bouche en bouche les instruisait tous. Un murmure confus s'éleva, ce qui fut suivi d'un battement de mains universel. Ces applaudissements n'étaient pas trop de mon goût; ils obligent les acteurs pour qui ils sont faits. . . .

Ma modestie commençait à s'alarmer de ce concert unanime. Je feignais quelque temps d'ignorer que j'en étais l'objet. Le parterre trop plein de bonne volonté, s'aperçut de l'effet que la pudeur opérait sur moi, il ne voulut pas absolument que ma gloire fût la victime de ma retenue. . . . on se poussait en foule du côté de ma loge, mon nom retentissait jusqu'au cintre. Les plus empressés se mettaient sur les épaules des autres pour me considérer de plus près; je les voyais accourir de l'extrémité de la salle, portés comme en triomphe, ils fendaient la multitude, s'approchaient, me disaient quelques douceurs impromptues, et fondaient en ma présence pour faire place à d'autres. Les acteurs sur la scène ne pouvaient obtenir audience, le désordre était général, je pouvais seule le faire cesser, il n'était pas juste que l'intérêt de ma gloire prévalût sur les plaisirs publics. Je me retirai malgré les efforts qu'on fit pour me retenir, en m'applaudissant avec encore plus de fureur.)[30]

In this extraordinary scene, Thérèse (somewhat facetiously) insists upon the fact that she did not take advantage of the admiration she received. Her first selfless act is to accept the preferential seating only for the sake of her fellow courtesans—giving them the honor of seeing someone from their ranks enjoy a position of distinction. She ends the passage equally altruistically, allowing the public good of continuing the play to take precedence over what was clearly a flattering experience for her. In addition, Thérèse's selfless example appears to influence her admirers, who, rather than compete with each other for her attention, help each other out: first by informing each other of her name, then by lifting each other up to her loge, and finally by generously backing away to allow others the same opportunity. Clearly, it seems Thérèse brings out the best in people.

In addition to mesmerizing crowds of men, the putains also use their access and influence to resolve injustices, especially economic inequity. Through her relationships with a wealthy *entreteneur* who pays her for sex and with a handsome young *greluchon* whom she often supports, the putain redistributes wealth. Like a lubricious Robin Hood, she takes from the rich (old, debauched aristocrats and hypocritical clergy) and gives to the poor (younger, talented, and more attractive men). Professionally, the putain is a model of capitalist values—marketing her charms as a successful businesswoman and modeling conspicuous consumption of luxury goods—but her private actions reveal socialist sympathies. She knows that the men who can afford to support her do not deserve the exclusive enjoyment of their money or her body, and she makes sure those commodities are more evenly distributed.

The putain's handsome secret lovers are not the only beneficiaries of her generosity.[31] And at the end of her memoir, Thérèse takes pity on the wife of one of her clients, after overhearing him refuse to give his spouse even a tiny allowance. Once the man leaves the room, Thérèse steps out of the cabinet where she was hiding to speak to the weeping wife: "We don't have time, Madame, for me to make awkward and misplaced excuses and for you to hear them. I have just witnessed the shameful way your husband has treated you. The loss of such a despicable heart is not worth your tears. I would like to offer you as a consolation half of my spoils." ("Nous n'avons pas le temps, madame, lui dis-je, moi de vous faire des excuses froides et déplacées, ni vous de les entendre. Je viens d'être témoin de la manière dont votre indigne mari vous a traitée; la perte d'un cœur aussi méprisable ne mérite pas vos pleurs. Je vous offre pour consolation le partage de ses dépouilles.")[32] And with that she hands half of the money she has just earned over to the desperate wife. Her final commentary on this last action of the novel: "How pleasurable it is to be generous!" ("Qu'il y a de plaisir à être généreuse!")[33] We find, then, in the putain memoirs a middle ground between the stereotypes of the avaricious whore and the unfortunate hooker with a heart of gold. Sex with a variety of men is in the putains' own best interests, certainly, but their sensitivity to the inequalities in their society also informs their choices.

The putain's sexual pursuit of justice takes more forms than financial gifts. She can also exact revenge. For example, while Thérèse is suffering from syphilis, she carefully avoids transmitting the disease to her handsome *greluchon* by teaching him the art of mutual masturbation until she is no longer contagious. Unfortunately, however, her young lover is still suffering—from the tyranny of a powerful older man. Too young to control his own inheritance, he must live off the meager allowance his stingy uncle doles out. The aspiring libertine is then forced to take out a loan from a famously unscrupulous banker who takes advantage of the situation to charge him an unfairly high rate of interest. Once Thérèse learns of these unfortunate circumstances, she decides to try and use her wiles to obtain a lower interest rate for her young friend. When the greedy banker refuses, Thérèse, knowing that she is still contagious, agrees to sleep with the banker, deliberately infecting him. Importantly, she gets no financial gain from the transaction; her *greluchon* is not in any way a paying customer, so his level of indebtedness to someone else has no effect on her. The vengeful act is nothing more than a way to settle a score.[34]

With her acts of generosity and her sense of justice, the putain's power over the men who desire her becomes nonthreatening. Because these prostitutes use the power of their allure—and the power of the pen—to ridicule and even harm only ridiculous, pompous, hypocritical, and undeserving men, they pose no danger to the public at large. Most men, including the presumed reader, need not fear the sexual power a woman like her can hold over them. She only mocks, infects, or humiliates the men who deserve it. The power that Thérèse enjoys has no more serious consequences for the public at large than the momentary delay of act 2 one evening at the theater.

In these novels, the putains create a strategic cycle of subversions. They reject and undermine the patriarchal order that would confine them and limit their possibilities. They use that rejection to sleep with and learn from men of all classes. This education in turn allows them to hone their skills to fully exploit the illegitimate powerholders of their society, thus further weakening the pillars of patriarchy in prerevolutionary France. The putains expose the artificiality and weakness in the inherited privileges of their society and propose a stronger, more valid social system. The primary beneficiaries of this meritocracy are, of course, the putains themselves. However, by supporting the public good they prove worthy of the wealth and power they earn.

In contrast, elsewhere in eighteenth-century texts, writers evoke the notion that the sexual powers of attractive women are a menacing agent of society's demise. Because women can arouse distracting and even corrupting sexual desire in men, it is in the best interests of society for women to be confined to the private domestic sphere, so the thinking went. But in the putain memoirs, female sexual power serves as more than an easy stereotype or a hollow justification for the patriarchal subordination of women. It is the way these novels connect the subversion of social class distinctions to a subversion of all hierarchies, particularly the increasingly asserted distinction between men and women.

The libertine utopia of the putain memoirs is more than the materialist paradise where the pursuit of sexual desires defies the moral and religious constraints that normally impede their physical pleasures. As *La Belle Allemande* demonstrates, the fantasy world the putain inhabits is one where social and economic inequalities can be corrected, individual autonomy is achievable, personal merit is rewarded, and the public good is ensured—all while and because libertines pursue their sexual desires and experience sensual pleasure. Through every sexual transaction, every snide observation, and every moment of triumph, the putain narrator, like Thérèse, creates an alternative society in which beautiful and savvy putains are the legitimate and deserving ruling class.

4

Margot la ravaudeuse, or The Libertine Public Sphere

The putains do not simply exercise a power over the men who desire them; they also control the spaces they inhabit. The heroine of *Margot la ravaudeuse* asserts: "If it's true that we are the very soul of pleasure, if it is true that pleasure follows us wherever we go, then aren't the places we occupy the most pleasurable on earth?" ("S'il est vrai que nous soyons l'âme des plaisirs; s'il est vrai qu'ils nous suivent partout, les lieux où nous présidons ne doivent-ils pas être les plus agréables du monde?").[1] The confident putain like Margot can enter and take over any space she likes. The pleasure she distributes becomes a power, like the sexual allure Thérèse refers to as her "empire of beauty," and accompanies her always, meaning the putain can thrive in any space.

To tease out how this power over "the places they occupy" works, in this chapter I will explore the role of space in the memoirs, in particular the putains' relationship to the new public sphere emerging in the eighteenth century. I will begin by highlighting the privileged position of space in libertine works like the putain memoirs and exploring the potential reasons for the numerous references to specific places in the novels. Then I step back from the novels themselves to examine key aspects of Jürgen Habermas's theory of the transformation of the public sphere in the eighteenth century and how the new distinction between public and private spheres represented an explicitly gendered divide. A few telling examples from literary and political discourses serve to convey the pervasive and emphatic demands for the sequestration of women to a private, domestic sphere. Returning to the putain memoirs, we will explore how the putains undermine this gendered understanding of space and how they use both public and private spaces for their own personal gain. Not only do the putains engage in the public sphere—through their presence in public places and in the deliberate act of publication—they also transform that public sphere into one that valorizes nonverbal communication as much as the written and spoken word. Finally, we see how their participation as sex workers in the economic public sphere of the marketplace reflects the same ambivalence toward the social and political changes in the eighteenth century that Laura Rosenthal lays out in her work on prostitution in British literature and culture. Unlike the discourses in Britain, however, the putain memoirs ignore the anxiety surrounding those changes, emphasizing only the potential for financial success the new public sphere offers to rational, self-disciplined individuals like the putains. The work of the putains—as sex workers and as creators of a libertine public sphere in their memoirs—promises profit for themselves but also greater freedom and benefits for all. Just as the putains, like Thérèse, use their power to correct social injustices, they also, like Margot, propose a utopian public sphere where all people can participate and contribute to the greater good.

Even though all the putains unabashedly move in and out of public places, the heroine of *Margot la ravaudeuse* is unique in the variety of her work in the public eye, as an outdoor clothing repairer, a model for artists, and a dancer at the Opéra, in addition to her occupations as a sex worker and an author. Certainly, all eighteenth-century prostitutes, as *filles publiques*, have a complicated relationship with space when it is divided into a public–private binary: they offer intimate access to their bodies to almost any member of the public willing and able to pay. Rosenthal observes, "Prostitution undermined the separation of the public and private spheres . . . for it placed in the marketplace the very thing—sexuality—understood to define the private sphere."[2] More than any other putain narrator, Margot displays the single-minded focus on profit over pleasure that leads to success in the libertine public sphere of the putain memoirs.

As the novel opens, we meet Margot, a young woman born to poor parents who was forced to work as a clothing repairer to supplement her family's income. She spends her days seated in a large barrel on the street, mending the torn socks and underclothes people bring to her. Like most putains, she becomes curious about sex at a young age, and she loses her virginity with a young groom early in the narrative. When Margot's mother learns that Margot is sleeping with the boy (and worse still, giving him money), her fury leads her to beat the girl. Outraged by this mistreatment, Margot runs away and finds herself in the Tuileries Gardens, where she meets Madame Florence, a madam who invites the penniless girl to stay in her home. Margot quickly discovers this home is a brothel, and it is here that her sexual education begins. In the brothel she develops professional expertise and flourishes, until one day when a group of thirty musketeers rush in demanding sex. Margot, as the only prostitute in the house that day, must service them all. Exhausted and somewhat overwhelmed by this episode, she decides to set out on her own and gets an apartment. Her education in sex continues during these early days through her many adventures living and working independently. In short succession, she faces a bout of syphilis, a stay in the Bicêtre prison, and a violent escapade with a jealous *entreteneur*. After this last episode attracts police attention, Margot hides with a neighbor, Madame Thomas, who introduces her to a lubricious and well-connected monk named frère Alexis. Frère Alexis in turn introduces Margot to the director of the opera, and her career as a dancer begins.

Margot's status as a public performer allows her to attract *entreteneurs* with ease. The rest of her career involves dancing at the opera and maintaining a steady stream of wealthy sponsors, with only one small setback in the form of another brief outbreak of syphilis. Margot's first *entreteneur* is a financier, and when he goes bankrupt, her reputation only improves for having "ruined" a man. She replaces him with a young German baron, until his father comes to Paris and takes him home. Her next *entreteneur* is an English lord with embarrassingly bad taste and manners. When he is forced to return to England, she finds a *fermier général* (tax farmer) to support her and after that an ambassador. After a while Margot breaks up with the ambassador because she has developed a kind of illness that no doctor can explain. Finally, one doctor diagnoses Margot with a surfeit of pleasure.[3] Fortunately for Margot, she has already amassed enough savings throughout her career to retire and enjoy a more peaceful existence with well-moderated pleasures. Importantly, she chooses neither a husband nor a long-term lover for company in this new, quieter life. Instead, she seeks out her own parents. Unfortunately, her father is deceased, but Margot manages to reunite with her mother, and all past grievances are forgiven. Together they set up a household, spending half their time in the country, half in the city. The ending to Margot's memoir, dividing her time between the isolation of the country and the bustle of the capital, is indicative of the putains' ability to blend public social interactions and the enjoyment of private pleasures in their lives and careers.

Throughout her memoir Margot, like all the putains, refers to the places she inhabits with remarkable specificity. First she lists the street where she is born (rue Saint-Paul), the street where she works as a *ravaudeuse* (rue Saint-Antoine), the path she takes when she runs away from her parents' home (le chemin de la Grève to the Pont-Royal to the Tuileries Gardens), and all the subsequent places she inhabits (a brothel on the rue Montmartre, an apartment on the rue d'Argenteuil, the Bicêtre prison, a room on the rue du Chantre, the fifth floor of a home on the rue Champ-Fleuri, and a new apartment on the rue Sainte-Anne). Many specific establishments are mentioned, including the café des Tuileries, the café Procope, the Glacière, the Palais Royal, and the Église des Quinze-vingts.

The specificity in these place names stands in stark contrast with the ambiguity of secondary characters' identities. The putain narrators are much more precise with the names of locations than of people. Most often the narrator reduces character names to initials or omits them completely, while making certain to give street names in their entirety. For example, one of Margot's first *entreteneurs* is listed by the abbreviated title of Monsieur de Mez***, the head of the theater where she works is called Monsieur de Gr*** M***, her lover from Germany is called simply "Monsieur le baron," and the English lover is just "Mylord." As in the police records pertaining to known prostitutes, places seem to have an elevated importance in the putain memoirs.[4] The practice of representing people with titles and initials, common in much of eighteenth-century literature, served to reinforce the verisimilitude of the text. Since these were "real" memoirs, the editor of course had to replace names with initials to protect the identities of the "real" people they described. Authors could name spaces and places, on the other hand, without the risk of being accused of slander.

Space also conveys a symbolic value in erotic literature, as libertine writers deliberately manipulate traditional connotations of certain places to heighten the titillation or subversion associated with their characters' actions.[5] For instance, Sarane Alexandrian notes that those places that should be "officially consecrated to good morals," such as convents, appear ironically in erotic literature as "centers of debauchery."[6] Other writers employ geographic metaphors to evoke images of a sexualized female body, as in Thomas Stretser's *A New Description of Merryland* (1740), which imitates the style of geography manuals and describes the genitals of a woman as if she were a country.[7] Also in vogue in the second half of the eighteenth century were directories like *Harris's List of Covent-Garden Ladies: or Man of Pleasure's Kalender*, which gave the addresses of London's prostitutes, and French guidebooks like *Les Bordels de Paris, avec les noms, demeures et prix* (1790). In a century that placed a premium on verisimilitude, these pamphlets listing prostitutes, their addresses, and physical descriptions, mimicked a form of writing generally accepted as true and allowed a reader the vicarious pleasure of reading about sexual women. The specific addresses gave the titillating descriptions a sense of reality and physicality, bringing the lusty whore out of the private realm of the imagination and into a real building on a public street.

This conflation of the private and the public is an important component of the subversive shock of erotic writing. Normally those acts and images that are proper, clean, and public stand in opposition to those that are considered improper, dirty, and private. The source of eroticism is, in Lynn Hunt's words, "the intrusion into the public sphere of something that was at base private."[8] The frisson of excitement from a sexually stimulating text like the putain memoirs comes from this conflation of the two spheres. Not surprisingly, then, the creation of pornography as a category of creative product was in response to a perceived need for a special private space to isolate certain obscenely erotic works, literally in the form of secret museums or special catalogs of books.[9] Although the putain memoirs predate the category and the term "pornography," their erotic content (whether explicit or euphemized) was already being associated with the private sphere of boudoirs and bedrooms. The writer of erotic prose like a putain memoir takes a private sexual moment occurring behind closed doors and turns it into a narrative that is presented in public though publication. The depiction of the sexual act crosses the public–private border, and it is this very transgression that makes erotic literature so titillating.

The prominence of spaces and places in the putain memoirs, then, signals this commonly held tension between the public and the private at the heart of eroticism and titillation. Importantly, however, the putain memoir novels evoke this simple formula of "private acts plus public expression equals erotic titillation" only to complicate its arithmetic. As we will see, in addition to crossing and re-crossing the purported border between that which is or should be private and that which is or can be public, the putains also undermine the very notion of such a border, calling into question the necessity and the inevitability of separating space in such a way. The narrators' appearances in and uses of both public and private spaces for both public and private acts successfully blur the boundary between the two, ultimately proving such divisions to be artificial and unnecessary in the pursuit of pleasure and financial security.

The precision with which places are identified in the putain memoirs also serves to establish the author's credibility, since the sites they mention were all hot spots in the Parisian demimonde. In the eighteenth century, sex workers and their patrons preferred certain places like the Palais Royal, but prostitution could be found in every neighborhood, from the main city center to the many faubourgs that surrounded it. Eighteenth-century readers would have immediately recognized addresses in the Saint-Honoré neighborhood and the faubourg Saint-Germain as residences belonging to the aristocracy. The Saint-Marcel, Saint-Jacques, and Saint-Victor neighborhoods were home to tradesmen and some of the poorest communities in Paris. Within the center of the city, the Marais neighborhood was home to fewer members of the fashionable aristocracy than it had been under Louis XIII and Louis XIV and was, by the mid-eighteenth century, home to the more old-fashioned and conservative residents of Paris.[10] A residence within the Marais, then, would communicate to the reader that the *entreteneur* selecting that location is decidedly unfashionable and passé.

The putain memoirs take place mostly within the highly trafficked, centrally located areas such as the Palais Royal, the Tuileries Gardens, and the Luxembourg Gardens, where many bordellos were located and real courtesans could be found taking leisurely promenades. Sexual activity was commonly considered a feature of the gardens, with solicitation and even services performed in the narrow pathways and dense copses of the parks.[11] Most working-class brothels were generally found closer to the city center, since convenient proximity to large numbers of potential customers was good for business.

Later, during the Revolution, another popular neighborhood was Butte des Moulins with the Maison Égalité. Prostitutes also frequently congregated in markets, cabarets, and taverns.[12] At the same time that central locations were the sites for most liaisons, many prostitutes, madams, and clients favored less conspicuous areas on the periphery and in the suburbs of the capital, such as the *guinguettes* on the outskirts of Paris. These taverns where the working classes went to relax and celebrate on Sundays and holidays were found in areas like the Porcherons suburb near Montmartre, and often attracted sex workers.[13]

Many wealthy men would also maintain a smaller home located around the periphery of Paris in the villages of Chaillot and Passy on the western edge of the city.[14] Sometimes plain buildings, other times expensive *hôtels particuliers*, these houses were where the wealthy took their *filles entretenues* or *filles à parties* (hired just for the night) to share late suppers. In these remote locations members of the upper crust could commit, in private, acts they would otherwise be embarrassed to perform.[15] However, these *petites maisons* quickly became famous, and maintaining one was often a sign of prestige and standing in the demimonde.

As the putains move up and down the social ladder, having sex with and learning from men from all stations, they pass through many of these neighborhoods. Two places, however, seem to dominate Margot's memoir: the Palais Royal and the theater. When Margot explains how the Palais Royal has become so closely associated with prostitutes that it almost belongs to them, her words convey reverence and a certain possessiveness: "The Palais Royal, a property we seem to have acquired by a deed as old as the establishment of the Opéra, is a garden of frankness where in total freedom we exercise the right to act like important women, to brave with impunity the eye of our spectator with our grand airs and our proud display." ("Le Palais-Royal étant un territoire dont la propriété semble nous être acquise par une prescription aussi ancienne que l'établissement de l'Opéra: c'est dans cette espèce de jardin de franchise que nous usons, en toute liberté, du droit de faire les femmes de conséquence, et de braver impunément l'œil du spectateur par nos grands airs et notre orgueilleux étalage.")[16]

Audacious courtesans were not the only attraction in the Palais Royal, however. Louis Sébastien Mercier describes it in his *Tableau de Paris* as a place of very public display, where "one can see everything, hear everything, know everything" ("on peut tout voir, tout entendre, tout connaître").[17] This large courtyard surrounded on four sides by an arcade housing shops with cafés, gardens, bazaars, and numerous "pleasure establishments" was a favorite spot for shopping for overpriced luxury goods, eating in restaurants, debating, or playing cards in cafés, but above all, a place to simply stroll while seeing and being seen.[18]

Visitors to the Palais Royal included all types of people, including aristocrats, philosophes, foreigners visiting Paris, stockbrokers, and lawyers. Because the Palais Royal was an exempt space where the king had no legal authority, many criminals fleeing justice would also congregate in the area for protection. Not surprisingly, this public space was also a popular site for the *filles publiques*. In fact, few respectable women frequented this "circus" because of the presence of so many courtesans. Again, Mercier warns: "A mother with her two daughters would not dare to cross this noisy path in the evening. A virtuous spouse, an honest citizen would not dare appear alongside of these obvious courtesans whose appearances, attitudes, clothing, and often even speech force them to flee, shuddering at the general corruption of both sexes." ("Une mère de famille n'oserait, le soir, traverser la bruyante promenade avec ses deux jeunes filles; la vertueuse épouse, la citoyenne honnête, n'oseraient paraître à côté de ces courtisanes hardies; leur parure, leur tenue, leurs airs, et souvent même leurs paroles, tout les force à fuir, en gémissant sur la corruption générale des deux sexes.")[19] As this passage from *Tableau de Paris* indicates, the Palais Royal was synonymous with vice, libertine behavior, and especially prostitution. Not surprisingly, this site appears in nearly all the putain memoirs as an essential place in which to be seen.

The putains also find the theater to be a useful and pleasurable site, perfect for the kind of attention they hope to attract and the kind of connections they hope to make. English Showalter describes the theater in eighteenth-century literature as "a public space, defined and enclosed, but with room for action and reaction, especially with the chance for direct interactions among all the people and objects present."[20] In the mid-eighteenth century, Parisian theatergoers had the choice of the Comédie française, the Opéra at the Palais Royal, the Comédie Italienne (which joined forces with the Opéra-Comique in 1762), as well as the small theaters set up at the *foires*, or fairs, especially at Saint Germain and Saint Laurent. Henri Lagrave estimates the average yearly attendance at the Comédie française to have been around 20,000, of whom 6,000 could be considered devoted fans who would rent a loge for a year at a time.[21]

The mania for the theater was not lost on the putains. Most often they refer to the performances they attend as "les spectacles" without mentioning a specific theater, opera, or play. Their performances in the audience are often more dramatic and entertaining than the production on the stage, as in Thérèse's two scenes at the theater. As a place of artifice, where performers pretend to be other people and convey emotions they do not really feel, the theater perfectly mirrors the trade of the prostitute. Because actresses and especially dancers at the Opéra were often kept mistresses, it was assumed that any woman appearing on the stage was available for hire. Therefore, audience members seeing women on stage would already be thinking about *filles entretenues*, in a frame of mind receptive to the putain's silent seductions from their loges or balcony seats.

When Margot and her fellow putains make themselves seen in the highly frequented sites of the Parisian demimonde, they are not simply seeking out new clients; they are also entering into a spatial product of what Jürgen Habermas has named the structural transformation of the public sphere. As Habermas describes it, the literary criticism performed in the salons—the Republic of Letters—developed from an intellectual practice into a culture of political criticism targeting the monarchy, and a new public sphere emerged. As debate and discussion came to be seen as more accurate and legitimate sources of judgment than the will of an absolute monarch, a new understanding of the public and private spheres emerged. No longer did the king and his administrative institutions constitute the public sphere, dictating what was best for the kingdom, with all the obedient, powerless subjects making up the private sphere. In the new authentic public sphere those subjects could come together in public places to debate and discuss issues to determine public opinion, which, because it was arrived at through rational thought and debate, was deemed more authentic than the decrees of the king. The new public sphere now consisted of those formerly private individuals, with the secret machinations of Versailles appearing more and more suspicious. The meeting places for these individuals to conduct rational, critical discussions began in the salons and spread into clubs (including Masonic lodges), academies, cafés, and intellectual societies as the literary public sphere developed into a political one.[22]

The new public sphere certainly allowed more participants than the previous public sphere, which included only the king and his advisors. Still, not everyone was welcome. To be precise, Habermas's authentic public sphere explicitly excluded women. As feminist historians and critics like Joan B. Landes have pointed out, Habermas seems to have been blind to the depth and significance of the gendered division of space.[23] As Landes persuasively argues, "the exclusion of women from the bourgeois public was not incidental but central to its incarnation."[24] The emerging authentic public sphere transformed the private sphere from the arena of all subjects to a site specifically domestic and reserved for women and children. The "people" from the private sphere who join together in the new public sphere are coded in eighteenth-century discourse and in Habermas's theory as masculine, despite the crucial role the wealthy and aristocratic women of the salons played in this transformative process. Furthermore, the division of space into public and private spheres—in the eighteenth century and at other times—coincides with the oppression and limitations placed on women.[25] In ancient Greece, for instance, men were to participate and interact in the *polis* while women, children, and slaves remained isolated in the domestic sphere of the home. Of course, the terms "public" and "private" are not neutral, and one should not neglect the long-established association of the public with that which is altruistic and in the interest of the entire community and the private with negative images of secretive and self-serving interests.

The idea that women should remain in the private domestic sphere, while not new to eighteenth-century France, had many influential supporters in literary and political discourses. The popular sentimental novel demonstrated how an admirable woman is one who stays chaste until marriage and remains sexually faithful to her husband, and it was understood that the best way to maintain first a young woman's chastity and then a wife's fidelity was to keep her body within the confines of the domestic sphere. The sites of the public sphere, such as cafés, clubs, and theaters, on the other hand, were seen as dangerous for women because of the necessary interaction among individuals there. Not only were women vulnerable to the potential advances of the men they encountered, but they themselves were often characterized as dangerously tempting. A public space where both men and women were present, so the thinking went, would be degraded by the presence of women, because the distracted men would no longer be able to work together for the public good.

The most popular and influential novel of eighteenth-century France, Rousseau's *Julie, ou La Nouvelle Héloïse*, adamantly argues for the confinement of women to the private sphere, not only because that is their "natural" domain, but because a smoothly and efficiently functioning society can only exist with the gendered division of space.[26] Rousseau conveys the contrast between the unfettered sexuality available in public spaces with the orderly productivity of the private sphere in a novel where the heroine virtually never leaves home. In fact, the same space, the estate at Clarens, represents alternately both public exposure and private security based on who is with Julie and what she is doing.

The contrast between the public and private in *La Nouvelle Héloïse* is perhaps best represented in the vegetal metaphors of the copse in which Julie and Saint-Preux share their first kiss—that critical and catastrophic first step—and the idyllic Élysée garden Julie cultivates as a married woman, properly reinstated in the patriarchal family, and firmly ensconced in the domestic sphere. As she and her husband show Saint-Preux around the haven of privacy and isolation confined behind thick walls and a locked gate, her former lover marvels at the lush greenery and pleasant brook running through it. The cool fertility of this garden, to which the three have retreated on an especially warm evening, is a fecund oasis compared to the barren, arid copse of their youth. Although the two young lovers took advantage of the cover of those small trees for their first tender exchange, the sparse foliage of their surroundings signaled Julie's exposure and vulnerability in that moment. Ironically, Julie's later garden blossomed during a marriage devoid of passion into a (re)productive and fruitful site, unlike the sterile space of her budding sexuality. The implication is that the flames of passion dry out and burn up the potential for procreation and the continuance of a legitimate and useful society. In an echo of the closing words of Voltaire's *Candide ou l'Optimisme* (1759), "Il faut cultiver notre jardin," the garden represents a quiet but sexless retreat from the vices of the world.

Rousseau was not the only author to connect women to the private sphere. Even in libertine and erotic literature of the time, texts that oppose the notion of female virtue tied to chastity, we find heroines most often in private spaces. The narrators of *Thérèse philosophe* and *Félicia ou mes fredaines*, despite embracing a libertine philosophy that allows them to follow their sexual urges proudly and without reservations, nonetheless lead a lifestyle that seems to resemble that of a traditional eighteenth-century wife. These women somehow manage to fall in love with (or at least feel a sincere desire for) a man who provides them with a comfortable life, and that affection makes monogamy easy for them. Neither Thérèse nor Félicia leaves the private domestic sphere of her home very often. They only encounter a few close friends, and throughout it all they remain completely dependent on the financial support of their lovers. In this fictional world, their economic dependence never poses a problem since the generosity of their lovers, like the desire these men have for the heroines, is never exhausted. Although as libertine heroines Thérèse and Félicia never expect their sexual relationships to be consecrated by a marriage ceremony or vows, their lessons in libertinage still all take place in the private sphere.

The division of space found in eighteenth-century fiction did more than merely reflect the political transformation of the public sphere. Through repeated examples in books, plays, and images, the gendered division of space developed into an epistemology central to the lives of everyday people. As readers admired characters like Rousseau's Julie, they came to see them less as characters or individuals and more as models to emulate. The putain memoirs, then, were a truly unique imaginative exercise, offering an alternative to the increasingly ubiquitous discourse warning of the personal and general disasters to come when women enter the public sphere. The full power of the dominant discourse, and the inevitable failure of the putain memoirs to replace it, will become apparent in the French Revolution. Despite the counter-narrative proposed in the putain memoirs, the rigid spatial dichotomy that was playing out in midcentury novels would become unquestionable truth thirty years later. Revolutionary propaganda, speeches, and legislative proposals reveal the pervasiveness of the gendered divide between public and private, established by decades of literary examples from both libertine and more mainstream authors.

For instance, the grand speeches of orators like Jean-Pierre-André Amar and Pierre Gaspard Anaxagore Chaumette at the National Convention in the fall of 1793 made clear the importance of motherhood and maternal duties in the lives of female patriots. At the October 30, 1793, session of the National Convention, Citizen Amar articulated what so many revolutionaries had been wondering: Do women have the right to be politically active in the public sphere of the new republic? After explaining that in general, and according to "universal opinion," women lack the moral and physical strength, as well as the selflessness, required to govern, Amar arrived at what he considered the most salient argument: Women should spend their time doing a different kind of work for the revolutionary cause. He asks: "Can women devote themselves to [the] useful and burdensome functions [of attending the sessions of the National Assembly]?" He answers: "No, because they would have to sacrifice the more important cares to which nature calls them. The natural private duties to which women are destined maintain the general order of society." ("Les femmes peuvent-elles se dévouer à ces utiles et pénibles fonctions? Non, parce qu'elles seraient obligées d'y sacrifier des soins plus importants auxquels la nature les appelle. Les fonctions privées auxquelles sont destinées les femmes par la nature même tiennent à l'ordre général de la société.")[27] And what were these "private duties"? They predominantly involved childrearing, as Amar clarifies: "to begin the education of men, to prepare the spirit and the heart of children for the public virtues, to direct them early on toward good, to raise their souls and teach them about the political cult of liberty" ("commencer l'éducation des hommes, préparer l'esprit et le cœur des enfants aux vertus publiques, les diriger de bonne heure vers le bien, élever leur âme et les instruire dans le culte politique de la liberté").[28]

Later, when a delegation of women wearing the red bonnet of the revolutionaries appeared at a session of the Paris Commune, Citizen Chaumette stepped forward to reiterate Amar's earlier concerns with this rhetorical question: "Since when is it decent to see women abandoning the pious cares of their households, the cribs of their children, to come to public places, to harangues in the galleries, at the bar of the senate?" ("Depuis quand est-il décent de voir des femmes abandonner les soins pieux de leur ménage, le berceau de leurs enfants, pour venir sur les places publiques, dans les tribunes aux harangues, à la barre du sénat?").[29] Once again, the opposition between private maternal duties and public political action forms the heart of the argument. The female space, marked by its domestic tasks such as rocking babies in their cribs, was incompatible with public places and the discussions and decisions of the new political process. Chaumette's speech coincided with the first laws banning women's political clubs and assemblies of more than five women in public. Thus, the arguments of Amar and Chaumette were more than mere rhetoric. By the end of 1793 women were explicitly excluded from the political assemblies and the new government structures, and their domestic and maternal duties served as the justification for that exclusion.

The examples from these political debates of 1793 demonstrate that by the time of the putain memoir's demise, the notion that women's "natural" destiny was in isolated, private spaces was firmly established. The words of these legislators attest to the eventual dominance of the discourses found in Rousseau's *La Nouvelle Héloïse* and other sentimental novels. Such was the cultural tide against which the putain memoirs swam. In fact, the scandal (and excitement) of the active, visible, and mobile putain stems in no small part from her defiance of increasingly rigid concepts of gendered space.

Whether they are attracting new customers or enhancing their reputations until they need a new one, the putains understand the importance of being out and about in public places, like gardens, theaters, and the Palais Royal. If the putains rarely solicit customers on the street, they nevertheless recognize the obvious need to advertise. Margot explains: "It is the established custom among us to make ourselves seen more frequently in public when our benefactors have left, so as to alert the clients that there is a vacancy and that we are available for hire. Following this wise custom, I presented myself in the most highly trafficked places." ("C'est un usage établi parmi nos sultanes de se faire voir plus fréquemment en public, quand leurs entreteneurs les ont quittées, pour avertir les chalands que la place est vide, et qu'elles sont à louer. Suivant cette sage coutume, je me produisis dans les lieux les plus fréquentés.")[30] The putains, like Margot, take an active role in recruiting new clients by making themselves seen. Their presence in these popular public places is no fortunate accident, but a deliberate act of self-determination. Just as the putains defy the patriarchal authority of a father or husband, and the social and religious codes of moral behavior, inserting themselves into public places is another form of defiance and an assertion of independence.

If the public spheres of the Palais Royal and the theater hold no horror for the putain, their homes likewise fail to provide the kind of isolation a typical eighteenth-century heroine would expect. For the putains, their homes, boudoirs, and beds are also their places of business. Unlike the wifely and maternal protagonist like Julie, who encounters only family members, servants, and longtime friends within the walls of her home, the putain entertains numerous lovers and customers in hers. Margot mentions several men who enter her home regularly with the full consent of her *entreteneur*: "A young wigmaker and a broad-shouldered baker's assistant were his alternating substitutes. The first one had the privilege of entering my bedroom whenever he wanted under the pretext of curling my hair. The second, as my bread supplier, had the same rights without M. de Mez*** feeling slighted in the least." ("Un jeune garçon perruquier, et un mitron à larges épaules étaient alternativement ses substituts. Le premier, sous prétexte de me faire friser, avait le privilège d'entrer familièrement dans ma chambre quand il voulait. Le second, à titre de mon pourvoyeur de pain, s'était acquis le même droit, sans que Monsieur de Mez*** en conçut le moindre ombrage.")[31] Margot emphasizes the legitimacy of her illicit affairs with a satirical use of legal terminology. The baker has the right to enter her room, and the wigmaker has received the same "privilège"—the term for the official permission from the king to publish a work. It is not clear whether her *entreteneur* is unaware of the mischief going on during the official visits of these men, or if he recognizes the precedence of a higher authority's consent and inherent professional rights. Whatever the case, he never tries to impede their access to his mistress. Margot's comment reminds us that the hustle and bustle in the home of a putain is a necessary part of maintaining her household and her appearance, and even when it leads to sexual infidelities, no one is seriously harmed.

As another part of her role as the mistress of a wealthy man, the putain often hosts large dinner parties. For instance, while supported by one *entreteneur*, Margot holds a sort of salon, which she compares favorably to that of Madame de Tencin: "I had to have night and morning eight place settings at my table, of which six were regularly occupied by poets, painters, and musicians, who in the interest of their stomachs, produced like slaves their mercenary incense to my Croesus. My home was a tribunal, where talent and art were judged with as much sovereignty as at Madame T***'s literary diner." ("J'avais soir et matin une table de huit couverts, dont six étaient régulièrement occupés par des poètes, des peintres et des musiciens, lesquels, pour l'intérêt de leur ventre, prodiguaient en esclaves leur encens mercenaire à mon Crésus. Ma maison était un tribunal, où l'on jugeait aussi souverainement les talents et les arts que dans la gargote littéraire de Madame T***.")[32] Her mockery of intellectual salon culture in this passage takes aim at the self-interest of its participants, those starving "slaves" offering flattery and wit for their own gain, as well as the legitimacy of the salon as an arbiter of taste and talent. The esteemed salon of Madame de Tencin in this passage is a *gargote*, a cheap restaurant, with no more legitimate power or "sovereignty" than the daily meals in the home of a former clothing repairer turned prostitute, dinners that were most likely rowdy (or worse, ironically and ridiculously reserved—Margot does not elaborate on the level of decorum at these meals).[33]

The other home where a putain who finds herself between *entreteneurs* usually returns, the brothel, is an even more crowded space. In the putain memoirs, these establishments are often presented as havens, a place for these women to go when they have nowhere else to turn.

Certainly, compared to living on the streets, a bordello is a very private and safe place. Nevertheless, the brothel is also quite open, in that (in theory) anyone can come in and demand service, provided they can pay. We find a rare depiction of this vulnerability in the scene where a regimen of soldiers bursts into the brothel where Margot works.[34]

Whether private apartments or brothels, the putains' homes do not provide a private sanctuary, nor do they want them to. The putains' subversion is not that of a woman venturing into masculine, public spaces to find customers, then retreating back to the feminine, private sphere for solace. In the libertine utopia of the putain memoirs, there are no boundaries. Their transgressions do not reinforce a boundary; their movements prove the immateriality of boundaries. Furthermore, the public and private spheres in the putain memoirs welcome both men and women. Lucrative, heterosexual liaisons are the goal and not a threat to the social order, so there is no need to separate the sexes into two different spheres. In fact, the putains are not only allowed to enter the public sphere; they thrive there.

The putains like Margot participate in the public sphere through more than their presence in public places and their rejection of private domesticity. One of the defining characteristics of the authentic public sphere that emerged in the eighteenth century is the importance of verbal communication. Witty, amusing, persuasive, and inspiring remarks spoken at meetings became essays, treatises, journal articles, pamphlets, and other publications. The public sphere was oriented around language—its textual production, discussion, and dissemination. There occurred a vastly expanded production of printed texts, or what Robert Darnton calls a heightened demand for the printed word.[35]

This new discursive economy, one characterized by a regime of words, printed and spoken, signaled a substantial shift from the visual symbolism of the monarchy. While the royal court consisted of private and public places—rooms that allowed for relative intimacy as well as large ballrooms and halls—the entire court constituted the public sphere because of who occupied it as well as the spectacle of power on display there. The absolutist public sphere was made sacred through visual, symbolic performances, including acts surrounding the king's body. With a view of authority manifested through the body politic, the king's bodily appearance held more significance than his voice as the locus of power. The ritualized pomp and ceremonies of Versailles with the imposing architecture of the palace created "visual representations of power [that] dominated all other forms of communication. . . . Power was enacted and tied to the king's person in a theatrical system of communication."[36] In contrast, the new cultural institutions, "coffeehouses, clubs, reading and language societies, lending libraries, concert halls, opera houses, theaters, publishing companies, lecture halls, museums, journals and newspapers," were "products of a swelling verbal and written culture."[37]

This other facet of the authentic public sphere, discursive rather than visual communication, is another realm the putains refuse to see as off limits. Many of the putains directly address the reader, or *lecteur*, and openly acknowledge that they are writing their memoirs to be published. In the opening pages of *Margot la ravaudeuse*, Margot speaks to her motivations and justifications for telling her story publicly: "It's not out of vanity, and even less out of modesty, that I'm exposing to the light of day the various roles I played during my youth. My main goal is to mortify, if it's possible, the pride of those who have made their little fortunes through means similar to mine, and to give the public a brilliant token of my appreciation, admitting that I owe everything I possess to their goodness and generosity." ("Ce n'est point par vanité, encore moins par modestie, que j'expose au grand jour les rôles divers que j'ai joués pendant ma jeunesse. Mon principal but est de mortifier, s'il se peut, l'amour propre de celles qui ont fait leur petite fortune par des voies semblables aux miennes, et de donner au public un témoignage éclatant de ma reconnaissance, en avouant que je tiens tout ce que je possède de ses bienfaits et de sa générosité.")[38] The words of her memoir, then, are a gift she is deliberately transmitting to her "public." For the putain, the reading public and her customers are one and the same.[39]

The prostitute narrators are as unafraid of publishing as they are of walking alone around the Palais Royal at night. *La Belle Allemande*'s Thérèse also proclaims her intention to publish and share her life story: "Me, give my story to the public? What a rare present! . . . So, I'm going to write a book. What a beautiful thing, writing a book, and how flattering for a person of my age to see herself in print and maybe even read with some curiosity! I cannot contain my joy." ("Moi donner mon histoire au public! Le rare présent! . . . Je vais donc faire un livre; la jolie chose que de faire un livre, et qu'il est flatteur pour une personne de mon âge de se voir imprimée, et peut-être lue avec quelque curiosité! Je ne puis contenir ma joie.")[40] Thérèse vainly considers her book to be a gift for her public, but the rest of the passage implies that it is more for her own pleasure that she writes. Her joy stems from the gratification of her reader's interest in the book as an extension of herself: when she gets a copy of the book, it will not be the words on the page she sees, but her own self. Just as she wants to be seen and admired at the theater or at the Palais Royal, her memoirs fulfill the same exhibitionist desire.

Because a virtuous woman was not seen or heard beyond the private sphere of her home, silence was the auditory version of physical confinement to private spaces.[41] Not long after Thérèse and Margot proudly publish their stories, Rousseau would describe in his *Lettre à d'Alembert* the admirable women from the mountains who keep silent in front of men in contrast to the lazy *salonnière* who is active only with her eyes and tongue.[42] A putain proclaiming her intention to publish was a refusal of the thinking behind Rousseau's definition of female virtue and a kind of verbal transgression.

At the same time the putains embrace public discourse, they also master the silent, visual communication utilized in the public sphere of the monarchy. With a glance, a smile, or a subtle gesture the putain effectively communicates availability and desire without speaking a word. The men the putains encounter understand the visual language of this libertine public sphere, but the prostitutes themselves are the ones in control, as Margot demonstrates during a rehearsal at the Opéra when a few carefully calculated gestures mesmerize the men watching her:

> No one has ever shown such a careful and imposing display of nonchalance. Lusciously enveloped under furs of ermine and sable, I had my feet in a covered box. . . . In this proud get-up, I was knitting with a distracted air and a golden shuttle. Sometimes I looked at my watch and made it go off. I opened each of my tobacco boxes one by one, and from time to time I brought up to my nose a superb crystal flask for the vapors that I didn't have. I leaned over to say insignificant things to my companions so that the curious gazers could judge the shapeliness of my limbs. In a word, I committed that evening a hundred little impertinences that enchanted my simpleminded spectators.
>
> (Jamais on ne se montra dans un négligé plus fastueux et plus imposant. Mollement enveloppée sous l'hermine et la martre zibeline, j'avais les pieds dans une boîte couverte . . . Dans cet orgueilleux appareil, je faisais d'un air distrait des nœuds avec une navette d'or. Quelquefois je regardais à ma montre, et la faisais sonner. J'ouvrais toutes mes tabatières l'une après l'autre, et me portais de temps en temps au nez un superbe flacon de cristal de roche pour des vapeurs que je n'avais pas. Je me penchais pour dire des riens à mes compagnes, afin que les lorgneurs curieux pussent juger de la tournure élégante de mes membres. En un mot, je commis ce soir-là cent impertinences, dont les benêts de spectateurs étaient enchantés).[43]

In this scene, even though she is taking a break, Margot nevertheless puts on a show. To witness her feigned boredom and simulated vapors she has a surprisingly large audience made up of her fellow dancers and other Opéra employees, as well as the *entreteneurs* waiting for their mistresses and unattached men looking for a new *fille entretenue*. Of all the curious onlookers of her performance, one man, a German baron whom a friend has brought to the rehearsal, is the most enchanted, as Margot reports: "I noticed with pleasure that my actions had plunged him into a sort of ecstatic rapture. . . . From the beginning to the end of the rehearsal, he had his two big eyes fixed on me like a pointer and seemed to experience an inner pleasure at my charms like one blessed." ("Je m'aperçus avec plaisir que mes gentillesses l'avaient plongé dans une espèce de ravissement extatique, . . . Depuis le commencement jusqu'à la fin de la répétition, il eut ses deux gros yeux fixés sur moi ainsi qu'un chien d'arrêt, et semblait jouir intérieurement de mes charmes à la manière des bienheureux.")[44] This public seduction is a success, and he becomes her next *entreteneur*.

The spaces of nonverbal communication in the putain memoirs are more than opportunities to highlight the prostitutes' skills of manipulation. They also permit another subversion of the king's authority. In addition to participating in a verbal public sphere in opposition to the visual one of the monarchy, the putains also usurp the power of visual representation. Like the ceremony of the *levée du roi*, gestures and objects hold serious symbolic value. The luxury items Margot manipulates are obviously gifts from previous *entreteneurs*, and her possession of them is proof of her desirability. Her aloof demeanor mimics the attitude of superiority of the aristocracy. Her gestures evoke desire and even obedience. The wealthy baron watching this scene of visual power is reduced to an animal—a panting dog—while Margot exhibits the ecclesiastic power to bless someone.

With their equally effective use of the new, authentic public sphere's verbal communication and the former public sphere's visual communication, the putains erase another purported boundary within Habermas's vision of the emerging public sphere. Communication through wordless, symbolic actions is no longer the sole purview of the monarch, and silence is not the inevitable fate of isolated women. Public discourses, conversations, and printed texts are viable tools for women as well as men.

In addition, the borderless public sphere found in the putain memoirs is more accessible than either the public sphere of the royal court or the new public sphere of the Enlightenment. The putains' public displays are visible to anyone present. While their flirtations and performances of feigned modesty in theaters are reserved for those men and women who have obtained employment in the theater, can afford tickets, or have tickets bought for them, the displays of their beauty and wealth also take place outdoors in parks and other open-air promenades where literally anyone can see them. To stroll through the Tuileries or around the Palais Royal one need not have a noble title, family wealth, or special favor from the king. Similarly, for their silent and seductive performances the putains do not need persuasive rhetorical skills or the kind of expensive, exclusive classical education necessary to make and understand references to the Roman Republic and its writers. Thus, the libertine public sphere in the putain memoirs is open to all.

This sphere does share a feature of the authentic public sphere of the eighteenth century: it is a site of economic activity, as buyers and sellers come together in public marketplaces to exchange goods and services. Laura Rosenthal's significant work on prostitution in eighteenth-century Britain provides valuable insights as to how the putains are able to thrive in this economic public sphere. She describes how the division of space into public and private spheres during the eighteenth century led not only to a gendered understanding of those spheres, but also to an urgent desire to "imagine the possibility perhaps more commonly experienced than absolute confinement to one or the other, of negotiating between these two spheres."[45] The putain memoirs, like the discourses on prostitution Rosenthal explores, fulfill that desire, as the narrators bring sexual acts out of the private sphere and into the public marketplace, effectively bridging the gap between the public and private.

In addition to being talented in the bedroom, eighteenth-century sex workers needed to succeed in the public marketplace, and depictions of prostitution in England and France began to reflect that reality. Rosenthal identifies how the image of the sex-crazed whore driven solely by lust, prevalent up through the seventeenth century, transforms into a more rational product of Enlightenment thinking, a professional with the business acumen and self-control necessary to turn a profit. As Rosenthal describes, "prostitution as the embrace of pleasure [is replaced by] prostitution as the sacrifice of pleasure to business."[46] The character Jenny Diver from *The Beggar's Opera* (1728) embodies well this change as she carefully separates sexual pleasure, pursued during "other hours [with] other men" from the business of prostitution.[47]

Margot also excels in this way and shares the lessons she has gathered on her path to success. For instance, Mme Florence begins her sexual education with a speech on the importance of money. She argues: "Everybody agrees, my pretty, that without money we are nothing. . . . Now, since we all like comfort, which you must agree requires money, it would be foolish to refuse to make money however one can." ("Il n'y a qui que ce soit, ma chère fille, qui ne convienne qu'on fait une forte triste figure en ce monde lorsqu'on n'est pas riche. . . . Or, comme il est tout simple d'aimer ses aises et le bien-être, ce qu'on ne saurait se procurer sans argent, vous conviendrez, je crois, que l'on est bien dupe de refuser d'en gagner quand on est à même de le faire.")[48] Margot later transforms lessons like this and the advice she received from other mentors, M. de Gr*** M*** and Frère Alexis, into a memorandum entitled "Advice for a Young Lady of the World." The eleven principles she lists begin with the suggestion that "any woman who wishes to achieve her ends must emulate the merchant and set her sights on her own interest and profits." ("Toute personne du sexe qui veut parvenir doit, à l'imitation du marchand, n'avoir en vue que ses intérêts et le gain.")[49] Of the remaining ten articles, seven focus on money, encouraging the potential putain to remember that "he who pays best wins out over his rivals" ("celui qui paie le mieux ait la préférence sur ses rivaux"), and always to "invest her money as it comes in and get a good return on her investment" ("placer son argent à mesure qu'il lui viendra, et s'en fasse de bonnes rentes").[50]

Margot clearly takes this financial advice to heart. References to specific sums abound in her memoir, appearing as frequently as references to places. For instance, we know how much she spent for the rendezvous with a stable boy when she lost her virginity (eight sols for the wine and two for the bread and cheese), how much she earned with her first trick (3 louis d'or), how much a jeweled cross given to her by the German baron cost (8,000 francs), how much she had saved by the time her English *entreteneur* left (an annual income of 12,000 louis), and how much she needs to comfortably retire (20,000 louis per year). Furthermore, Margot is very careful with her own money. Despite pushing more than one *entreteneur* into bankruptcy, Margot clarifies, "I never buy anything on credit." ("Oh! Non, ce n'est pas ma coutume de rien prendre à crédit.")[51]

Margot is also careful in the kind of men she chooses for sexual pleasure. While most putains escape the tedium of their unsatisfying *entreteneurs* in the arms of secret *greluchons*, Margot eschews these relationships that imply romantic feelings and often cost the putain money. Imagining the reader's curiosity, she explains: "I should have responded a while ago to a question that readers will doubtless have asked themselves many times over. How is it that Margot, whose libidinous nature resembles that of the Empress Messalina, could consent to see men for money, men who were for the most part no great shakes in bed? . . . I always had in my employ, but please this must remain secret, I have always had in my household a young vigorous footman." ("Il y a longtemps que j'aurais dû répondre à une question que mes lecteurs m'ont indubitablement faite plus d'une fois en eux-mêmes. Comment est-il possible que Margot, qui est née avec un tempérament de Messaline, ait pu se contenter de gens qu'elle ne voyait que par intérêt et qui la plupart n'étaient rien moins que des Hercules dans les travaux libidineux? . . . J'ai toujours eu à mes gages . . . Mais que ceci, je vous prie, soit sous le secret. J'ai toujours eu un jeune et vigoureux laquais.")[52] Margot goes on to explain that she recruits these men based on their appearance, preferring those "exactly the same in body and mind as the peasants portrayed by Marivaux: naive and light-hearted" ("exactement de la tournure d'esprit et de corps du paysan que l'ingénieux et élégant Monsieur de Marivaux nous a peint d'un coloris si naïf et si gai"), and educates them herself on how best to please her.[53] These relationships are a "reasonable system" that saves her from the emotional stress of a jealous or unfaithful lover and keeps her "appetite for lasciviousness in check" ("pour modérer les feux de l'incontinence").[54]

To be sure, the pleasurable breaks her footmen provide are necessary. More than any other putain, Margot describes the work of a prostitute as difficult and onerous:

> When I take the time to reflect on the cruel and bizarre treatment a prostitute has to put up with, I can scarce imagine a viler condition, including that of a galley slave or courtier. Is there anything more disgusting than having to satisfy the fantasies of any Tom, Dick, or Harry? To smile at a detestable old fart, to caress someone everyone finds repulsive, to lend our bodies to every imaginable vice, in a word, to hide one's true feelings behind an impenetrable mask in order to laugh, to sing, to drink; to hand oneself over to the wildest excesses, nay, to the most degrading and humiliating acts of wickedness, most often against our will and with extreme reluctance? Those who imagine that the life of a prostitute is a bed of roses don't know the half of it. . . . Let me say it again. Our life might seem alluring: nothing could be more humiliating.
>
> (Quand je fais réflexion aux épreuves cruelles et bizarres où se trouve réduite une fille du monde, je ne saurais m'imaginer qu'il y ait de condition plus rebutante et plus misérable. Je n'en excepte point celle de forçat ni de courtisan. En effet, qu'y a-t-il de plus insupportable que d'être obligée d'essuyer les caprices du premier venu; que de sourire à un faquin que nous méprisons dans l'âme; de caresser l'objet de l'aversion universelle; de nous prêter incessamment à des goûts aussi singuliers que monstrueux; en un mot, d'être éternellement couvertes du masque de l'artifice et de la dissimulation, de rire, de chanter, de boire, de nous livrer à toute sorte

> d'excès et de débauche, le plus souvent à contre cœur et avec une répugnance extrême? Que ceux qui se figure notre vie, un tissue de plaisirs et d'agréments, nous connaissent mal! . . . Je le répète; tout agréable que paraisse notre état, il n'en est ni de plus humiliant, ni de plus cruel.)[55]

Despite this vivid depiction of the degrading treatment even a successful putain must endure, Margot never regrets her choice of profession. She is certainly aware that few other options would have led to her being able to retire independently wealthy, unencumbered by a husband. More than lamenting her fate, this passage reveals the true key to her success. It is not an attractive appearance, not a lascivious nature, and not even carefully honed sexual skills that ensure success in the business of prostitution. A putain must above all have the self-discipline to hide her disgust and feign pleasure and the self-control to limit her side dalliances to a "reasonable system" she can control.

Margot's professional philosophy here demonstrates how the French putains avoid the anxiety surrounding an unrestrained marketplace that Rosenthal identifies in British depictions of prostitutes. In the British context, while the figure of the prostitute did provide an example of someone more realistically blending the public and private spheres (more than, say, a virtuous wife and mother), it also captured the vulnerability of the individual to an anonymous and "unforgiving marketplace."[56] In the tragic stories of penitent prostitutes and cautionary tales Rosenthal analyses, we find the possibility of abandonment and destruction of the individual when the boundaries between the public and the private spheres are blurred, boundaries that in the British context also protect personal and national identities.

The reason for the dissonance between the situation Rosenthal describes and the case of the French putain memoirs is perhaps more generic than national. Clearly, the French putain memoirs are not tragic stories of fallen and abandoned women. Only two (Javotte and Suzon) of the thirteen narrators of putain memoirs die in prison, and their stories have a lighthearted and amusing tone that belies the heroines' horrific end. The putains are never repentant, rarely penniless, and seldom abandoned. Rather, it is Margot's mother—the woman who married and raised at least one child, turning over her ravaudeuse barrel to her daughter so she could remain in the private domestic sphere—who ends up alone and in prison. The putain like Margot who can exhibit self-control and self-sacrifice, who can separate her own sexuality from the roles she plays and the acts she performs, is indeed empowered in the public marketplace of the new commercial society.

The same can be said of Cleland's *Memoirs of a Woman of Pleasure*, the British prostitute narrative that most closely resembles the putain memoir, and which, as Rosenthal admits, offers a "utopian model of business in which each transaction refines, pleases, and continues to perfect both parties."[57]

In the world of the putain memoirs, the marketplace is not unforgiving, and the individual only prospers when the boundaries between the public and private spheres are blurred. Indeed, the character of the prostitute does, in Rosenthal's words, "embody a new kind of commercial identity that can empower or threaten the individual through self-control, self-sacrifice, and self-division in marketplace exchanges," but in the putain memoirs we only find the potential empowerment and none of the threat.[58]

Despite her occasional cynicism describing the lifestyle of a putain and the sang-froid she exhibits in separating business and pleasure, Margot still contributes to the libertine utopia we find in all the putain memoirs. Like the other narrators, Margot describes a fantasy world where women are able to defy the legal and social limits imposed on them through their presence in public places, their rejection of the private, domestic sphere, the publication of their thoughts and observations, their revalorization of visual communication, and their active participation in the economy. All these efforts require a freedom real women could not expect. In pursuing their careers, the fictional putains help build a new libertine public sphere, one that serves their own best interests, no doubt, but that also erases boundaries for other people. As a site of interaction and communication among individuals, the libertine public sphere is open to all people, regardless of sex or class.

The image of the putain that we find in *Margot la ravaudeuse*—someone who embodies the eighteenth-century version of sex work by understanding "prostitution as commercial exchange rather than sensual indulgence" and rational enough "to endure dispassionate sex"—is not at odds with the lusty and feisty putain who mocks impotent aristocrats and exposes hypocritical priests.[59] Margot loves sex as much as the other putains. However, in her memoir she reveals more of how the putains manage their subversions. The courage to claim her own kind of public sphere and the self-discipline to leverage the opportunities she finds there are qualities to be found in all the putains. With her explicit advice and unflinching dedication to her own financial future, Margot follows through on her promise to "expose to the light of day" her path to success, a path that took her out of her father's home, through a myriad of public places, and into a life of satisfaction, wealth, and most importantly, independence.

Margot la ravaudeuse beautifully demonstrates what the putain memoirs do best: erase barriers. Just as the genre blurs lines between pornographic and philosophical content, libertine and erotic labels, verisimilitude and ironic self-awareness, so too do the heroines undermine social divisions based on birth, class, and gender. At a time when the Enlightenment was opening up new avenues for organizing, governing, and understanding society—epistemologies that created as many injustices as they corrected—the putain memoirs spanned the distance between the old and new. The putain narrator recognizes the utility and effectiveness of the monarchy's visual, symbolic expressions of power, while also rejecting the ancien régime's patriarchal social order based on inherited wealth and privilege. At the same time that her own success depends on manipulating and pleasing men with power and money, she unabashedly criticizes those people and institutions through her written words published in the new authentic public sphere. In other words, the putain succeeds in both the old and new public spheres, proving that the transformation of the public sphere was not sudden, dramatic, or complete.

The putains like Margot reveal a world without boundaries. There are no lines separating good from bad, a virtuous woman from a fallen one. The private sphere is not a haven of safety and comfort for women, and the public sphere holds opportunities, not inevitable dangers. When the putain tells her story with brutal honesty, she is pulling back the curtain to reveal these fictions. The lesson the putains teach is that the barriers based on class and gender only serve to maintain the privileges of an undeserving few at the expense of society's best and brightest—men and women with enough intelligence and rational self-control to harness their passions and seize the opportunities for prosperity found in the marketplace.

5

La Cauchoise, or Dear and Venerable Sisters

Without a doubt, the narrators of the putain memoirs are self-defining and self-sufficient. They are models of individual success achieved through their own talents and skills and without recourse to family connections. This independence from the patriarchal system is a hallmark of the putain memoir genre. These narrators, however, are far from living and working in isolation. Instead they create, maintain, and benefit from a network of relationships with other women. Sometimes these women serve as mentors, sometimes as partners-in-crime friends sharing in their escapades, and sometimes, as we find in *La Cauchoise*, these women are lovers.

In this chapter I build on the argument from chapter 3 that the putain memoirs criticized and undermined the patriarchal order with their depictions of men in power—fathers, aristocrats, and wealthy non-nobles—as foolish, impotent, and greedy, and thus not worthy of the benefits they enjoy. I will show here that in addition to wielding a kind of power through her sexuality and using that power to redistribute wealth and pleasure, as Thérèse does, the putain can also offer up an alternative social structure to the patriarchal hierarchy she critiques. And the patriarchal order in *La Cauchoise* is not simply unjust; it is dangerous. In a startlingly realistic and graphic manner, the heroine of *La Cauchoise* shows the vulnerability of *filles publiques* and the violence they potentially face in their relationships with men. Convents serve as prisons where fathers have the absolute authority to lock up their daughters with no more accountability than the king issuing *lettres de cachet*. Furthermore, the narrator of *La Cauchoise* describes in frank detail a threat facing eighteenth-century prostitutes and sex workers today: violent clients. In three remarkably graphic examples of sexual assault, *La Cauchoise* makes clear the vulnerability of women engaging in intimate acts with strangers.

After uncovering the unpleasant, sometimes brutal, but financially necessary heterosexual relationships in *La Cauchoise*, we will then turn to the fulfilling and helpful relations the putain finds with the women in her life. *La Cauchoise*'s La Dumonci has a close friend, a seamstress who is savvy in the libertine demimonde they occupy and who re-enters her narrative in key moments. And just as Margot benefits from the tutelage of the first madam who takes her in off the streets after she runs away from her family, La Dumonci finds a mentor and teacher in an older woman, Sister Prudence, who teaches her the art of sexual pleasure and secures her release from imprisonment.

What we find in *La Cauchoise* that is unique is the explicitly sexual relationship these two women enjoy. Building on the considerable work of scholars of female same-sex relations in the long eighteenth century, I argue that the sapphism in *La Cauchoise* serves as more than a titillating scene for male voyeuristic pleasure, and more even than a signal of anxiety about the growing sense of political and social changes that threatened the patriarchal order and male dominance.[1] While the relationship between La Dumonci and Sister Prudence contains elements that support both interpretations, their couplings also depict a genuinely pleasurable experience that completely excludes men physically and metaphorically. The result is less a menacing threat to the reader and more an appealing possibility for a safe and satisfying life where relationships with other women present a utopian alternative social structure that bypasses men and male-centered institutions.

Finally, we turn to *La Cauchoise*'s deliberate evocation of a sisterhood among putains, but also of all women. Even as the putain memoirs reveal patriarchal power centers, and men in general, as not only impeding women who pursue economic independence and personal pleasure, but also as posing violent and dangerous threats, these stories rarely work as simple cautionary tales, steering would-be female readers away from the perilous life of a putain. *La Cauchoise* provides examples of how to disarm the threats women face through a powerful source of strength and protection: other women. La Dumonci declares this unofficial network as a kind of professional sisterhood, one that she is proud to be a part of. This sisterhood transforms the story of *La Cauchoise* from a personal journey of growth and survival, formed from self-defense tricks handed down from friend to friend, into a political proposal indicting ancien-régime patriarchy and offering an alternative system.

In fact, by the time of *La Cauchoise* (first published in 1783) the putain memoirs seem to focus less on critiques of the ancien régime—although debauched nobles and lascivious clergy certainly populate this novel as well—and more on articulating their utopian alternative to eighteenth-century social and political structures. As other voices proclaim domestic labor and modesty to be essential qualities for women in an egalitarian society, the authors of the putain memoirs like *La Cauchoise* describe a very different alternative. A mere six years before the *cahiers de doléances* would convey the complaints of the French to their king, *La Cauchoise* proposed a fictional world in which women joined together to protect themselves from the tyranny of kinglike fathers, husbands, and jealous lovers.

The narrator who shows us this libertine dream of female fraternité never gives her first name, and all we have are the pseudonyms she goes by for protection, including "La Dumonci." The story of *La Cauchoise* contains many of the themes of previous putain memoirs, but also provides more graphic details and some violent episodes. The narrator explains that she spent her childhood in a small village in Normandy until age fifteen, when she is quickly seduced into becoming the mistress of a young bourgeois playboy who rents her a room in Le Havre. When he catches her being unfaithful to him, he arranges for her to be raped by a group of men and then has her arrested. As part of her punishment, she is sent to a convent, but this confinement becomes a source of liberation when she meets a nun, Sister Prudence, and the two develop an intimate friendship, which proves to be the most satisfying relationship of the book. After teaching La Dumonci about masturbation, dildos, and anal sex, Sister Prudence, knowing her young lover's taste for le monde, generously arranges for her to be released and sends her to Paris.

La Dumonci arrives in Paris knowing no one. She quickly meets a man who promises he can find high-paying clients for her sexual favors. After "restoring her virginity," he introduces her to a financier who provides her with a beautiful, lavish apartment, and this relationship proves to be financially, if not sexually, satisfying to La Dumonci. Fortunately, she soon finds a handsome count who fulfills her sexual needs while the financier continues to support her. All goes well until she and the count humiliate an abbot who then informs the financier of his mistress's infidelity. Forced to sever ties with her beloved count, the practical La Dumonci takes solace in the security of her financier's money, until she makes a terrible gaffe at the theater—insulting a woman who turns out to be a princess—and her financier cuts her off completely.

It is then that La Dumonci becomes serious about her profession, declaring she will have sex with anyone and everyone who will pay. Among her many customers is a colonel in the infantry, who takes her to his garrison in Rouen where she contracts her first case of syphilis. Contracting and transmitting venereal disease is a recurring theme through the rest of her story, which she ends in the Latin Quarter admitting that she is once again infected and deciding to use this break from work to write her memoirs. She recognizes that what little beauty she had has faded and that it will soon be time to become a procuress, but she regrets nothing.

Before exploring the benefits that the putains like La Dumonci find in female friendships, I will first examine their counterpoint: the unfulfilling and often damaging relationships the narrators have with the men in their lives, both family members and lovers. As we have seen, the heroines of these novels critique and discredit notions of family lineage and patriarchal power structures. La Dumonci begins her narrative with an example of the same kind of criticism of the hierarchical and patriarchal social system of the ancien régime as we found in *La Belle Allemande*. Like Thérèse and other putain narrators before her, La Dumonci proudly denies having any kind of illustrious family heritage and asserts that the status of her ancestors and family is not at all important. Even though many of her fellow prostitutes claim to be related to noble and influential people, La Dumonci disdains such pretension, explaining that a putain should scorn her birth and her family, having no other ambition than the satisfaction of her passion and the cultivation of a few "useful and agreeable acquaintances" ("des connaissances aussi utiles qu'agréables").[2] As we will see, these acquaintances will include not only the wealthy men who purchase her charms, but also the female friends and lovers who will occupy an important place in her life.

Not only is family unimportant for social status; in La Dumonci's case we see that her own parents clearly had nothing to do with her success. She describes her mother and father as completely disinterested in their daughter's education and prospects, hoping only to draw some profit from her labors. When they realize that her natural penchant for laziness will not serve them at home, they decide to send her to the city with eggs and butter to sell. There she discovers a more lucrative career better suited to her tastes. Certainly, her parents never expected her to discover prostitution at the markets; La Dumonci figures out for herself how to transform the interest a young man shows her into a successful means of support. From the vantage point of late in her career, writing her memoirs, she recognizes and explains that all the wealth, fame, and success that she has gained is through her own work and talent, and the favors and advice of friends.

The putains' mothers occupy an ambivalent position in their lives, being at once a symbol of parental control and of solidarity as a fellow woman. For example, in *La Cauchoise*, while neither parent has given La Dumonci her riches or her happiness, at least her mother has done nothing to impede her pursuit of wealth and satisfaction. Her father, on the other hand, is depicted as oppressive and pitiless. After La Dumonci's first trip into the city, she complains to her parents about the male attention she received there (the kind of attention she will quickly learn to enjoy and exploit). In this conversation, we see that her mother shows some concern for the girl, whereas her father is completely unsympathetic and unbending: "Once I returned to my father's home, they asked me how I found the city. 'Really awful,' I replied to my mother who had asked me. 'Why so?' asked this good woman. 'Oh, the men there,' I immediately answered, 'made me turn all red.' That little sample shows how naive I was then. I finished by saying that I would no longer go into the city, but my father would hear nothing of it and made me go back a few days later." ("Revenue chez mon père, on me demanda comment je trouvais la ville; bien vilaine, répondis-je à ma mère qui m'interrogeait. Pourquoi donc dit cette bonne femme? Ah, ces messieurs-là, repartis-je aussitôt, m'ont fait devenir toute rouge: qu'on juge par cet échantillon, de ma simplicité: je finis par dire que je n'irais plus à la ville, mais mon père n'entendit pas cela, et m'y fit retourner quelques jours après.")[3]

Even though both her parents are inadequate in the upbringing they give her, La Dumonci's mother at least appears to offer some sympathy and concern. She is the "good woman" who is interested enough to ask what is wrong after her daughter's first visit to the city. It is specifically only the father who insists on sending her back later, not in hopes that she might find a career or lovers, but because he is uninterested in her discomfort and only wants to make use of her labor. Later her father alone re-enters the story to send her to the convent, and when Sister Prudence tries to get her parents to let her out of the convent, it is the father who refuses.

La Dumonci even pauses in her narration to speak directly to her rejection of her family when she moves out for good:

> My readers, seeing me separated from my parents in this way, must no doubt expect me to present for them the pain they felt in losing me and the lengths to which they went to find me. I believe that I am, however, completely excused from going into such detail. To be clear, from the moment I started staying with the seamstress, my parents meant nothing to me, and I never heard anything else about them. If I thought about them from time to time, it was just to feel sorry for their fate in the hopes of improving it for them some day and to thereby fulfill my natural obligations and to obtain their pardon for my escapades. My situation seemed a lot sweeter than theirs.
>
> (Mon lecteur, en me voyant ainsi séparée de mes parents, s'attend sans doute que je vais lui peindre leur douleur de m'avoir perdue, et les soins

> qu'ils ont pris pour me recouvrer: je me crois totalement dispensée d'entrer dans un tel détail: à parler clair, du moment que je fus chez la couturière, mes parents ne me furent plus rien, et je n'entendis plus parler d'eux. S'ils m'occupèrent quelquefois l'esprit, c'était uniquement pour plaindre leur sort, dans l'espoir de l'améliorer un jour et de satisfaire par là aux devoirs de la nature, et mériter de leur part une indulgence plus que papale pour mon escapade par les sentiments de mon cœur; mais mon état me paraissait alors bien plus doux que le leur.)[4]

This is her last comment on her blood relatives, until her father reappears in her story. Any desire she has to help them financially or otherwise—her "natural obligations"—seem to arise, not out of filial love or affection, but out of a sense of guilt for the prosperity and pleasures she enjoys compared to the modest means of her parents. Furthermore, this concern is most likely short-lived, since even when she becomes wealthy and well known, she makes no mention of sending money, gifts, or any kind of assistance home to "improve their condition." Unlike Margot, who reconnects with her mother at the end of her story, La Dumonci never contacts either parent. Clearly, the debt she owes them as their offspring is of little importance within her set of values.

La Dumonci's relationships with men throughout her story seem to follow the model established with her father. Such unpleasant and dissatisfying depictions of our heroine's relationships with men is another way in which she undermines traditional, patriarchal society in this novel. Her first lover is a wealthy young dandy who seduces her with his incessant demands. But this is no example of sweet first love. La Dumonci finds this boy, who takes her virginity, quite unattractive, with his "blue eyes buried beneath a huge, bumpy forehead, an extremely short nose, a pallid complexion, and covering it all abundant smallpox scars" ("des yeux bleus enfoncés dans un front relevé en bosse, un nez extrêmement court, un teint livide et, pardessus le tout, force marques de petite vérole").[5] Again we find a reference to *la petite vérole*, conjuring *la vérole*, or syphilis. The effect this image creates is one of contagious ill health.

Furthermore, this man has difficulty taking her virginity because of the odd shape of his penis, which is "far bigger at the top than at the bottom" ("plus gros par le haut que par le bas,") and she jokes that this size would have been more appropriate for some rich old dowager ("eût été excellent pour quelque douairière").[6] Before being able to penetrate her, he ejaculates a few times on her legs from the effort: "He plugged away at my poor twat for a long time, but it refused to open its lips. My lover had already made several very copious libations on my thighs that had not caused me even the slightest emotion." ("Il s'escrima longtemps contre mon pauvre joujou qui ne desserrait pas les lèvres. Mon amant avait déjà fait plusieurs libations, et très copieuses, sur mes cuisses, qui ne m'avaient pas causé la plus légère émotion.")[7] Although she eventually enjoys sex with him, she assures the reader that it wasn't long before her "lover was no longer enough to satisfy all [her] desires" ("mon amant ne put plus suffire à satisfaire tous mes désirs").[8]

The lighthearted mockery in these passages soon gives way to a more somber tone. When this young fellow discovers that the narrator has been unfaithful to him (by passively submitting to the aggressive advances of an impassioned soldier), his character proves to be just as ugly as his face, and he plans a cruel revenge. The jealous lover hides his anger with coolness while he arranges a gang rape of his mistress. In an uncharacteristically violent and unpleasant scene, La Dumonci recalls how the young man who was supposed to be her "protector" took her to a deserted building:

> That same instant I saw eight brawny thugs emerge out of an adjacent closet. Among them I could distinguish a soldier, a wigmaker's apprentice, and a bookseller. . . . Imagine my surprise when the soldier came up to me and said:
>
> "Let's go, sweetheart; don't put on any airs, for God's sake! I've got a hard-on like a monk and, goddammit, I'm as good as my captain." He immediately took me in his arms and threw me on the bed. I cried out for help but in vain. My lover was deaf to the sound of my voice. Two other men wanted to hold down my hands.
>
> "Oh no," said the soldier, "I want to fuck her whether she likes it or not, and I intend for it to be without anyone's help."
>
> He had hardly finished saying these words in a hellish tone when he grabbed both my hands in his left hand and pinned them on my head. He separated my thighs with his knee, and with his right hand planted his cock in my cunt. After that he moved around like a real grenadier, fucking me three times without pulling out. Then he said to the others, with a triumphant and mocking tone:
>
> "Your turn, gentlemen. Do the same if you can."
>
> No matter how much I cried and tried to resist, the champions exploited me three times each, one after the other.
>
> (Dans le moment même je vois sortir d'un cabinet voisin huit drôles des mieux bâtis, entre lesquels je distinguai un soldat, un garçon perruquier

> et un compagnon libraire. . . . Quelle fut ma surprise quand le soldat vint me dire: allons, mon cœur, point de façons, sacredieu! je bande comme un carme et, mordieu! je vaux bien mon capitaine. Il me prend à l'instant dans ses bras et me jette sur le lit. Je criais en vain au secours, mon amant était sourd à ma voix. Deux de ces messieurs voulaient me tenir les mains; Oh! que non, dit le soldat, je veux la f**tre malgré elle, et je prétends que ce soit sans le secours de personne: à peine eut-il achevé ces mots d'un ton infernal, qu'il me saisit les deux mains de la main gauche et me les joint sur la tête. D'un coup de genou il me sépare les cuisses, et me plante de la main droite le v*** dans le c***; il s'agite après cela, en vrai grenadier, me f***t en plein trois fois de suite sans déc**ner, puis il dit aux autres, d'un air triomphant et moqueur: à vous, Messieurs, faites-en autant si vous le pouvez.
>
> J'eus beau pleurer et vouloir faire la réservée, ces champions m'exploitèrent chacun, l'un après l'autre, trois fois.)[9]

The frightening and graphic tone of this sexual assault sits in sharp contrast to the pleasurable and lighthearted descriptions of group sex elsewhere in this novel and in other putain memoirs. For example, later in her career La Dumonci will entertain six young men at the same time, but the tone of that scene is humorous with an amused emphasis on her ingenuity. In Fougeret de Monbron's *Margot la ravaudeuse*, the narrator complains of having to service an entire regiment in one day and after this incident even decides to leave the brothel where she was working. But in her case the complaint is that too much pleasure is too much. There is no mention of La Dumonci's pleasure anywhere. In fact, she mentions her cries twice. In addition, these men objectify her, "exploiting" her as if she were a natural resource. As much as she is denied the agency of consent each time she is raped, she is also denied a human voice with her lover's apparent deafness to her words. After this scene, her former lover delivers her to her father, who places her in a convent. Thus, before she meets Sister Prudence, we have seen what has been the total of La Dumonci's heterosexual experiences: a vengeful, pockmarked youth, a well-endowed captain who abandons her as soon as their affair is discovered, and eight rapists.

After her release from the convent, La Dumonci's next heterosexual encounter is less horrifying, but just as dissatisfying. When she finds a pimp in Paris, he demands that he be allowed to try out La Dumonci himself before he will find clients for her. Once again, the narrator experiences an unpleasant sexual experience with a man, the pimp being hardly able to maintain an erection: "My rascal gave it as much as he could. I must admit frankly that I found absolutely no pleasure with him. In fact, you be the judge whether it was even possible to get any: he was just barely hard. He was like all the other pimps, who bed as many women as they deliver. He had already screwed four that same day." ("Mon drôle s'en donna le plus qu'il put. J'avoue franchement que je ne trouvai aucun plaisir avec lui: en effet, qu'on juge s'il était possible que j'en prisse! A peine bandait-il; il était comme tous les autres maquereaux, qui exploitent autant de femmes qu'ils peuvent en livrer: il en avait besogné quatre ce jour-là même.")[10]

She seems to save her strongest criticism for the man who supports her throughout most of the story, her *financier entreteneur*. Like her first lover, he is anything but attractive. The first thing she notices about him is the "amplitude of his portliness" ("l'ampleur de son embonpoint)", in other words, he is obese.[11] She explains to the reader, "He was, I tell you, frighteningly ugly, to the point that I was a little scared." ("Il était, dis-je, laid à faire peur, ce qui m'effraya un peu.")[12] Later, presumably as the charm of his money begins to wear off and her lack of any attraction to him gives way to aversion, her criticisms become even harsher. The adjectives she uses to refer to him range from insulting (as "round, "fat," and "imbecilic") to judgmental and horrifying ("brutal" and "wicked").[13] There are also three longer passages in which she expresses her feelings. In one she asks the reader for forgiveness for not going into more detail about the financier, saying that talking about him would bore her to death, and that men like him are only meant to provide the money they must pay (because no one would sleep with them otherwise) and to leave as quickly and as often as possible. In another scene, she describes as mere annoyances his attempts to seduce her and to display his affection: "He found me in bed and began by telling me good morning. Then he tried, for whatever it was worth, to show me a few little signs of his tenderness. Then he came to cajole me while I got ready. After a thousand annoyances, or rather a thousand examples of childishness, he told me that he knew the whole truth [about my fidelity]." ("Il me trouva au lit, il commença par me dire bonjour, et tâcha de me donner, vaille que vaille, quelque petites marques de tendresse. Il vint ensuite me cajoler à ma toilette, où, après mille agaceries, ou plutôt mille enfantillages, il me dit qu'il savait la vérité à fond.")[14]

Finally, she describes the night before her financier leaves for a trip to the country: "A week later, my financier left for the country. He gave me the most tender of farewells because the last night I slept with him before his departure he fucked me four times. That is to say, my poor jewel sucked four times in the same night one of the vilest cocks that I have ever encountered in my whole life." ("Huit jours après, mon financier s'en fut à la campagne; il me fit des plus tendres adieux, car la dernière nuit que je couchai avec lui avant son départ pour ce voyage, il me baisa quatre fois en plein; c'est-à-dire que mon pauvre bijou suça quatre fois dans cette même nuit un des plus vilains v*** que j'aie vus et maniés dans toute ma vie.")[15] Despite all the money he gave her, this relationship was hardly a pleasant experience for her.

The next man who supports her, the colonel in the infantry who takes her to Rouen, fares only a little better. She ridicules this man who has what she calls "the folly of some men when they attach themselves to whores, as do all the great men in Europe and their 'monkeys' who are even more disdainful on that front" ("la folie des hommes quand ils ne s'attachent qu'à des putains, comme sont en Europe tous les grands, et leurs singes encore plus méprisables qu'eux à cet égard").[16] His extreme physical desire for her is annoying as she describes it: "As for me, I would have been perfectly happy without this excessive love, without this fury, if I may, for fucking." ("Quant à moi, j'aurais été parfaitement heureuse sans l'amour excessif, sans la fureur, je puis dire, du f**tre.")[17] Not only is this relationship purely transactional for La Dumonci, she wisely remains a bit leery of this intense patron, as we discover when she contracts a venereal disease, probably from a man other than the colonel: "If it wasn't a sure thing to trust my colonel when I was in good health, it was all the more natural for me to fear him immensely after having given him a pox like the one I was carrying." ("S'il n'était pas sûr de se fier à mon colonel étant en bonne santé, il était bien plus naturel à moi de le craindre infiniment après lui avoir donné une vérole semblable à celle que j'emportais.")[18]

After undergoing a cure for her venereal disease, La Dumonci encounters another terrible man, someone she calls in retrospect a *croc*, meaning a fang or a dangerous hook. The reason for this menacing imagery becomes apparent when he threatens to have her sent to prison for refusing to perform fellatio on him. This man speaks to her in the worst language, calling her a *garce* (bitch), a *foutue garce* (fucking bitch), and a *bougresse* (slut).[19] Furthermore, he does not even give the narrator the payment he promised. Instead he sends her insulting poems informing her that he gave her a venereal disease. To sum up her experience, she advises that prostitutes must try to avoid this type of man, "one of these detestable animals, the ferrets of brothels, without whom a whore would be only too happy" ("un de ces détestables animaux . . . furets de bordels . . . sans eux une putain serait trop heureuse").[20]

Finally, the last man she describes in the book brings yet another violent encounter: a near-rape scene recalling the treachery and violation she experienced through the machinations of her first lover. A frustrated young monk bursts into her home and attacks her:

> He grabbed me by the head, and then, throwing me on my bed, he bit me like a dog and got ready to plunge in mercilessly the full length of his fuming, lathering dagger. I could only prevent this by grabbing his fucking engine and twisting it really hard. The instrument was so affected that it cried out its spite into my hand, and with so much unction that he flooded my cunt and thighs in a torrent of fuck. I was able to disarm him that way, with a vigorous punch. And I sent away my apostolic Priapus as dissatisfied as when he arrived.
>
> (Il m'empoigna par la tête puis, me jetant sur mon lit, il me mordit comme un chien, et se disposait à m'enfiler sans miséricorde de toute la longueur de son *braquemart* écumant de fureur, ce que je ne pus empêcher qu'en empoignant son b**gre d'engin, et le lui tordant très fortement: l'instrument en fut si fort affecté qu'il s'avisa d'en pleurer de dépit dans ma main, et avec tant d'onction, qu'il m'inonda le c*** et les cuisses d'un torrent de f**tre. J'achevai pour lors de désarçonner, par un vigoureux coup de poing, mon priape apostolique, et je renvoyai enfin le moine aussi peu satisfait que quand il était venu.)[21]

Although the scene recalls her earlier sexual assault, with the narrator thrown on the bed, this passage differs when the would-be victim returns his violence in self-defense, grabbing, twisting, and punching. This time it is not the woman who is crying out, but her attacker's member. The scene ends with La Dumonci empowered and the monk slinking away, dissatisfied and wounded.

Importantly, La Dumonci dehumanizes each of these three men—the colonel who resembles other "monkeys" devoted to whores, this monk who bites her like a dog, and the "croc," whom she not only calls a "ferret," a mere rodent, but whom she identifies only synecdochally as the tooth of an animal. This man is a feral beast whose entire identity is reduced to the fangs he uses to wound and devour. From her cruel, vengeful first lover to the would-be rapist at the end of her narrative, La Dumonci feels nothing but disdain, disgust, and some fear for these men who feel entitled to use and abuse her body.

The one man who does bring her genuine pleasure is a young count whom she makes her *greluchon* during her time with the financier. In contrast to her *entreteneur*'s hideous face and body, this lover is handsome, "tall, well-built, with prominent black eyes, underneath two eyebrows of the same color, full cheeks, red lips, a shapely leg" ("grand, bien bâti, des yeux noirs à fleur de tête, surmontés de deux sourcils de la même couleur bien fournis, des joues remplis, des lèvres vermeilles, une jambe faite au tour").[22] This description is almost feminine in its resemblance to the listing of physical attributes of the putains in these novels. The count is also somewhat objectified in that it is purely his attractive appearance that matters. The narrator quickly qualifies: "I would love to praise his wit, but alas he had none." ("Je souhaiterais avoir à faire l'éloge de son esprit, mais il n'en avait pas.")[23] Furthermore, her relationship with him is in fact quite limited. She knows she can never go to him for financial assistance: "The count was not the kind to support me. Even though he was rather rich, he was one of those original men who like pleasure but who can never resolve themselves to buying it or paying for a piece of ass." ("Le comte n'était pas d'humeur à m'entretenir; il était, quoiqu'assez riche, de ces hommes originaux qui aiment le plaisir, mais qui pourtant ne sauraient se résoudre à acheter, à payer un cul.")[24] In fact, this initially blissful relationship ends up causing La Dumonci the greatest pain, and after this man breaks her heart, she vows never to love again and to have sex only for money.

Female characters finding true love only to have their hearts broken is, of course, a common theme in many genres of literature. Similarly, it is not surprising that these subversive and critical narrators mock and disdain their wealthy clients. What are remarkable, however, are the rich and satisfying relationships they describe having with other women. In contrast to the steady disappointment and dissatisfaction she finds with men, the putain's experiences with other women are the ones that she most enjoys.

While the first woman in La Dumonci's life, her mother, seems to play a minimal role in her development and career, the seamstress she meets after leaving her parents' home will become an important part of her life. In fact, she refers to the new phase of her life on her own as "the moment I started staying with the seamstress." She does not call it "once I lost my virginity" or "as soon as I met my lover," or in any other way reference her boyfriend. Instead, it is her roommate, a woman who will hold a special place in her heart later on, who represents this period of her life and the break with her family.

This woman is more than a symbol of change for La Dumonci and certainly more than a landlord. Once La Dumonci's treacherous lover discovers her infidelity and suspects the seamstress of facilitating it, he orchestrates La Dumonci's rape and also plans to have her and her friend sent to a convent the next day. La Dumonci is fully aware of his intention, but after her assault he keeps her under his constant surveillance, so she is unable to warn her friend. La Dumonci hardly laments her own abuse and impending imprisonment, but is instead tortured by the fact that she cannot warn her friend:

> My treacherous lover . . . took me home rather than taking me back to my father, but he never left me alone for a moment. I don't know if he did that to keep me from talking to the seamstress, whom I would surely have told about my experience and whose fertile genius—made so by her long experience in the world, her pains, and her pleasures—would have found a solution to the horrors that threatened us. She could have called on her good friends, and with a prudent and necessary escape we could have plotted our revenge with ease. . . .
>
> The unmerited treatment that he had just made me endure, his threats, and I believed, the lack of pleasures that I would have in the convent, which I thought of as my tomb, upset me. All these things filled my soul and my mind with the saddest and most melancholy mood. My underhanded lover was, on the contrary, charmingly upbeat, so that the seamstress, who had no idea to what to attribute all that she was seeing, was excessively intrigued. I picked up on her nervousness without being able to tell her anything. She looked for ways to get it out of me, but in vain. She could never succeed. How nice it would have been, how happy I would have been to be able to warn her of the danger that was looming for her and for me!
>
> (Mon perfide amant . . . me reconduisit chez moi au lieu de me ramener chez mon père, mais il ne me quitta pas un seul moment: je ne sais s'il le fit pour m'empêcher de parler à la couturière, à qui je n'aurais pas manqué de faire part de mon aventure, et dont le génie fertile en expédients eût apporté, par son long usage du monde, de ses peines et de ses plaisirs, un secours aussi prompt que salutaire aux malheurs qui nous menaçaient, par l'assistance de ses bons amis, et au moyen d'une retraite aussi prudente que nécessaire dans ce moment critique, après quoi nous aurions pu prendre notre revanche à notre aise. . . .
>
> Ainsi, le traitement indigne qu'il venait de me faire, ses menaces, et, je crois plus encore la disette de plaisirs que j'allais éprouver dans le couvent, que j'envisageais comme mon tombeau, me troublèrent; toutes ces choses répandirent dans mon âme et dans mon esprit l'humeur la plus triste et la plus mélancolique. Mon parjure amant était au contraire d'une gaieté charmante: quel contraste! Aussi la couturière, qui ne savait à quoi attribuer tout ce qu'elle voyait, était-elle excessivement intriguée: je m'apercevais de son inquiétude, sans pouvoir néanmoins l'instruire de rien. Elle cherchait les moyens de me dissiper, mais en vain, elle ne put jamais y réussir. Qu'il

m'eût été doux! que j'aurais été heureuse de pouvoir la prévenir sur le malheur qui la menaçait comme moi!)[25]

The narrator is confident that her friend—who already displays concern and sympathy for La Dumonci's unease—would not only have been a compassionate confidante to whom she could communicate the pain of her sexual assault, but also a capable friend with the necessary ingenuity and network of friends to get them out of their predicament. A true friend like the seamstress has both "the fertile genius" and the "good friends" to remedy a predicament. In contrast with the men in her life, La Dumonci sees this female friend as a source of aid, as a confidante who will understand her worries, and as a fellow victim. This kind of bond is much stronger than anything she felt for her kin or for her male sexual partners.

When La Dumonci is sent to a convent along with her dear seamstress friend, she again expresses her selfless sympathy for her friend: "I was accompanied there by my poor seamstress, whom I pitied more than myself. I've always cherished her since then. You'll see the proof of that later on, and you'll have to admit that, generally speaking, even a putain can still have an excellent heart." ("J'y fus accompagnée de ma pauvre couturière, que je plaignais plus que moi. Je l'ai toujours chérie dès lors; on en verra des preuves dans ces Mémoires: et l'on doit d'ailleurs convenir, généralement parlant, qu'une putain a toujours le cœur excellent.")[26] It is through her actions toward a female friend, and not toward a lover or client, that this hooker will prove to have a heart of gold.

After her release from the convent, La Dumonci's first thought is again of that seamstress, who has unfortunately not been freed. Years later, at the height of her good fortune, La Dumonci finds this same friend sick and badly abused at the hands of two cruel soldiers. The woman's situation appears dire. Three days later this unfortunate woman shows up at her door, and La Dumonci describes their conversation in an unusually touching passage:

> She finally came by around ten o'clock in the morning to throw herself at my knees. I made her stand up and I embraced her cordially. After that I had her sit down next to me, despite her frightful state. Without proper underwear and without clothing, . . . a sad and shameful air seemed to be blocking her heart. She wanted to speak, but you could see that confusion held her back and cut off her speech. I noticed that very quickly, and to put her at ease and to get her to confide in me, I had her take off her rags and gave her what she needed to cover herself properly. When this sad and regrettable ceremony was finished, I told her some very affectionate things, the last of which was:
>
> "I insist, my good friend, that you stay with me forever."

"Oh!" this girl said to me with a big sigh, "you're giving me back my life."

This sigh, which came out naturally, broke the dam, and in the next moment my seamstress painted me such a touching picture of her misfortune that I had to beg her not to go on. . . . But let's end this topic, because it's making me cry, and let's get back to talking about me.

(Elle vint enfin, sur les dix heures du matin, se jeter à mes genoux; je la fis relever et je l'embrassai cordialement; après quoi je la fis asseoir à côté de moi malgré l'état affreux où elle se trouvait: sans linge et sans habits, . . . un air triste et honteux semblait barrer son cœur. Elle voulait parler, mais on voyait que la confusion la retenait et lui coupait la parole. Je le remarquai bien vite, et pour la mettre plus à son aise et l'inviter à me donner sa confiance, je lui fis poser ses haillons et lui donnait tout ce qui était nécessaire pour la couvrir. Quand cette triste et fâcheuse cérémonie fut terminée, je lui dis bien des choses affectueuses, dont les dernières furent:

—Je veux absolument, ma bonne amie, que vous restiez toujours avec moi.

—Ah! me dit alors cette fille en poussant un grand soupir, vous me rendez la vie!

Ce soupir, échappé tout naturellement, rompit la digue, et dans l'instant ma couturière me fit une peinture si touchante de ses malheurs que je fus obligée de la supplier de ne m'en pas dire d'avantage. . . . Mais finissons cet article, car il m'arrache des larmes, et revenons à parler de moi.)[27]

The depth of her feelings toward this woman is obvious. Even taking into consideration a certain amount of hyperbole and *sensibilité* common in eighteenth-century fiction, we find a degree of emotion in this passage that cannot be found elsewhere in her memoirs. What seems at the start of this passage to be merely an opportunity to impress the reader with her own generosity quickly reveals a genuinely painful memory. La Dumonci's reaction to the "terrible things" that she hears is almost visceral. Even now, years later, in telling this story she trembles in horror and admits that the memory of this good woman makes her cry. Her reaction to the seamstress contrasts starkly with her feelings toward her family. Unlike the guilt she feels toward her parents, which she apparently does nothing to atone for, she is able to assist, and indeed is thrilled to help her friend enjoy her last remaining days.

In many ways this unfortunate friend represents a tragic alternate fate that La Dumonci herself could have known. Ironically, the woman whose savvy and connections could have saved them earlier in her story becomes the one in dire need of our narrator's aid. Whereas the seamstress's cruel clients have made her suffer, it is La Dumonci's generous clients who are providing her with shelter. Also, the seamstress was twenty-nine when she died, but La Dumonci refers to her age as just having finished her twenty-eighth year. Perhaps this turn of phrase is to recall La Dumonci's own age at the time of writing her memoirs, which she states earlier is twenty-eight. Using the same number to refer to her current age and the age at which she was most closely linked to this woman points to their connection. Clearly, she identifies with this woman on a strong level.

While living as the financier's mistress, La Dumonci takes solace with her lover, the handsome count, but also with a woman she repeatedly calls "ma chère amie" (my dear friend), another man's mistress named La Duttey. Again, there is a level of identification with this fellow prostitute, this time in the similarity of their assumed names. This woman is a good friend to La Dumonci, as the narrator states: "I could trust her entirely." ("Je pouvais me fier entièrement à elle.")[28] There is also an ambiguously sexual element to their friendship. This woman serves as the liaison between La Dumonci and her lover, and each time she must break off with the count, she is also forbidden to see her friend. It is as if her sexual relationship with the count is somehow transmissible to the friend who enables their rendezvous.

Once her *entreteneur*'s initial suspicions are allayed, however, he allows La Dumonci to see them again, and she rushes to pay a surprise visit to La Duttey to announce the news. She is not at all surprised or jealous to find the count spending time alone with La Duttey. First, she asks the count to kiss her, then she states: "The count complied beautifully, as did my good friend. But they just couldn't get over their surprise. Both of them, *equally* charmed to see me, were looking to find the cause for this joy" (my emphasis). ("Le comte me répondit fort bien, ainsi que ma bonne amie; mais ils ne pouvaient revenir de leur surprise. . . . tous deux, également charmés de me voir, ils cherchaient la cause de ce bonheur.")[29] While the kiss or embrace the narrator receives from her lover may have contained a different degree of sexual passion than the one from her friend, such a difference is nowhere indicated in the text. And even though the narrator could very well be describing a different kind of joy in each person that is simply equal in its intensity, the placement of these two friends—one of whom occupies an unequivocally sexual role in her life—in parallel positions concerning her return at the very least allows some ambiguity.[30]

A relationship that is not at all ambiguous for La Dumonci is her sexual apprenticeship under the tutelage of Sister Prudence. The narrator attributes all her professional progress as a libertine to this nun who took her under her wing: "I was a simple fucker when I entered this holy house, but I had, when I came out, all the talents of a true putain. I did the opposite of Mary Magdalene, who, being a debauched public woman, became repentant because she was forced by the horrible state to which her libertine life had reduced her. In my case, I achieved perfection in whoring thanks to the excellent models before me—examples that I took to heart." ("J'étais une simple f**teuse quand j'entrai dans cette sainte maison, mais j'avais, lorsque j'en sortis, tous les talents d'une vraie putain. J'ai fait tout le contraire de sainte Madeleine qui, de débauchée et femme publique qu'elle était, devint repentante parce qu'elle y fut forcée par l'état affreux où son libertinage l'avait réduite. Quant à moi, je parvins à la perfection du putanisme à force d'avoir d'excellents modèles sous les yeux, et des exemples dont j'ai fait mon profit.")[31] In what will be her only unequivocally homosexual relationship, the affection and devotion La Dumonci describes between these two women will far exceed simple lust: "I admit that I owe a lot to a certain kind sister who took care of my education. I would never have amounted to anything without her." ("J'avoue que je dois beaucoup à certaine bonne sœur qui prit soin de mon éducation. Je n'aurais jamais rien valu sans elle.")[32] Her female lover gives her not just pleasure, but an education and even her worth.

At their first meeting, Sister Prudence makes clear the mutual benefits of their relationship: "Tell me honestly, do you like this convent? . . . I can guess your answer. So then, if you want to be my good friend, I will be the one to get you out of here. But first I must try you out; I wouldn't want to send you out into the world without any talents. You appear to have an excellent base; we just have to cultivate it. I'll take care of that, and with pleasure. Come see me every day, and you will certainly be happy with me." ("Dites-moi franchement: aimez-vous ce couvent? . . . je devine votre réponse. Eh bien, si vous voulez être ma bonne amie, ce sera moi qui vous en ferai sortir. Mais avant cela il faut que je vous éprouve: je serais fâchée de vous renvoyer dans le monde sans talents. Vous paraissez avoir le fond excellent, il ne s'agit que de le cultiver. J'en prendrai le soin avec plaisir. Venez me voir tous les jours, vous serez sûrement contente de moi.")[33] Beneath the flirtatious tone of their meeting lies an assurance that theirs is to be a mutually beneficial relationship. La Dumonci will be Sister Prudence's *bonne amie* and in exchange Sister Prudence will teach her skills useful for a prostitute and in addition will ultimately secure her release from the convent. Sister Prudence gets the pleasure of a young and eager lover, and La Dumonci will gain her freedom. Unlike the similar transactions she would later have with men, this deal brings her pleasure on top of the benefits of the exchange. The two women develop a satisfying sexual relationship despite the older nun's body, which the reader soon discovers to be sagging and faded.

Over the course of their next several meetings Sister Prudence tells her the story of her life and adventures. Like a good pupil, La Dumonci asks for explanations of anything she does not understand and in this way becomes knowledgeable in no time. Although this language of education and training is of course meant to be amusing, and the entire depiction of her lascivious nun-lover plays into the common anti-Church rhetoric frequently found in libertine literature of the time, the information Sister Prudence imparts is nonetheless useful for La Dumonci. The "training" she receives from Sister Prudence (no matter how sarcastically the term may be intended) allows her to excel in her profession and become wealthy, famous, and successful. Having received barely any education from her parents—who taught her nothing more than how to read and write—La Dumonci relishes and benefits from the practical lessons this friend gives her. These gifts prove to be worth more than what any male client ever pays this savvy whore.

La Dumonci not only gains knowledge and skills, but she is also able to leave the convent thanks to Sister Prudence's intervention. As the two women spend their time enjoying sexual pleasures, Sister Prudence is keeping up her end of the bargain behind the scenes by trying to obtain the freedom of her young pupil, first by asking her father to allow her to leave (which he coldly refuses) and then by convincing the superiors that the young woman has reformed. This aging and fading libertine generously helps her friend escape the convent. No man in La Dumonci's life ever displays such selflessness. The narrator recognizes Sister Prudence's rare qualities, and in addition to the detailed depictions of their sexual activities and the enormous pleasure La Dumonci receives from them are signs of true devotion. La Dumonci is never faithful to any of her male lovers, including her beloved count, but in the convent she sees only Sister Prudence.[34]

Even though the graphic depiction of sex between these two women could be read as satisfying a voyeuristic desire in heterosexual men to sneak a peek at two beautiful women pleasuring each other, La Dumonci cuts off this fantasy with a frank description of Sister Prudence's aging physique. The nun is considerably older than La Dumonci, who describes her bosom as having "a leathery bluish-gray tint" ("une peau livide et tannée") and her body in general as "withered, nasty, and gloomy" ("fanée, vilaine et maussade").[35] Unlike the corpulence of her *financier entreteneur* or the misshapen penis of her first lover, however, Sister Prudence's physical shortcomings do not at all compromise La Dumonci's pleasure in her arms. Rather, the unattractive description functions more as an unexpected realistic detail that shocks the male reader out of his fantasy of two nubile and lustful women exposing their perfect bodies for the reader's pleasure. Instead, this "withered" and "nasty" body eliminates the possibility of male pleasure in their couplings. The pleasure is the women's alone.

The idea that women can create happiness, satisfaction, and indeed pleasure at the total exclusion of men, a principle manifesting in many of the relationships in *La Cauchoise* and in the other putain memoirs, is expressed most clearly in one of La Dumonci's sexual encounters with Sister Prudence involving a double-headed dildo:

> For a long time, we had been using the kind of dildo everyone is familiar with. I put it in the sister, and Sister Prudence did the same for me. But we could never experience the same pleasure at the same time, and that was exactly what we would have liked. So what did Sister Prudence do? She asked one of her tinsmith friends to make her a dildo sixteen inches long with a penis head on each end and with a spring in the middle which could shoot out the milk we put in there and send it flowing into the two wombs at the same time. The intelligent tinsmith accomplished his mission perfectly. Sister Prudence covered the tin with crimson velvet and attached as much hair as possible to the middle. You can see by this attention to detail the care with which Sister Prudence studied and followed nature's example. All this was done in less than eight days.
>
> The moment came to try it out. Oh, how sweet it was for the nun and me! For us it was the most solemn holiday. I was supposed to meet her at two o'clock, and I didn't miss it. I found the sister in her shift, and the milk was warming up.
>
> "Let's go sweetheart," she said. "Quick, do like me and get on the bed."
>
> I didn't have to be told twice. I got undressed in the blink of an eye. Sister Prudence, who had filled the dildo, said, jumping on the bed, "Finally, we are going to have the same pleasure as if we were man and woman." And with that she took the artificial doctor and put one end in my cunt and the other end in hers.
>
> "Hold me," she added. "Kiss me. Good . . . push hard . . . move your ass around . . . that's it . . . good! . . . so do you feel that?"
>
> It hurt a little when she put this machine in my cunt. Sister Prudence had had it made to the size of hers, which could have passed for a carriage entrance. But after a lot of thrusting, it was able to penetrate. Then I felt

all my parts being tickled in excess. The sister, seeing me so animated, reached behind herself and flipped the spring. In this way, the milk mixed with the hot spermatic fluid that came out and filled our two cunts. Good God, what pleasure we felt!

("Nous sous servions depuis longtemps du godemiché tel que tout le monde en connaît. Je le mettais à la sœur, et sœur Prudence me rendait la pareille, mais nous ne pouvions ressentir le même plaisir toutes deux en même temps. C'était là cependant ce que nous aurions voulu. Que fit sœur Prudence? Elle donna ordre à un ferblantier de ses amis de lui faire *un godemiché long de seize pouces*, qui fût *terminé par deux têtes de v**t, avec un ressort dans le milieu*, qui, du même coup, fît couler dans les deux matrices le lait qu'on devait mettre dedans. Le ferblantier intelligent s'acquitta parfaitement bien de sa commission. La sœur revêtit ce fer-blanc d'un velours cramoisi, sur le milieu duquel elle attacha le plus de poils qu'elle put. On voit, par cette attention, avec quel soin sœur Prudence étudiait et suivait la nature. Tout cela fut fait en moins de huit jours.

Le moment de l'épreuve vint. Qu'il fut doux pour la nonne et pour moi! C'était pour nous un jour de fête la plus solennelle. J'eus rendez-vous à deux heures, et je n'y manquai pas. Je trouvai la sœur en chemise, le lait chauffait, *allons, mon cœur, me dit-elle, fais-en vite autant que moi et mets-toi sur le lit*: je ne me fis pas prier, je fus déshabillée en un clin d'œil. Sœur Prudence ayant rempli le godemiché: enfin, dit-elle en sautant sur le lit, nous allons avoir le même plaisir que si nous étions homme et femme: elle pose aussitôt le docteur artificiel, d'un côté dans mon c***, et se met elle-même l'autre bout dans le sien. Serre-moi, ajouta-t-elle, embrasse-moi, bien . . . pousse fort . . . remue le cul . . . il y est . . . bon! . . . eh bien! le sens-tu? . . . Je souffris un peu quand cette machine m'entra dans le c***. Sœur Prudence l'avait fait tailler sur le sien, qui pouvait passer pour une porte cochère. Après bien des secousses, il put pourtant pénétrer. Je sentis alors toute mes parties chatouillées à l'excès: la sœur, me voyant fort animée, passa la main derrière elle, lâcha tout à coup le ressort: le lait se mêla par ce moyen avec la liqueur spermatique qui sortait à toutes deux toute bouillonnante de c***. Grand dieu! quelle volupté nous ressentîmes!)[36]

On the one hand, this passage appears to valorize the pleasures of heterosexual intercourse; the "finally" in the phrase "we are going to have the same pleasure as if we were man and woman" implies they have been waiting for and wanting this kind of heterosexual pleasure, which must surpass that of any other acts they have shared. Further, when the narrator praises

Sister Prudence for making certain that the special dildo she has built resembles as closely as possible a real penis, she hints at craving the body of a man.

However, as Ula Klein's work on the dildo in eighteenth-century literature demonstrates, this kind of lesbian encounter represents more of a threat to masculinity than a celebration of men.[37] Her analysis of English dildo poems and female husband narratives identifies the dildo as a material marker for lesbianism that provokes anxiety at the possibility of women achieving pleasure at the total exclusion of men. While Klein presents a variety of examples that include some depictions of the dildo as a "paltry substitute" for the male member, in *La Cauchoise* Sister Prudence's invention is a near-perfect replica in La Dumonci's opinion. Both the tinsmith's skill (or "intelligence") and Sister Prudence's careful attention to detail in its design ensure that this "artificial doctor" resembles a real penis as closely as possible. In fact, this suitable replacement is created in eight days, only two more than God needed to create the original man and his penis.

Once the two lovers put the dildo to use, it proves to surpass the prowess and virility of any one man. Not only is it able to penetrate two women simultaneously, its size and design manage to stimulate La Dumonci "in excess." Furthermore, this dildo serves as much more than a successful stand-in for a real penis. A key ingredient in the pleasure it creates is the fluid used in its mock-ejaculation. Tellingly, Sister Prudence fills it with milk—a substance that only females can produce.[38] Indeed, the word *lait* here is in stark contrast with the usual term in these novels for fluid released in an orgasm: *liqueur*. It is at precisely the moment when this milk is emitted and mixes with the women's own sexual fluids (described as "spermatique") that the narrator cries out the orgasmic phrase "Good God!" (Whether this is a citation of her cry from the scene or a cry of pleasure in remembering and writing about this moment is unclear, and irrelevant here.) This sexual encounter at once inverts sexual reproductive roles and erases gender difference. The inversion occurs with the two women who secrete spermatic fluid while it is the penile object that emits maternal milk. And unlike in heterosexual relations or even in sex acts between two women with a regular dildo, in this case neither woman is exclusively penetrated or exclusively penetrating. There is no difference in the genders of the two partners nor in their sexual roles. The result is, if not mutual orgasm, at least success in enjoying the same pleasure at the same time. Even though the two women claim to want to have sex the way a man and a woman do, what they really want is this sexual equality, feeling the same pleasure in the same way.

The satisfying sex between La Dumonci and Sister Prudence demonstrates the possibility of achieving pleasure at the total exclusion of men. What we do not find in this novel is homosexual desire meant as a negative example to reinforce the primacy of heterosexuality, as scholars have identified in other texts. Certainly, the sexual training La Dumonci receives helps her become a better putain who presumably offers a more satisfying experience to her male clients, and it is true that she finds sexual pleasure with some men later in her narrative. But as a putain memoir with none of the implications of a conventional romance narrative, *La Cauchoise*, in the words of Elizabeth Wahl, does not reinforce the reader's "sense of sexual sufficiency by demonstrating that even a woman of lesbian inclinations must inevitably turn to men for sexual satisfaction."[39] This particular woman of lesbian inclinations turns to sex with men primarily for money, not pleasure. Further, her relationship with Sister Prudence is specifically exclusive, negating the possibility of the kind of *ménages à trois* Chris Roulston identifies in many eighteenth-century novels, involving a husband, his wife, and her best friend. Even though these female friendships are tinged with sexuality, they still maintain and reinforce the heterosexual, bourgeois marriage—something none of the putains, least of all La Dumonci, aspires to secure.[40] In other words, it is the specific lesbian relationship that we find in *La Cauchoise* and the putain's lifestyle in general that make such an interpretation of the same-sex desire inapplicable here. Furthermore, the vivid depictions of her dissatisfaction with men and thus with penises both before and after her "education" with Sister Prudence does not at all support the theory that her lesbian encounter only serves to make La Dumonci better appreciate a penis. It is not until she finds her count that she has any kind of satisfying sex with a man.

Outside of her scenes with Sister Prudence, the narrator advocates sincerely for a greater acceptance of same-sex desire. There are several instances in which La Dumonci defends first lesbian sexuality and then sodomy, and despite the irony elsewhere in the novel (and throughout the putain memoir genre), these passages read as genuine expressions of support. In the first she explains: "I heard someone claim one time that there can be no pleasure between two people of the same sex getting together. I promise that those making such claims are false doctors. They just need to experience it. Personal experience in such matters is worth more than all the reasoning in the world. Besides, there is nothing so surprising in two women being attracted to each other." ("J'ai ouï soutenir quelquefois qu'il n'y a point de plaisir entre deux personnes de même sexe qui s'unissent: je promets que ceux qui sont de ce sentiment sont de faux docteurs. Qu'ils l'éprouvent seulement. L'expérience, en ces choses-là, vaut mieux que tous les raisonnements du monde. Il n'y a rien d'ailleurs de tant surprenant dans ce goût de deux femmes l'une pour l'autre.")[41] La Dumonci continues with the anecdote of two famous lesbians at the French court, "a lady of the highest class" ("une dame de la plus haute condition") and her favorite, L. P. de L., a thinly veiled reference to Marie Antoinette and La Princesse de Lamballe.[42] Although accusations of homosexuality were common in the critical pornographic pamphlets attacking the queen in prerevolutionary France, La Dumonci's defense of this lady's desire for a woman, as well as the argument preceding it, appear genuine.[43]

This reference to rumors disparaging Marie Antoinette is a reminder of the political context in which *La Cauchoise* was written. Published just a few short years before the storming of the Bastille, a putain memoir like La Dumonci's reveals many of the tensions of the time; and as several scholars maintain, larger social, economic, and political tensions have often been expressed through heightened attention to same-sex relations between women. In *The Sexuality of History: Modernity and the Sapphic, 1565–1890* (2014), Susan Lanser argues that representations of sapphism and accounts of lesbianism appeared in Europe throughout the early modern period and the Enlightenment, both as a part of and as a means of working through the challenges and changes of that "long period of reform, revision, revolution, and reaction."[44] Lanser explains how the sapphic became "entangled with" conflicts regarding "authority and liberty, power and difference, desire and duty, mobility and change, order and governance."[45] Each of these binaries is also a site of the putain heroines' rebellions: in their memoirs they demand financial and sexual liberty, they usurp power from those who do not deserve it and redistribute it to worthier people, they eschew filial obedience and maternal duties to pursue their own desires, they enjoy physical and social mobility throughout their careers, and they propose new social orders to replace the unjust and dangerous systems under patriarchy. That sapphic subjects would appear in such memoirs seems inevitable. That the putain memoirs of the 1780s are the most explicitly sapphic is also logical, given that, as Lanser demonstrates, "the sapphic seems to have mattered most when specific societies or social spheres were on the verge of certain kinds of change or engaged in certain kinds of struggle."[46] Few places in European history were more on the cusp of radical change than France in the 1780s.

England in the long eighteenth century also saw massive shifts in the economic and social realms, changes that Lisa Moore, in *Dangerous Intimacies: Toward a Sapphic History of the British Novel* (1997), links to a proliferation of literary portrayals of sapphism. Moore attributes this coincidence to the "unprecedented disruption in England's legislative and economic systems" at that time.[47] In Moore's analysis, however, the stories of lesbian love serve not to undermine or replace the traditional order but to reinforce it as the dominant narrative and affirm the virtue of the domestic, bourgeois Englishwoman. In the novels she explores, representations of lesbianism provide examples of, and temptations to, sexual immorality that the virtuous heroines manage to refuse and thereby legitimate the heterosexual "bourgeois hegemony."[48] In other words, during this time of upheaval, authors deployed stories of lesbian love as the immoral alternate path for the heroine to reject in order to reinforce the naturalness and virtue of heterosexual (matrimonial) relations.

In discussing the lesbian heroine or *tribade* in French prerevolutionary literature, Jeffrey Merrick similarly emphasizes the binary of "natural" versus "unnatural." Like Lanser and Moore, Merrick identifies the tribade as a threat to the established order, as these relationships between women were categorized as bisexual, mercenary, and betraying their natural inclination and duty to reproduce.[49] Ultimately, lesbianism "disrupted the patriarchal and familial order of French society by diverting or extricating women from marriage, which institutionalized their 'natural' subordination to men and their 'natural' procreative function."[50] This observation echoes David Halperin's argument that "sexual relations among women represent a perennial threat to male dominance, especially whenever such relations become exclusive and thereby take woman out of circulation among men."[51]

Elizabeth Wahl also locates tensions regarding female homosexuality in the reproductive function that lesbians may abandon. She posits that "by the end of the eighteenth century, cultural anxieties about sexual relations between women had become inextricably connected to fears about the collapse of a capitalist patriarchy that was dependent upon the participation of women in its reproductive economy." Not only are heterosexual, procreating women essential for sustaining the patriarchal order, they are also less likely to assemble into groups or communities to advocate for women's rights. According to Wahl, "representations of sexualized intimacy in satire and in pornography tended to link the dangers of female homosexuality with the dangers of female community and women's aspirations for intellectual and personal autonomy, particularly as more and more individual women were identified in both satiric and erotic discourses as 'sapphists' or lovers of other women."[52]

To be sure, La Dumonci's story explicitly links lesbianism and communities of women. This putain enjoys strong relationships with several specific women, and she also has a symbolic relationship with all other sex workers. She sees herself as a member of a group, a professional collective with similar tastes, goals, and fears. Early in her narrative this narrator references other members of her profession, calling them "my dear and venerable sisters" ("mes chères et vénérables consœurs").[53] While the comment that follows this apostrophe is a critique—the narrator claims that some other putains try to imply a noble or influential father to heighten their allure—the meaningful relationships with women and other putains that she goes on to describe will belie the apparent sarcasm here. The term for "sister" here is also telling. Rather than choosing the word *sœur*, connoting a blood relation that would legitimate the nuclear, paternal family, she calls her comrades her *consœurs*. The play on words here is lost in translation, but the prefix *con* is also a vulgar term for the vagina. Thus, the narrator's *consœurs* are her "fellow sisters," her "co-sisters," and her "sisters of the cunt."

In addition to "my dear and venerable sisters," she makes several references throughout the text "my dear sister putains" ("mes chères consœurs les putains")[54] and "the women of my station" ("les femmes de mon état").[55] In addition, La Dumonci often speaks not as an individual, but as a member of a group with its own principles. Throughout the novel the narrator repeatedly pronounces specific rules or generalizations (fourteen in all) about prostitutes, as if to educate the reader. For example, she asserts that, "generally speaking, a putain always has an excellent heart" ("généralement parlant, une putain a toujours le cœur excellent");[56] "it's in Paris that a putain has plenty of elbowroom" ("c'est [à Paris] qu'une putain a véritablement ses coudées franches");[57] "everyone knows that besides the pleasures of the bed, a putain likes nothing more than traveling" ("on sait de reste qu'une putain, sauf les plaisirs du canapé, n'aime rien tant qu'à voyager");[58] and, when speaking of a hospital, "A putain fears nothing more than this hotel of misery" ("Une putain ne craint rien tant que cet hôtel de misère").[59]

The networks among these *consœurs*—mutually beneficial relationships between or among women working toward the common goals of greater freedom and prosperity for each—create a kind of female fraternité, to anticipate the lexicon of the Revolution. As Carole Pateman rightly observes, the term "fraternity" has come to be "a metaphor for the universal bonds of humankind, for community, solidarity or fellowship," while remaining a highly gendered word and idea.[60] From revolutionary France to university campuses, a fraternity is a brotherhood only of men. I choose to call the complex relationships among women in the putain memoirs a female fraternité, rather than, for instance, a sorority, in order to at once recall and question the gendered origins of a word that ostensibly signifies a more universal group bond. These women display all the solidarity and fellowship of fraternal bonds, and their relatively selfless support of their friends and fellow putains anticipates the republican virtue of fraternité that accompanies *liberté* and *égalité*.

Of course, there is a certain sense of self-deprecating sarcasm on the part of the narrator in these instances. The humorous tone implies that a sense of professional solidarity would be ridiculous among women who have sex for a living, yet the truth hides just beneath the joke. The quality of La Dumonci's relationships with La Duttey, the seamstress, and above all Sister Prudence does indicate a genuine sense of community. Rather than seeing other prostitutes as competition—and the putains rarely express a sense of rivalry or jealousy toward their *consœurs*—La Dumonci views them as colleagues with a great deal in common to unite them. The shared experience she imagines among all whores allows her to make these generalizations applicable to all the female members of her group.

A sense of professional solidarity can be seen as early as 1745 in *La Belle Allemande*, which begins with Thérèse commenting on the "profession" she shares with the heroine of the first putain memoir, Frétillon. Later in her story Thérèse is mistaken for a woman of distinction and is seated in a prominent loge at the theater. Although she contemplates correcting the confused usher, she quickly changes her mind and proudly accepts the dignity she is offered on behalf of all the women of her "station." By allowing herself to be seated prominently with the respectable women, she is usurping a privilege normally denied to all of her fellow kept mistresses. In that moment she represents all the women of her profession.

La Dumonci sees herself as a part of a community of prostitutes, but she is also a successful member of a network of female friends. Whether as mentors, confidantes, lovers, or rescuers, the women of this novel come together to create a new kind of social body. In contrast with the men in her life, La Dumonci sees the women within her network as a source of aid, as companions who will understand each other's worries, and even sometimes as fellow victims. The variety of roles these women occupy for each other goes beyond the categories of "female friendship," "lesbian lovers," or even the intentionally vague labels used by scholars of early modern sexuality such as "romantic friendship" or "intimate relationships." Whatever it is called, this same-sex bond among the *consœurs* of her life is much stronger than anything La Dumonci feels for her family or for her male sexual partners.

The rich and satisfying relationships the putains share with the women in their lives—be they their *consœurs*, their maids, their madams, or their mothers—uncover a fluidity in female same-sex relationships that recalls both Eve Sedgwick's description of male homosocial desire and Adrienne Rich's lesbian continuum. In *Between Men: English Literature and Male Homosocial Desire* (1985), Sedgwick identifies literary examples of male relationships that are close and intimate and express in subtle ways an erotic ambivalence. Sedgwick in fact developed this idea of male homosocial desire as a complement to what she saw already existing among women: a paradigm of female relationships that float seamlessly from the sexual to the social without taboos,[61] a phenomenon Adrienne Rich calls the lesbian continuum. Under this term, Rich describes all relationships among women—mothers, sisters, friends, and lovers—as the same kind of connection with differences only in the degree of eroticism.[62] The putains participate in a network of female homosocial relations that are not only rewarding and satisfying for them, but also mutually beneficial in a way that anticipates the fraternité of the French Revolution.

In addition, the homosocial bonds Sedgwick describes not only permit an ambiguous eroticism among men; they also serve to promote men's interests. College fraternities, male-only golf clubs, masonic organizations, and other clubs—in fact many descendants of Habermas's authentic public sphere of the Enlightenment—support the kinds of "good old boys' clubs" that advance the careers of men and protect them from the consequences of their misdeeds. In the same way, the networks of female relationships in the putain memoirs allow the women to help each other thrive, whether through getting each other out of scrapes, supporting each other financially in times of need, or introducing each other to the good procurers and potential clients. Importantly, the putains and their madams never try to hold their fellow prostitutes back. Like the real madams of eighteenth-century Paris, these women felt no animosity when one of their *filles* left to become the mistress of a wealthy man. The madam who successfully placed of one of her own with an important man only improved her renown and reputation. And in the novels, any time the putains need extra support between *entreteneurs*, their former madams welcome them back to the brothel with open arms. While this kind of generosity and selflessness may be part of the utopian libertine fantasy in the novels, it nonetheless reveals the solidarity among female sex workers, and all women in these narratives.

Another term for what Sedgwick calls homosocial bonds is one of the three philosophical pillars of the French Revolution: *fraternité*. Robespierre was the first to proclaim liberté, égalité, and fraternité as guiding principles of the French Republic, but the concept of brotherhood—men working together for the common good—was much older. Fraternité requires and enables the masculine variety of virtue: strong men coming together in a public space to work together. Both the kind of virtue required (strong men) and the necessary presence in a public place immediately make fraternité impossible for women, according to the prevailing understanding of gender at the time. As a means of governing, however, fraternité was an attractive alternative to the authoritative monarchy the French had experienced. Lynn Hunt has described the French Revolution as the destruction of a social network with political power based on family connections attainable through birth or marriage with a father/king at its apex. This model was replaced in 1789 with one based on equality and fraternité, that is, the mutual benefits from friendships and political alliances among men.[63]

The female fraternité depicted in these novels is another way to critique the increasingly restrictive limitations of ancien-régime society and its rigid social and gendered boundaries. Along with humiliating descriptions of powerful and aristocratic men, examples of women who exhibit unchaste behavior and masculine virtue, as well as complicated uses of public and private spaces, these novels also contain glimpses of a utopist fantasy world in which members of a group come together to pursue their personal liberty, to seek personal satisfaction, and still manage to promote the public good.

Certainly, prostitutes like La Dumonci were a threat to traditional bourgeois marriage and that particular kind of patriarchy. But these are not tales of caution. There are no warnings to the reader that his wife or daughter may abandon heterosexuality for a depraved convent full of "tribades." Instead these stories offer a sense of excitement, titillation, and amusement. La Dumonci and her sisters, her *consœurs*, do not reproduce humans, and they do not reproduce the ancien-régime society based on marriage and family connections. Instead, they advocate universal solidarity through fraternité, in which one's talent and imagination—as embodied in Sister Prudence—are more important than how one was born, be it as a woman or as a lower-class member of the third estate. The social structure that is encoded in their subversive sexuality is much more appealing to them than the paternalistic one they are experiencing. In fact, it is not until the Revolution gets under way—when these same formerly disenfranchised people who composed and enjoyed the putain memoirs become the lawmakers and sources of power—that nonreproducing women become threatening. Once the citizens of the new Republic want their new society to reproduce, the figure of the subversive prostitute begins to lose its appeal.

6

Histoire de Juliette, or The Rejection of Motherhood

Perhaps the most salient trait of the putains, the quality at the heart of all their subversive actions, is their rejection of motherhood. All the putain narrators share a conspicuous lack of interest in becoming mothers. But avoiding pregnancy and abandoning children are not just necessary sacrifices for professional success as a prostitute. Certainly, the putain who is free from the dangers of childbirth and the burdens of dependent children is in a much better position to manipulate gullible *entreteneurs*, to assist her consœurs, and to voice pointed criticisms at the powerful classes in ancien-régime society through witty memoirs. But in eighteenth-century France, when a female protagonist the reader is meant to support and admire rejects her reproductive destiny, her choice carries enormous symbolic weight.

We have seen how the putain extracts herself from the patriarchal family, with its despotic fathers and husbands, to form a new network of social support, thereby undermining the purported "naturalness" of gendered roles and power distribution within nuclear, biological families. If we view the political upheaval in eighteenth-century France as a family romance, as Lynn Hunt suggests, the unmarried, childless putain effectively writes herself out of the drama. The mothers and daughters of Freud's mythic tribe cease to serve as the coveted objects of desire, hoarded by the father, sparking the murderous jealousy of the sons, who, after slaying the unjust father, must invoke an incest taboo to prevent further violence.[1] Instead, in the putains' family romance, the women march away from the masculine struggles for power and sexual dominance to create their own utopian society—one where men do not determine the identity or role of a woman but merely provide her with material wealth and pleasure. As Lynn Hunt and others have argued, the end of the French monarchy represented a political patricide. It follows, then, that the appeal of the putain memoirs for fifty years marked a fantastical matricide. In that libertine utopia, no specific mother was symbolically executed. Instead, it was motherhood in general, as the desired and inevitable destiny of all women, that was eradicated.

The demise of the putain memoir genre at the end of the eighteenth century coincides with the diminished allure of a motherless libertine utopia. To explore the connection between those two changes, I will turn to Sade's 1797 *Histoire de Juliette*. After demonstrating the novel's ties to the putain memoir tradition—despite being significantly longer and more violent—I then turn to Juliette's emphatic and repeated rejections of motherhood, culminating in the murder of her own daughter. With the support of the larger scholarly discussion of mothers in Sade's fiction, a close reading of that final crime scene will uncover the ultimate supremacy of the maternal role, and how Juliette's apparent rejection of motherhood is in fact a reaffirmation of the centrality of motherhood to a woman's identity. By the time of the Marquis de Sade, even the most independent and successful putain cannot escape her maternity.

Without attributing the demise of the putain memoir genre directly to Sade, I will show how his ultimate female libertine exposes the putains' rejection of motherhood as their greatest transgression of all, a transgression the French reading public no longer found amusing. Indeed, the libertine utopia of the putain memoirs, in the context of the chaos and violence of the French Revolution, longer no offered an appealing fantasy but instead a destabilizing threat. A comparison of the putain memoirs with a fictional prostitute narrative from the nineteenth century, *La Dame aux camélias*, reveals just how much the situation had changed. The putain memoirs were a product of their time, and by 1800 that time was over.

Donatien Alphonse François, Marquis de Sade, a name that immediately evokes libertinage, penned his own version of the putain memoir with the *Histoire de Juliette, ou Les Prospérités du vice*. Although her name suggests an ironic reference to Rousseau's Julie, who successfully overcomes her passionate desires to fulfill society's—and her father's—expectations, Juliette more closely resembles the fictional putains like Thérèse, Margot, and La Dumonci. Her story includes many of the themes found in the putain memoirs, albeit taken to the gruesome extreme typical of Sade. The *Histoire de Juliette* first appeared in 1797 as an addendum to a new edition of Sade's already popular *Justine, ou Les Infortunes de la vertu*. In the second half of this mammoth ten-volume work, Sade introduces us to Juliette, the evil sister of the famously virtuous and long-suffering Justine. Unlike her sister, who steadfastly refuses to abandon her moral principles even in the face of torture and misfortune, Juliette wholeheartedly embraces a life of vice and crime and enjoys endless success and satisfaction thanks to that choice. Like the other putains who came before her, Juliette's sexual initiation occurs at around thirteen or fourteen, in her case while living in a convent as a *pensionnaire*. Delbène, the superior of her convent, not only teaches her homosexual pleasures like those that La Dumonci learned from Sœur Prudence; she also brings men into the convent for Juliette's education and her own pleasure.

When Juliette's parents die, leaving her and Justine penniless, the sisters must leave the convent, and Juliette goes immediately to work in a Parisian brothel. There she meets her first *entreteneur*, a thoroughly evil and philosophical man named Noirceuil. She moves on to a few other patrons, from whom she learns more and more ways to pursue vice. When she displeases one *entreteneur* by slightly hesitating at his idea to destroy the population of France, she must flee Paris and his wrath. In the provinces, she marries a wealthy man, gives birth to a daughter in a move to secure her hold on his fortune, and then poisons her spouse. She leaves the child and heads to Italy, where she passes herself off as a wealthy courtesan. After seven years of traveling, she returns to Paris, where she and Noirceuil renew their relationship and kill her daughter. After she finishes her narrative, Juliette watches her sister Justine die, struck by lightning. Juliette, the reader is assured, remains happy, wealthy, and powerful until her own peaceful death.

As is typical of Sade's fiction, his novel *Juliette* takes the themes of a familiar genre to a wicked extreme. In this case the genre is the putain memoir, with heroines who openly admit to exchanging sex for money, who relish the power they wield over men they consider inferior, who move about with utter disregard for boundaries, and who prefer relationships with like-minded friends over the arbitrary bonds of biological family. Like Thérèse at the opera, Juliette learns to enjoy her power over others. She has no respect for family lineage and relishes getting the better of those she disdains. However, whereas the other putains content themselves with duping, financially ruining, and occasionally infecting the men they target with venereal disease, Juliette more often prefers outright murder.[2]

Like Margot, Juliette moves about in whatever spaces will best suit her needs. The private domestic sphere clearly holds no appeal for her. With an eye ever toward her own interests and personal profit, she never allows tender feelings to distract her from her pursuits. Juliette has no trouble finding sexual partners whom she renders as compliant as Margot's footmen to satisfy her urges so she can remain levelheaded in her quest for power and wealth. The difference between Juliette and Margot is again one of degree. Margot explains that she needs an annual income of 20,000 livres, and once she reaches that sum, she will retire, while Juliette's lust for money and power has no limit. In addition, Margot assures the reader that she takes good care of the footmen she employs for her sexual needs. Juliette, on the other hand, does little to feed, clothe, and house the men and women she uses for pleasure, preferring to torture, violate, and, once her desire is sated, abandon—if not murder—them.

Like La Dumonci, Juliette finds truly gratifying relationships with other women, relationships that are explicitly sexual and mutually beneficial (at least for a time). Indeed, Juliette's friendships with Clairwil and Durand contain echoes of La Dumonci's closeness to the seamstress and Sister Prudence. But unlike La Dumonci and the other putains, the fraternité she spends the novel learning to join is a masculine fraternity of the powerful.

A scene from early in Juliette's story—in fact, her first "street crime"—captures many of these features of the putain memoirs and highlights how Juliette distorts those themes to horrific effects. After listening to long speeches from her libertine mentors urging her to disregard laws and any moral considerations for the rights of others, Juliette ventures out on her own to put her lessons into practice. This event alone recalls Margot's decision to leave Madame Florence's brothel, Thérèse's determination to govern herself, and La Dumonci's escape into the world and out of the convent. All three heroines strike out independently, utilizing the education they have received to make their way. Similarly, Juliette explains:

> Wishing to put both my daring and my savagery to the test, I got into man's attire and, a brace of pistols in my pocket, went out alone, stood in a back street, and waited for the first comer, with the aim of robbing and murdering him for my pleasure. I was leaning against the wall; I was in that state of inner turmoil great passions provoke . . . and then I heard sounds of lamentation. I sped in the direction whence they came, they were groans; I approach, 'tis a poor woman huddled upon a doorstep.
>
> "And who are you?" I inquired, drawing close to the creature.
>
> "The most unfortunate of women," is her tearful reply; and I observe that she cannot be over thirty years of age; "and if you are death's messenger, you bring me glad tidings."
>
> "But your difficulties are of precisely what kind?"
>
> "They are frightful," she said, and as she sat up, the lamplight revealed her mild inviting features. "Yes, few have ever been so unlucky as I. We've had no work for a week, no money, we had a room in this building, we weren't able to pay the rent, nor able either to buy milk for the baby—they've taken it away from me and put my husband in jail. I too would

have been arrested had I not run away from those monsters who treated us so brutally. You see me lying on the threshold of a house that belonged to me once, for I have not always been poor. In those days, when I could afford to, I helped the needy; will you do for me now what I used to do for them? I do not ask much."

A subtle glow stole through my veins as I heard those words, savored that accent. Oh, by God, I said to myself, what an occasion for a delectable crime, and how the idea stung my senses.

"Get up," said I. "I'm a man as you can see. You have a body left, don't you? I intend to amuse myself with it."

"Oh, Sir! Here am I beset by sorrow and distress—can such a state kindle lust?"

"It kindles mine all right; so do as I tell you, else you'll regret it.

And taking strong hold of her arm, I forced her to stand still while I proceeded to an investigation. It brought agreeable things to light, those skirts harbored charms very fair, very firm, very appetizing.

"Frig me," I ordered, conveying her hand to my cunt, "I am a woman, but one who stiffens for her own sex. Put your fingers in there and rub."

"Oh, Lord! Leave me be, leave me be, I shudder at all these horrors. Though poor, I am honest; don't humiliate me, for pity's sake!"

She endeavors to break away from me, I seize her by the hair, raise a pistol to her temple: "Be off, buggeress," I say, "off to hell with you, and tell them there that Juliette sent you."

And she fell, blood gushing from her head.

(Voulant éprouver à la fois mon courage et ma férocité, je m'habille en homme, et je vais seule, deux pistolets dans mes poches, attendre dans une rue détournée, le premier passant qui tomberait sous ma main, dans la seule vue de le voler et de l'égorger pour mon plaisir. Appuyée contre le mur, j'étais dans cette espèce de trouble causé par les grandes passions. . . . des lamentations se font entendre . . . Je vole au bruit; je distingue des plaints; j'approche: une pauvre femme, couchée en travers d'une porte, poussait les gémissements qui venaient de frapper mon oreille.

—Qui êtes-vous? dis-je, en m'approchant tout à fait de cette créature.

—La plus infortunée des femmes, me répond en pleurant cette malheureuse, qui ne me parut pas avoir plus de trente ans; et si vous m'apportez la mort, vous me rendrez un bien grand service.

—Mais de quel genre sont vos revers?

—Affreux, sans doute, répondit cette femme, en se relevant assez pour me laisser apercevoir, à la faible lueur des réverbères, des traits très doux et intéressants, oui . . . oui, ils sont affreux mes revers. Il y a huit jours que nous manquons d'ouvrage; nous n'avons pu payer le faible prix de la chambre que nous occupions dans cette maison, ni le mois de nourrice de notre enfant . . . On a conduit cette misérable créature à l'hôpital, et on a mis mon époux en prison; la fuite seule m'a préservée de la rage des monstres qui nous traitaient avec tant de rigueur; vous me voyez étendue sur le seuil de la porte d'une maison qui m'appartint autrefois: je n'ai pas toujours été malheureuse. Plus à mon aise, hélas! je soulageais les pauvres: me rendrez-vous ce que j'ai fait pour eux?

Un feu subtil se glisse à ces mots dans mes veines. . . . Oh! sacredieu, me dis-je, quelle occasion d'un crime détestable, et comme il irrite mes sens!

—Lève-toi, dis-je à cette femme, tu vois bien que je suis un homme, je veux m'amuser de ton corps.

—Oh! Monsieur, suis-je en état d'exciter des désirs au sein des larmes et de l'infortune?

—C'est ce qui enflamme les miens; presse-toi donc de m'obéir.

En la saisissant par un bras, je la contrains à se prêter aux recherches que je veux en faire. On ne se doute point de ce que je trouvai sous ces jupons-là: des chairs très fermes, très blanches et très rebondies . . .

—Branle-moi, lui dis-je, en lui portant la main sur mon con, je suis une femme, mais une femme qui bande pour son sexe et qui veut se branler avec toi.

—O ciel! laissez-moi . . . laissez-moi. Toutes vos horreurs me font frémir: je suis sage, quoique dans l'infortune, ne m'humiliez pas à ce point.

Elle veut échapper, je la saisis par les cheveux, et lui appliquant le bout de mon pistolet sur la tempe:

—Va, bougresse, lui dis-je . . . va dire aux enfers que voilà le coup d'essai de Juliette.

Elle tombe noyée dans son sang.)[3]

Despite its violence, this scene reveals how much Juliette has inherited from her putain consœurs. She unabashedly walks out into the public sphere seeking out the kind of encounters virtuous women are taught to flee. The weeping woman suffering in poverty recalls the wife Thérèse encounters at the end of her story and with whom she shares half of the money she has just received. She also resembles La Dumonci's seamstress friend, escaping the clutches of "monsters" and sharing her tragic tale. In her moment of despair this woman returns to the home she once inhabited, desperately seeking the private sphere of her former domestic space and reaffirming her roles as a wife and mother even if her husband and child are gone. In this way, the pitiful woman emphasizes by contrast the putains' independence and self-reliance. But unlike Thérèse and La Dumonci, Juliette expresses no sympathy for this cowering, unfortunate woman. Instead her only reaction is sexual desire, which quickly turns to a murderous impulse. When she shoots this woman, Juliette enjoys her first solo murder, a slaying of not just one woman, but the domestic ideal of womanhood that the putains have long been resisting. More specifically and more importantly, Juliette kills a mother. This matricide—for even if this woman is not Juliette's own mother, she nevertheless is killing a mother—takes the renunciation of motherhood in the putain memoirs to its ultimate extreme. With her first cold-blooded street crime, Juliette is, like the putains who preceded her, emphatically rejecting motherhood, as she will repeatedly do throughout her narrative.

The heroines of the putain memoirs owe their freedom partly to their refusal to marry and form permanent primary relationships with men. Without the obligation to submit to a powerful husband's control, the unmarried putain is free to pursue wealth and offer her friends or consœurs solace and protection. Even more beneficial to the putain is her refusal to be a mother. Although a few putains do accidentally get pregnant, motherhood is never, ever a role to which they aspire. As we have seen, the putains have ambivalent feelings regarding their own mothers. The networks of female relationships one finds in the novels rarely include mothers selflessly helping daughters, and the putains are seldom close to their mothers. Furthermore, almost all the putains' subversive acts, from enjoying multiple sexual partners and moving about in public places to creating mutually beneficial relationships with other liberated and libertine women, are possible precisely because they are not mothers. In the putain memoirs, at least, an admirable woman is one who expresses her social value without producing or raising children.

Like all libertines, the putain finds her personal pursuit of pleasure at odds with the responsibilities of childrearing. In addition, as sex workers the putains face professional and personal situations where pregnancy and motherhood are impractical, if not impossible. The physical constraints of pregnancy and the duties of childrearing would certainly limit their ability to solicit new customers. Furthermore, these reproductive functions formed the basis of arguments for the confinement of women to the domestic sphere. By not having babies, the putains render moot some of the arguments that were meant to keep them out of the public sphere. Unencumbered by suckling infants, the putains can work and move about with ease.

Despite their rampant sex lives and virtually no mention of birth control, Margot, Thérèse, and La Dumonci never report a single pregnancy. The illogical failure of these texts to take into account the real consequences of sex is surprising. The narrators, otherwise so proud of their frank descriptions of desires and activities that are taboo, and otherwise so methodical in their philosophical explanations of sex, never say how they avoid getting pregnant. As attentive as Thérèse's mother is while developing her daughter's beauty and desires into marketable charms and while teaching her how to be a savvy businesswoman, she never includes contraception in her education. Margot begins her career under the careful tutelage of Madame Florence, but the instructions this mentor offers focus more on how to simulate virginity than how to avoid pregnancy. Even Sister Prudence's lessons, so essential to La Dumonci's professional success, would seem to have neglected this topic. The fact that the putain narrators detail some very specific tricks of the trade they learn from these female mentors (creams to simulate an intact hymen and blueprints for a two-headed dildo, among others) makes the exclusion of such a crucial topic in their texts remarkable.

Sade's Juliette is the only putain who describes an occasional use of birth control; all the others remain silent. Perhaps the reader is to assume that the other putains were asking their clients to use the eighteenth-century form of condoms but discreetly refrained from describing this step of the seduction process. Or perhaps the writers of the putain memoirs adhered to a belief of the time that frequent sexual intercourse led to sterility in women. More likely, these male authors simply failed to appreciate the high stakes women faced when sexually active. The worst consequence eighteenth-century men faced from sex was a venereal disease, and these maladies appear in almost every novel. But the concerns of a pregnancy simply did not worry these writers.[4]

The dearth of pregnancies reveals a flaw in the kind of materialist philosophy the putain memoirs employ. Throughout these novels materialist philosophy justifies sexual desires and acts. Like much of libertine literature, the putain memoirs argue that libidinous libertines are simply following the impulses that their bodies receive and perceive.[5] In other words, what is prudishly and erroneously condemned as immoral behavior is just a natural function of the human body. Without using the word "biology," libertines like the putains justified their sexual behavior as simply following a biological drive that they were unique only in openly acknowledging and obeying. One would expect, however, that such frank "realism" would acknowledge the logical outcome of frequent sex: the occasional pregnancy.

If the putains are just following nature's dictates by having sex, logically they should also be reproducing from time to time.

In the end, the necessary suspension of disbelief on the part of the reader allows these authors to create a utopian literary world in which getting pregnant is—for whatever reason—not a hindrance for women. In such a world the putain can be just as libertine as men and fear nothing more than the same consequences men faced. In choosing which of nature's dictates to follow—the pursuit of pleasure but not the drive to procreate—the putains are able to inhabit the same world as male libertines, which, it is important to note, is something no real eighteenth-century woman could do.

Arguably, the entire oeuvre of the Marquis de Sade contains a vehement rejection of mothers and motherhood. In his works mothers are often the favorite victims of the villainous libertines. Torturing and defiling what is considered in mainstream French society to be sacred and revered are the hallmarks of Sade's writing, but the repeated examples of maternal debasement, particularly in the *Histoire de Juliette*, hint at a special significance to his vilification of mothers. Whether neglectful or attentive, mothers in Sade's works meet a gruesome and tragic fate. Some of the more striking examples include Madame de Mistival, Eugénie's mother in *Philosophie dans le boudoir*, who is anally raped and deliberately infected with syphilis before her anus and vagina are sewn shut, as well as the mothers of two of Sade's most violent libertines, Bressac (in *Justine*) and Minski (in the *Histoire de Juliette*). Each villain recalls with glee violating and murdering his mother. As Jane Gallop observes, the mother is a "privileged victim" in Sade's writing, and many of Sade's libertines consider the murder of their own mothers as "their greatest accomplishment."[6] Caroline Weber also identifies this tendency toward what she calls "scenarios of maternal degradation" in the *Histoire de Juliette* in particular.[7]

There has been much speculation among Sade's biographers and literary scholars as to the source of Sade's perverse attention to mothers. Certainly, the especially cruel tortures enacted upon mothers represent much more than the straightforward hatred they seem to suggest. Many believe the special status of the mother as a prized victim reflects a feeling of respect or even veneration for mothers. Marcel Hénaff, for one, attributes the desire to destroy the Mother (Hénaff uses the capital M) to her status as master/mistress of the domestic sphere and guardian of the daughter's virtue. As such the Mother represents that which the libertine wants to subvert and pervert.[8] Hénaff also sees the vivid depictions of violence toward mothers as a means for "the revolted, fascinated, 'incestuous' and 'criminal' son" to desire the hated Mother through her profanation.[9] The detailed anatomical descriptions of the tortures the maternal body endures permit a form of eroticism otherwise unacceptable in the Sadean world. Tellingly, mother–son incest is the only familial combination not defended in Sade's fiction.[10]

As a point of entry for exploring the vilification of mothers in his works, biographers of Sade often note and analyze his ambivalent feelings toward the mother figures in his real life compared to the fates of mothers in his fiction, as well as the simultaneous sense of awe and hatred toward mothers his own actions and words displayed.[11] Despite a lack of significant historical evidence, Sade's biographers are usually quick to point to the absence of Sade's own mother, Marie-Eléonore, as a crucial factor in the young writer's (unhealthy) development.[12] Many point to the moment when the five-year-old Donatien was sent to live in Provence with his grandmother while his mother remained in Paris, and see this event as an indication of her lack of interest or maternal concern. Maurice Lever's description of Marie-Eléonore as "remote, absent, [and] indifferent" is widely accepted.[13] While the accuracy of such a description and of the possible effects her distance could have had on her son are as yet impossible to know, the typical narrative of Sade's life proceeds from this premise to posit that as a young adult, Sade found surrogate mothers to fill the void—including Madame de Saint-Germain and Madame de Raimond, two friends of his father, and la Présidente de Montreuil, his own mother-in-law. This last mother figure changed in his eyes from fairy godmother to wicked stepmother when she arranged for Sade's indefinite imprisonment in 1772 with a lettre de cachet. It is thought that, from this point on, much of the venom of the marquis's pen is directed toward this pseudo-mother, who becomes his powerful arch-nemesis.

These readings of the life of the Marquis de Sade reflect the kind of narrative that the putain memoirs problematize. The implicit idea is that, had Sade's mother nurtured him more, and had she resembled more closely Rousseau's Julie, the author's penchant for depicting torture and violence could have been attenuated. Instead of a mother attached to the private, domestic sphere and concerned only with her son's well-being and development, Sade had—like many of the putains—an absent and presumably inattentive mother.

If Juliette is Sade's putain producing a discourse of feminine independence, there is a significant flaw in his plan: Sade's vicious and successful putain is herself a mother. For this reason, more than any other fictional putain, Juliette must distance herself from her role as a mother in an explicit way if she is to obtain her share of the enormous power she sees her network of friends enjoying. Juliette allots a great deal of space in her memoir to undermining the value of motherhood in principle and avoiding pregnancy and marriage in her own life. She accepts and tacitly agrees with her mentors' many long discourses decrying reproduction and procreative sex, claiming that France is already dangerously overpopulated.

For instance, her first teacher in her education of evil, Delbène, gives a thirty-page speech to her young pupils in which she corrects many of their received ideas, including the notion that sex should be for procreation: "It is erroneous that propagation is supposed to be one of Nature's laws, if we imagine such nonsense our pride alone is to blame. Nature permits propagation, but one must take care not to mistake her tolerance for an enjoinder. Nature stands in not the slightest need of propagation; and the total disappearance of mankind—this being the worst consequence of a refusal to propagate—would grieve her very little." ("C'est à tort que l'on suppose que la propagation est une des lois de la nature: notre seul orgueil nous a fait imaginer cette sottise. La nature permet la propagation, mais il faut bien se garder de prendre sa tolérance pour un ordre. Elle n'a pas le plus petit besoin de la propagation; et la destruction totale de la race, qui deviendrait le plus grand malheur du refus de la propagation, l'affligerait si peu.")[14] Nature's lack of concern toward reproduction tellingly resembles the insouciance of the putains; Delbène's "Nature" is simply dispassionately uninterested.

Delbène continues her lesson and asserts that, beyond demographic concerns, a female libertine should avoid reproduction and motherhood for her own sake. Delbène is not the only libertine to denounce procreative sex, but she is the most direct when she explicitly warns Juliette: "Do not breed. Nothing gives less pleasure than childbearing. Pregnancies are damaging to health, spoil the figure, wither the charms, and it's the cloud of incertitude forever hanging over those events that darkens a husband's mood. There are a thousand means to avoid conception, five hundred more to forestall childbirth." ("Ne faites jamais d'enfants, rien ne donne moins de plaisir; les grossesses usent la santé, gâtent la taille, flétrissent les appas, et c'est toujours l'incertitude de ces événements qui donne de l'humeur à un mari. Il est mille moyens de les éviter.")[15]

While Juliette makes no comment on Delbène's advice, either as its recipient or as the narrator recounting the speech, we can assume she takes these words to heart, because she is careful not to hinder her sexual pleasures (or to legitimize them in standard eighteenth-century thinking) by allowing them to lead to pregnancy. She is pregnant only twice throughout her lengthy memoir, the first time after committing incest with her father. After killing her father, Juliette also kills his potential progeny by terminating her pregnancy. Before her second pregnancy Juliette marries a wealthy man out of financial need. She insists that she decided to have a child while married to him only to solidify her claims to her husband's money, and she is proudly uncertain whether the child is his. She devotes only one paragraph to the birth of her only child, Marianne, whom she abandons after a few months when she needs to leave France. She never gives little Marianne a second thought for six years until she returns to France. When Juliette does return and reclaims her daughter, she makes certain to emphasize her lack of maternal warmth for the child: "No child could have been prettier than she; but Nature was mute in me, libertinage had extinguished its voice. . . . I am obliged to say that in embracing Marianne I felt absolutely nothing stir in me but the pulsations of lubricity." ("Il était impossible d'être plus jolie; mais la nature était muette en moi; le libertinage l'avait éteinte. . . . Je n'éprouvai, je dois en convenir, d'autres mouvements, en embrassant Marianne, que ceux de la lubricité.")[16]

One would think that advice similar to Delbène's speech on avoiding pregnancy would have formed a part of the practical education most of the putains received, but that is strangely not the case. No other putain explicitly mentions advice on how to avoid pregnancy or even warnings that there exist such things as unwanted pregnancies. Delbène, in contrast, explicitly mentions the practices of birth control and abortion, even if she does not delve into the details of their methods in the speech Juliette recalls.

The reason for the contrast could perhaps be attributed to the varied lengths of the memoirs. Juliette's story is considerably longer and more detailed than those of the other putains. Some details the other narrators choose to omit are bound to appear here. To be sure, Sade is more methodical in many of his long, detailed descriptions of scenes and events than any of the putain memoir authors, and he is well known for taking popular ideas to their logical extreme (and often beyond). For instance, we find in his *Philosophie dans le boudoir* that Sade's version of the liberty the revolutionaries sought becomes the freedom to steal and kill. It is not surprising, then, that this particular author would explain more precisely how female libertines could enjoy their pleasure without consequences. Additionally, Sade's preoccupation with maternity is certainly part of this difference; an author who writes so vividly about torturing mothers would also logically devote a great deal of ink to passages that discourage women from becoming mothers. Seen in this light, Juliette's concerted efforts to efface her maternity throughout the novel become more examples of, in Weber's terms, "scenarios of maternal degradation."[17]

Juliette shares the practical and concrete reasons to avoid pregnancy that motivate all the putains: pregnancy and childbirth would limit her sexual availability, at least for a time. But in the *Histoire de Juliette*, the possibilities open to the childless putain encompass more than just uninterrupted sexual pleasure. For Juliette, rejecting motherhood grants her real power and a network of powerful friends.[18] This power, however, is not simply the "empire of beauty" that Thérèse and Margot enjoy—receiving gifts and adoration from important men overcome with desire. Juliette's is the power of life and death over others. Juliette learns how to achieve this wealth and control alongside her villainous friends and colleagues, like Noirceuil and Durand, working for each other's mutual benefit in a kind of evil *fraternité*. During the long story of Juliette's apprenticeship into vice, she encounters numerous debauched rogues and libertines, many of whom seem to know each other already. It is as if they all belonged to a club of evildoers; and, as Juliette discovers, they do have a secret club—the Sodality of the Friends of Crime. This formal society is made up of wealthy and powerful men and women who join together to enjoy secret sexual liberties and to inflict pain and suffering upon underlings brought in for this purpose.[19]

Not surprisingly, Juliette quickly learns that admission into the Sodality requires renunciation of any wish to reproduce, and thus the power she wishes to enjoy there is incompatible with motherhood. The rules of the group explicitly forbid reproduction and thus, for the female members, motherhood. Article 26 of the society's statutes explains exactly what should happen if the sexual activities of the Sodality accidentally result in children: "Children resulting from Sodality unions will be, at birth, immediately placed in the *crèche* and subsequently in the nursery annexed to the seraglios, later—at the age of ten for boys, of seven for girls—to become inmates thereof." ("Les enfants faits dans la Société seront aussitôt placés dans la maison du noviciat des sérails, pour en devenir membres, dès qu'ils auront atteint l'âge de dix ans pour les garçons, de sept pour les filles.")[20] Nevertheless, the article continues, the careful plans to raise and make use of these children is not an encouragement to create them. Instead, too many pregnancies can lead to a woman's expulsion from the secret society: "But a woman addicted to childbearing will not be tolerated by the Sodality, propagation being utterly alien to its spirit and aims; true libertinage abhors progeniture; and the Sodality therefore disfavors it." ("Mais une femme ou une fille qui serait sujette à faire des enfants, serait promptement exclue: la propagation n'est nullement l'esprit de la Société; le véritable libertinage abhorre la progéniture; la Société le réprime donc.")[21] The questions Juliette must answer during her interview for initiation into the Sodality imply the same message as Juliette's evidently correct answers indicate:

> "Have you had offspring?
> —No, none.
> —Do you intend to refrain from having them?
> —I shall do everything in my power to avoid them.
> —You therefore dislike progeniture?
> —I detest it.
> —Were you perchance to become pregnant, would you have the courage to abort?
> —Certainly."
> ("Avez-vous fait des enfants?
> —Jamais.
> —Protestez-vous de vous en abstenir?
> —Le plus que je pourrai.
> —Vous détestez donc la progéniture?
> —Je l'abhorre.
> —S'il vous arrivait de devenir grosse, auriez-vous le courage de vous faire avorter?
> —Assurément.")[22]

By responding appropriately and renouncing her reproductive powers, Juliette is able to join this confederation, which has not only sexual power over underlings during their meetings but far-reaching political power in France.

Juliette's admittance to the Sodality grants her access to the club's debauched activities, but more importantly to its powerful members. Like the other putains, Juliette feels more sympathy and affection for these friends—for the members of her fraternité—than for any member of her family, even her own daughter. For instance, when Juliette reconnects with her former *entreteneur* turned friend, Noirceuil, she describes their reunion in startlingly tender terms. She calls him her "stout and cherished friend" ("cher et bon ami")[23]—an uncommon expression of sincere affection on the part of Juliette—and Noirceuil welcomes her back to France "with every sign of happiness" ("avec la plus grande marque de joie").[24] He promises that henceforth he will share all of his growing success and power with her, as he states: "Juliette, be certain that I shall never take a step upward without enabling you to rise alongside me." ("Juliette, . . . sois bien certaine que je n'y monterai jamais sans t'y élever avec moi.")[25] These are sincere expressions of affection that never appear in Juliette's descriptions of interactions with her sister, father, or daughter.

Juliette's preference for her male and female libertine friends over her family is another form of the putains' rejection of family lineage and filial bonds. Like Thérèse and La Dumonci expressing disdain for women who try to vaunt their family ties and ancestors, Juliette's rejection of her family is another way to distance herself from motherhood. What sets Juliette apart, of course, is the hyperbolic evil of her friends and the extraordinary power they hold. La Dumonci is confident her seamstress friend could prevent them from being sent to a convent; Juliette knows her friends could wipe out the population of France. Thérèse has the ability to stop the show with an appearance at the theater, but Juliette can literally stop the hearts of the people she controls. At the center of each of these examples of a kind of power—a power to influence the behavior and lives of other people. The power the putains seek and use is the power to convince a man to spend everything he has to keep her by his side, the power to secure a better rate of interest for her lover, and in the world of Juliette, the power to end a life. The one power the putains do not want, however, is the power to create life. In fact, for Juliette that power is exactly what she must renounce if she is to join the Sodality of the Friends of Crime. Her initiation vows make clear the trade-off all putains face. In Sade's fictional world, the power to create life is incompatible with the power to destroy life, and Juliette wholeheartedly prefers the latter.

What makes a mother—that is, someone with the power to produce a new human being—at once awe-inspiring and repugnant for a libertine like Sade? Many critics employ the metaphor of Mother Nature to explain the source of these ambivalent feelings toward maternal power. For instance, Jane Gallop describes Sade's view of mothers as two versions of Mother Nature, both that which is considered good and proper in conventional thinking (such as heterosexual intercourse for procreation) and, on the other hand, all that can and does occur in nature, including the perverse monsters Sade's heroes celebrate.[26] Whereas the first Mother Nature is despised and ultimately vanquished by the Sadean hero, the second is revered and always emerges triumphant. In many ways, Gallop's image of the two forms of Mother Nature also applies to the contrast between the putains and the heroines in sentimental novels. As libertine heroes, the putains actively reject what is good and proper (the first Mother Nature), the better to follow and praise the instincts inspired by the other Mother Nature—those that better suit their interests and pleasures.

Gallop refers to this second "monstrous" Mother Nature as the phallic mother—a mother whom the child never discovers to have been castrated. This castration—the child's discovery that its mother has "lost" her penis and the accompanying anxiety and disdain that ensue—is not something the reader recognizes in meeting the putain. Through a variety of means, the putain escapes the constraints that other women face and thereby retains her phallus, and the powers of speech, movement, and control that it represents. Her refusal to remain confined to the domestic sphere allows a penetration into public spaces just as phallic as their penetration of other women via dildos. Thus, in Gallop's reading of mothers in Sade's works we find some indebtedness to the "phallic mothers" of the putain memoirs.

Like Gallop, John Phillips connects the mother in Sade's writing to nature, when he ascribes the violence toward mothers in Sade's writing to this connection between the fictional mothers and Mother Nature, describing the latter as a phallic woman, "an awesome force to be worshipped, and yet, at the same time, the image of maternal indifference to be vilified and annihilated."[27] As in the work of most of Sade's biographers, we find in Phillips's reading echoes of the eighteenth-century discourse positing an attentive mother as the norm (or "natural") and the indifferent mother as an object of hatred.

Connecting motherhood to nature of course implies adherence to a long tradition of reinforcing gendered binaries, and much of Sadean scholarship seems to follow suit. In Phillips's interpretation, the maternal is threatening because it represents the invisible yet irresistible sexual power women were believed to hold over men, a power that because of its arbitrariness and lack of logic remains beyond the control of men.[28] Phillips views the mother as directly representative of nature and thus a powerful figure, with the ability not only to destroy life but more impressively to create it. This reproductive power makes the mother a more formidable and appropriate rival than the father for Sade as artist/son.

Similarly, Caroline Weber stresses the mother's procreative power as that which makes her the hated rival of the son in Sade's works. For Weber, nature and the mother have an "intolerable, inimitable power to create," which causes "rivalrous hostility and violent envy" in the libertine son.[29] This hatred finds its outlet in the tortures enacted upon the mother's body. In Sade's Oedipal triangle, then, the son's jealous rage is directed toward the mother rather than the father, who, along with his law, is easily thwarted and deposed.[30] Nevertheless, at the heart of this hostility lies respect for a worthy adversary.

The point of tension that we find in these scholars' analyses reflects two distinct forms of female power: the power to sexually arouse (men) and the power to create life. To continue Gallop's metaphor, the first Mother Nature—representing all that is good—has the latter form of power, while the "phallic" Mother Nature has the power to arouse and manipulate. That Juliette and indeed all putains prefer the influential, "phallic" power over the reproductive, maternal form of power is not surprising when we consider all the limitations constraining people who can create life. Not only were women expected to remain in the domestic private sphere, but with the French Revolution they were denied access to the critical debates and procedures shaping their republic precisely because women could (and, according to the philosophy of many revolutionaries, *should*) create new citizens. Juliette distances herself from her reproductive power with her early matricide street crime and with her denials of her own maternity. Notably, it is by selling her body to all that Juliette is able to escape the patriarchal family structure that uses women as a means of exchange and ensure her own fortune.[31] Similarly, it is as a prostitute that Juliette meets Noirceuil and Saint-Fond, her two male mentors.[32]

The mother-whore binary is certainly not unique to Sade's works or the putain memoirs, but by denying their putain heroines the power to create life, the authors of these novels enabled them to enjoy other powers: the power to arouse sexual desire, certainly, but also, as we have seen, the power to settle old scores, the power to reward worthy men, the power to mock hypocrites, and the power to control an adoring crowd at the opera. The power they exert never needs to be isolated and is never especially threatening, precisely because it is so clearly different from the procreative power of mothers. With Juliette, however, we find a new version of the putain, one who is in fact very threatening and dangerous. For most of her story Juliette conforms to the putains' rejection of motherhood. As we have seen, Juliette repeatedly affirms the many speeches of her fellow villains denouncing motherhood as anathema to the goals and pursuits of true libertines. But if Juliette's first street crime—the murder of a mother—establishes a safe distance between herself and mothers, her final cruelty—the infanticide of her daughter—is less clear.

In her last and arguably most horrifying crime, Juliette helps her friend and mentor Noirceuil murder her daughter, Marianne, by burning her alive. Before this scene, Juliette has agreed to help Noirceuil enact his ultimate fantasy. In a performance that mocks all at once prohibitions against incest, the sacrament of marriage, and the patriarchal family, Noirceuil dresses as a woman in order to marry his young son. Then in a second ceremony, where he is dressed as a man, he weds his other son, who plays the part of the bride. On the same day Juliette, dressed as a man, marries her daughter, and later is a bride to her own young protégée Fontange, who is, of course, cross-dressed as the groom. After these doubly inverted ceremonies, all the wedding parties retire to Noirceuil's estate where, along with Noirceuil's two henchmen, Juliette's two *tribade* servants and two female prostitutes hired especially for the occasion, they begin lavish and gruesome sexual tortures.

At first there is an understanding that despite the theatrics, Marianne will not actually be killed. But after mutilating Fontange and killing the prostitutes and his own two sons, Noirceuil's murderous desire cannot be stopped. Nevertheless, recognizing Juliette's parental rights, he stops to ask her permission to have his way with Marianne. At the same instant, Noirceuil's henchmen bring her to orgasm, and Juliette loses all her previous hesitation and concedes, crying out: "She is yours." ("Je te la livre.")[33] Noirceuil rapes the little girl then throws her into the fire. Juliette, now a full participant in the infanticide, gleefully pokes the child back into the flames until she is burnt to death. Even though the entire episode is Noirceuil's idea, and he issues orders directing the events throughout, Juliette performs two significant acts: she gives her daughter to Noirceuil rather than simply acquiescing to his earlier request that she sell Marianne to him, and she ensures her daughter's death, pushing the child over and over back into the fire.

Juliette commits many crimes throughout her story, but the murder of her daughter seems to be the most serious and most significant, as its placement at the end of the novel and as the last elaborately staged orgy suggests. Juliette has ample opportunities to kill her daughter earlier in the narrative—for instance, during the months they are together before Juliette flees to Italy. Or she could have brought the child along to torture during her travels. Instead, Sade seems to save the murder of Marianne as Juliette's final accomplishment.

The other significant aspect of this crime—what makes the scene of Juliette's infanticide stand out from the other scenes of cruelty and horror in the novel—is the fact that it depicts Juliette, not as a rebellious young daughter defying her own parents and the social order they represent, but as a mother herself. Ironically, Sade's most perfect female libertine at the height of her success and at the culmination of her training chooses to recall her own inclusion in the category of Sade's most "privileged victims," mothers. While Juliette is denied the opportunity to murder her own mother and to enjoy what is for libertines like Minski and Bressac the "greatest accomplishment," in this scene she is nevertheless able to destroy maternity. Even though her mother is already dead at the outset of her story, Juliette is able to recall her own role as a mother and then emphatically renounce it. In killing her daughter, she in a sense kills a mother: her own maternity.[34]

And yet Juliette's final renunciation of her maternal power in the infanticide scene is not, in fact, a straightforward rejection. Throughout the planning and execution of the final orgy, she repeatedly expresses sincere hesitation, which would appear to contradict all her previous actions and the principles of her long training denouncing motherhood. In direct conflict with all her previous assertions that Marianne means nothing to her, Juliette refers to her daughter repeatedly as "poor," "adorable," and "precious."[35] In response to Noirceuil's proposal of the event, Juliette asks, "And Noirceuil, you wish to have my poor adorable little Marianne, [whom I adore], become one of the victims in these hideous orgies?" ("Et vous voulez, Noirceuil, que ma malheureuse Marianne, que j'adore, devienne, sans doute, une victime de ces épouvantables orgies?")[36] During the tortures, Juliette expresses worry for her daughter, despite the promise Noirceuil has given her not to harm the girl: "Surveying these preparations, I felt just a little apprehensive for my precious Marianne and was moved to remind Noirceuil of the assurances he has given me." ("Un peu effrayée de ces apprêts pour ma pauvre Marianne, je m'avisai de rappeler à Noirceuil les promesses qu'il m'avait faites.")[37] Juliette's hesitations do not go unnoticed. Noirceuil recognizes her concern but hints at his true intentions with his reply: "Strive to find the strength to endure the misfortune you seem to dread." ("Tâche de trouver dans les luxures qui vont nous enivrer assez de forces pour supporter le malheur que tu sembles craindre.")[38] Noirceuil's desire overcomes his previous promise to Juliette, and he seizes the little girl with "the very speed of light" ("avec la promptitude de l'éclair"), and Juliette recalls, "My poor Marianne's shrill screams are all the warning I receive of the dreadful outrage perpetrated against her." ("Les cris aigus de ma *pauvre* Marianne sont les seuls avertissements que je reçois de l'outrage affreux qu'elle essuie.")[39] Juliette refers to Marianne as "poor" ("malheureuse") one last time after relinquishing her maternal rights to Noirceuil: "No sooner does he hear these words than he decunts, takes hold of the poor child in his two wicked hands, and hurls her, naked, into the roaring fire." ("Il n'eut pas plus tôt entendu ces mots, qu'il déconne, saisit cette malheureuse enfant et la jette, nue, au milieu des flammes.")[40] The pity Juliette displays in this scene is the closest she comes to conforming to contemporary notions of maternal care.

To call someone *malheureuse* or *pauvre* is to empathize and imagine oneself in the very position of the unfortunate soul. In the libertine world Juliette by now inhabits, empathy is a weakness. Nowhere else in the novel do we see such reluctance without remorse on the part of Juliette. She makes no apologies for her hesitations during this act, as opposed to other moments earlier in the text when her hesitation before an evil deed is criticized. A slight hesitation before the plan of her powerful patron, Saint-Fond, to destroy the entire population of France costs her his affection and protection and forces her to flee and regret her momentary lapse. Yet Juliette unabashedly admits to Noirceuil during the final orgy, "You make me shudder" ("tu me fais frémir"), when it was exactly this reaction, "un frémissement," that caused her near-downfall earlier in the novel.[41] Of course she is speaking here with Noirceuil and not Saint-Fond, and a degree of frankness is permitted between close friends. Weakness, however, is never allowed, and it is astonishing that Juliette should so openly admit her anxiety. Juliette's almost obsessive repetition of "poor" and her expressions of hesitation are clearly unconscious, for as a by now well-trained libertine her rational philosophy should never waver in the pursuit of pleasure. When these words of concern escape during the scene, it is a repeated reminder of Juliette's maternity.

Through her entire story Juliette is successful at separating herself from motherhood in order to free herself to enjoy the real power and pleasures of a libertine. In this process, her femininity is rarely a problem. Juliette can and does cast it aside when she needs or wants to perform the heinous crimes and the sex acts that men do.[42] And until this last scene Juliette is able to renounce her status as mother and assume the full rights and privileges of the fraternité of libertines.

Juliette's avowal of her hesitation and her verbal slips of maternal care during this infanticide are a new development in the putain memoirs. Few other putains have children, and no other putain ever expresses concern for her child. For all her oaths never to reproduce and to loathe progeny, Juliette is the only putain to recall and emphasize her maternity in such a way. Tellingly, once this putain's inescapable maternity is revealed, no more putain memoirs appear. Never again would a French author adopt the voice of a confident and independent putain critiquing the underserving beneficiaries of wealth and privilege. Never again would fictional sex workers recount their mischievous excursions in and around public places, arm in arm with the women who shared their profession and their sense of irreverence. By the time of the French Revolution such narrators were no longer possible—even in the mind of the Marquis de Sade. Juliette's verbal slips in this climactic murder scene were not what caused the end of the putain memoirs, but they do point at the cultural shift that made women refuting motherhood and pursuing libertine pleasure unimaginable.

Bound up in that cultural shift of the 1790s is a deliberate emphasis on building a future that can survive and thrive. But personal sacrifices in the present moment for the benefit of future generations is not a virtue lauded in the putain memoirs. For all their egalitarian impulses and supportive friendships, the putains are never thinking about what kind of world their children or grandchildren will inherit, and this disinterest in future generations becomes outright intergenerational conflict in the work of Sade. Frances Ferguson's work on Sade in *Pornography, the Theory* (2004) highlights this theme among his criticisms of the new French Republic expressed in *La Philosophie dans le boudoir.* The problem, for Sade, is that the abstract rights upon which the republic is founded "barter the only experience one can actually have—the experience of persons and objects in the present—for the abstraction in which both children and potential children become the justification for political decisions."[43] In other words, the French Republic—allegorically represented as a woman named Marianne—is the child of current citizens who are expected to make sacrifices to ensure her future prosperity. Not surprisingly, the libertine Juliette defies this expectation and makes certain her Marianne never grows up.

Even the less homicidal putains are unwilling to trade their own bodily experiences to generate and cultivate a future generation. No putain narrator describes launching her daughter into the profession or introducing her to a female fraternité of consœurs. They may not literally kill their progeny as Juliette does, but they put an end to their family lines no less effectively. The putains anticipate Sade's "attack on the Enlightenment's privileging of the child" in their refusal to sacrifice their independence, identity, and experiences for the sake of producing a future person.[44]

However, as Ferguson persuasively argues, the very "intergenerational obligation and intergenerational inheritance" that Sade so vehemently attacks in his writing is precisely the justification often used to protect Sade's works from censorship. One reason to preserve something we find abhorrent is that we owe a "cultural debt" to potential, as-yet unborn readers. The belief is that there exists, in Ferguson's words, "an obligation to preserve even what one may hate for the love that some future generation may have for it."[45] So, even though Sade's libertines may refuse to acknowledge the utility of future generations, someone somewhere has to value the needs of potential progeny for a text, a body of work, or a genre to survive. In dismissing the possibility of reproducing human beings in their stories, the putains abandon the possibility of extending their literary bloodline.

Clearly, the world into which the Marquis de Sade's horrific putain memoir, *Histoire de Juliette*, appeared was quite different from the France of its predecessors. By 1797 the nicks and barbs inflicted on the ancien régime by the voices of opposition had combined with other tensions and instabilities to topple the monarchy in an explosive revolution, the violence of which grew as the leadership radicalized, until the French became weary of the constant upheaval and bloodshed. By 1797 economic and political stability were more attractive than subversion, as France began its steady slide back to more authoritarian forms of government that would eventually lead to Napoleon's empire and then the restoration of the monarchy. Already by 1797 the frustrations and fantasies at the heart of the putain memoirs had disappeared.

After the *Histoire de Juliette*, no new novels with the structures and themes of the putain memoirs appeared. A few titles, including *La Belle Allemande*, were reprinted early in the nineteenth century, but most faded into obscurity. A century later, the publishing company La Bibliothèque des Curieux uncovered a number of erotic works from the eighteenth century, including a few putain memoirs, and published them with short introductions consisting of a few details concerning the texts' publication history and speculation as to authorship. These editions were not widely circulated or read, and in 1925 Robert Briffaut, one of the two brothers who founded La Bibliothèque des Curieux, was arrested for an affront to good morals ("outrage aux bonnes mœurs"). In the 1960s the publishing house Tchou reissued some of these editions.

Despite the burgeoning scholarly interest in the oeuvre of the Marquis de Sade beginning in the late 1960s, there were few editions of eighteenth-century libertine erotic works in French until Raymon Trousson's 1993 anthology *Les Romans libertins du XVIIIe siècle*, a collection of novels including *Margot la ravaudeuse*. Seven years later, the prestigious Pléiade series issued the first volume of a two-volume anthology entitled *Romanciers libertins du XVIIIe siècle*, edited by Patrick Wald Lasowski, which includes two putain memoirs, *Mémoires du Suzon, sœur de D** B . . .* (anonymous, 1778) and *Confessions d'une jeune fille* (alternate title for *Anandria ou Confessions de Mademoiselle Sapho*, Pidansat de Mairobert, 1789). English editions of the putain memoirs have been completely impossible to find, except for Austryn Wainhouse's 1967 translation of *Juliette* and Édouard Langille's 2015 translation of *Margot la ravaudeuse*.

By and large, however, the putain memoirs have remained in the shadows, mostly ignored in French literary scholarship. It would be easy to attribute the end of the microgenre to the repulsive image of the putain in Sade's *Juliette*. La Dumonci's informal and supportive network of female friends becomes in *Juliette* the Sodality of the Friends of Crime, who financially ruin families, murder, torture, and enslave people for their own accumulation of wealth and amusement. Whereas the earlier putains fortuitously avoid pregnancy and eschew motherhood, Juliette more explicitly rejects her maternal role by burning her own daughter alive. The subversions of the putain memoirs are always harmless and humorous, until Sade carries them to a gruesome extreme.

Unlike her predecessors, who are described as rebellious but harmless (and even virtuous in the help they give to other women, to young men needing promotions in society, and even sometimes to jaded, debauched aristocrats looking for satisfaction), Juliette is a horrible menace to society. The reader of most putain memoirs can easily rejoice in the heroines' flaunting of conventional mores and be, if not inspired, at least amused by their independence; but Juliette's readers must clearly face more conflicted feelings. Even though Juliette commits horrific crimes, she, like her consœurs before her, does achieve her goal: to become a successful practitioner of her own brand of personal liberty and enjoy all the satisfaction and rewards her actions can bring.

As a subject of study, the fictional sex worker of eighteenth-century France has been overshadowed by her nineteenth-century sister.[46] The two versions of *filles publiques* bear little resemblance, as seen in Victor Hugo's tragic character Fantine from *Les Misérables* (1862) embodying the tragic fate that befalls a woman forced by circumstances to sell her body. Another fictional prostitute, the titular heroine of Émile Zola's *Nana* (1880), shares some characteristics with the eighteenth-century putains, particularly in her displays of a mercenary attitude toward sex. Like Thérèse and La Dumonci, she learns to keep her emotions out of her sexual relationships after suffering from a broken heart. Additionally, she combines lesbian desire, professional camaraderie, and genuine concern for a friend in her relationship with Satine. And like all the putains, she is enormously successful at manipulating male desire with carefully choreographed appearances in public places.

But there are also crucial differences. Nana never shares her perspective directly with the reader; her voice is absent. All other actions and words are filtered through the anonymous narrator, who presents her as an aberrant, dangerous monster—a product of her genetic heritage, environment, and society, to be sure, but nonetheless crudely animalistic in her desires and instincts. Nana seems to lack the self-awareness and the appreciation of irony we find in the putain memoirs. And in the case of Nana—as well as Hugo's Fantine—the courtesan meets something rarely mentioned in the putains' tales: a tragic and gruesome death. Even when the nineteenth-century courtesan elicits (and often deserves) the reader's empathy, she is still punished for her moral transgressions, and her narrative ends with the prostitute safely removed from society and the moral order protected and reaffirmed.

Perhaps no nineteenth-century courtesan embodies the differences between fictional sex workers in the eighteenth and nineteenth centuries as well as Marguerite Gautier, the heroine of Alexandre Dumas fils's 1848 novel, *La Dame aux camélias*.[47] The courtesan in this novel (better known in its operatic adaptation, Verdi's *La Traviata*) is as marginalized and potentially destabilizing as her predecessors, but otherwise bears little resemblance to the feisty and irreverent putains. Gone are the biting social critiques, the disregard for patriarchal privileges, and the professional pride of the eighteenth-century putains. The predominant complaints of this nineteenth-century novel are the laments for the plight of women forced to sell their bodies—couched in the implied assumption that no woman would choose such a career willingly—voiced by the male frame narrator.

This loss of the prostitute's voice is perhaps the most striking change in nineteenth-century prostitute narratives. First-person narration disappears, and the reader's access to the heroine is filtered through a male narrator. Even in those rare moments when Marguerite speaks, her words are always framed textually by the mediating presence of a trustworthy male witness, either her lover or the male narrator to whom he recounts his tale. Like her literary doppelgänger Manon Lescaut, who haunts the entire narrative, Marguerite remains always out of the reader's reach, her voice always filtered.[48] The only words the reader receives directly from the courtesan are those in letters to Armand directly quoted in the novel. Even if we choose to take the two male intermediaries at their word (that they have faithfully copied her letters word-for-word), the situation in which she writes is so tragic, and her tone is so full of regret, that even her mini-memoir here represents further submission to the patriarchal system that condemns her rather than the defiance we find in the putain memoirs.

Marguerite shows none of the pride in writing her story that we see in the putains. Gone is the uncontainable joy that Thérèse feels in writing a book or the gratitude Margot shows her public; this sex worker only writes out of despair at losing the man she loves. She is gravely ill as she writes and uses these last days of her life to compose several tear-stained letters to the man she loves but has been forced to abandon. True, she recounts a short personal narrative in those letters, but not of her whole life—not even of her adult life and career since the loss of her virginity—but only a recounting of her thoughts and actions since their split. She has no intention of offering the public her story, either as a way of thanking them for their support or of exposing the hypocrisy and duplicity of her clients. Her letters are addressed to one man, and their content is comprehensible only within the context of their relationship. Unlike the memoirs of the putains, her writing cannot stand alone; readers require the twenty-four preceding chapters of explication that her lover Armand and his friend provide. Marguerite is a far cry from the independent eighteenth-century putain in many ways, not the least of which being her reliance on male narrators for textual support.

Marguerite never proudly and openly calls herself a putain, a whore, or a prostitute the way La Dumonci did. She feels only shame and sorrow. These memoirs of her final days are not the triumphant account of her rise to wealth and renown, but the wretched details of a painful and lonely descent, serving only to explain why she refused to see the man she loves. But unlike Thérèse and La Dumonci, who make a deliberate choice to pursue more lucrative sex rather than suffer the penury and eventual heartbreak of a romantic relationship, Marguerite's decision is not her own. Instead, she is merely acquiescing to the request of Armand's father—literally submitting to patriarchy. She has broken off her relationship with the young and otherwise honorable Armand, not because he is too poor to support her (which he is) or because he insists on her fidelity (which he does), but because this courtesan wants to shield him and his family from the stain of associating with a fallen woman. She is only turning to writing to try and explain her reasons and demonstrate her selflessness to Armand.

Nevertheless, Marguerite is a sex worker, although it appears she is never reduced to working in a brothel or streetwalking; she enjoys the good fortune to occupy the position of a *fille entretenue* who takes on occasional *passades* for extra money. Still, she does make use of public spaces to arouse interest and attract potential lovers. Like Thérèse, her attendance at the theater draws a great deal of attention. When Armand first meets her, it is at the theater, and after their introduction he cannot take his eyes off her, as he admits: "I couldn't possibly tell you what was playing. All I can remember is that from time to time I looked over at [her] loge . . . where the faces of new visitors appeared one after another." ("Vous dire ce que l'on jouait me serait impossible. Tout ce que je me rappelle, c'est que de temps en temps je levais les yeux sur [sa] loge . . . et que des figures de visiteurs nouveaux s'y succédaient à chaque instant.")[49] Armand is not alone in preferring Marguerite to the performance on the stage. In this case, however, we have no idea whether Marguerite enjoys the homages these men show her as much as Thérèse did. Nor does she receive the hyperbolic round of applause requiring her to leave in order for quiet to resume and the show to continue.

Marguerite makes other public appearances in the form of leisurely drives down the boulevard des Champs-Elysées. Her promenades contrast with the carriage rides Margot describes in the Bois de Boulogne with her English *entreteneur* in that these appearances seem to be an unpleasant task for Marguerite. Again, we have no indication in her letters, in her quoted discourse, or in the explanations of the two narrators that she enjoys showing off her wealth and the success it implies. In fact, her display, like all the forms of ostentatious consumption (such as expensive clothing, furniture, and jewels), plunges her into debt and is nothing more than a necessary means of communicating to new men that she has been and is desired by other men. What were savvy business and marketing decisions for the putains are unfortunate and debilitating burdens for Marguerite. For Marguerite, public promenades that advertise her status as an available prostitute (albeit as a wealthy courtesan) are onerous obligations and reminders that she can never be honorable enough to be with the man she loves. The emotional distress they cause is as painful as her physical suffering from her illness.

Marguerite is much more at ease enjoying the domestic idyll she shares with Armand during their time together in the house in Bougival. In an attempt to leave her life as a courtesan behind and devote herself entirely to Armand, Marguerite leaves Paris for this suburban village and sets up a simple domestic household with him there—one that would rival Julie's peaceful isolation at Clarens, but in a more passionate, loving relationship. During this romantically described moment of bliss the lovers share, Marguerite seldom leaves the confines of this home and its garden. Her circumspect behavior appears to improve her physical health as her symptoms subside, and she seems genuinely content tucked away in this private space, renouncing luxury in order to devote herself to one man. In short, Marguerite demonstrates a preference for the private sphere that no putain ever feels.

The nineteenth-century prostitute narratives also lose the protofeminist complaints about sexual double standards or the injustices of unfair privileges in a hierarchical society. Indeed, the two older, wealthy men Marguerite encounters, Armand's father and the benevolent count who provides her with financial support but asks for no sexual favors in return, appear as virtuous, compassionate, honorable men deserving of the power and privilege they enjoy. When Marguerite deceives the count by pursuing her affair with Armand, there is no satisfaction in fooling the rich old man and rewarding the deserving young one, as we are accustomed to finding in the putain memoirs. In fact, both Armand and Marguerite express remorse that their love for each other requires that they betray this kind benefactor. Clearly, *La Dame aux camélias* does not subvert, but instead reinforces, the patriarchal order.

Similarly, this novel lacks the eroticism that characterizes the putain memoirs. There are virtually no erotic descriptions in this text, and every sexual encounter is shrouded in silence. The first time Marguerite and Armand make love is no exception. As the moment draws near, we see the two lovers in her bedroom, Marguerite tellingly dismisses her maid, and the chapter ends. The next chapter begins the next morning. Their entire night of passion is effaced and replaced with the blank space on the page and the benign chapter title "XII." In contrast, the vivid description of Marguerite's hideous decaying corpse being exhumed and relocated spares no graphic detail. Sexual pleasure is erased and substituted with disease and decomposition. At the same time, the materialist explanations for the characters' sexual urges are replaced with a medicalized discourse in which passion is an unhealthy, feverish state.[50]

The dual traditions of libertine subversions and erotic descriptions that intersected so powerfully in the eighteenth century through the stories of prostitutes, *filles publiques* who used their sexuality to defy stifling mores in favor of personal pleasure, disappear from those stories by the nineteenth century. Most significantly, we have lost that essential hallmark of erotic (and later pornographic) writing in use from Aretino to Sade: the sex worker's voice. While the putain authors took the titillating practice of a woman describing her own sexual desires and experiences and put it to use to criticize abuses in the ancien régime and to propose a more just—if entirely impossible—alternative ideal, authors like Dumas merely employed the prostitute as an empty puppet who served as an example of the tragedy that can result from a society's collective lack of compassion. Their heroines neither undermine existing power structures nor imagine new ones. The marginalized prostitute of nineteenth-century French literature is not the fearless putain with a story to tell, but the hollow illustration of her author's pity for the unfortunate.

As Sade's Juliette demonstrates, by 1797 readers were no longer amused by the independent putain—Thérèse deliberately infecting unscrupulous lenders with syphilis, or Margot bleeding dry a string of lascivious and foolish foreigners. A narrator like La Dumonci who showers her lovers with scorn and saves any genuine affection and sympathy for her fellow female libertines had become disturbing, if not monstrous.

With the French Revolution, the putains' moment ended. Clearly these narratives were a product of a particular literary and historical moment. These novels mark the intersection between titillating erotic writing and subversive libertine literature at a time just before the discourse in support of female domesticity and maternal virtue became inextricably linked to opposition to the ancien régime. By the middle of the eighteenth century, materialist philosophy was sufficiently well known to be able to justify the libertine's pursuit of sexual pleasure, but the biological realities of sex were not yet the authors' concerns. The dual forces of the royal censor and the cultural clout of the salons left many authors feeling a strong desire to undermine rather than reinforce the status quo. The authentic public sphere was beginning to emerge, but its differentiation from the domestic private sphere was not yet an entirely impermeable gendered barrier. At a time when various forces were converging to establish the sexual and social roles of men and women as clear and distinct, these novels present a momentary glimpse of sexual pleasure as a universal experience. The barriers between social classes in prerevolutionary France, boundaries associated with the inescapable destiny of one's birth, prove nonexistent in these texts. The culturally constructed requirements of modesty and domesticity were not yet so solidified that an independent and successful woman would be unthinkable.

The temporal and geographic constraints of the putain memoir genre are precisely what make these novels important. They turn a spotlight onto the complexity of this unique moment. The shift from a monarchy where class distinctions dominated to a republic where (at least in the minds of the Revolution's leaders and orators) gender distinctions ensured social order was not at all seamless. Rousseau's gendered utopia was not the only alternative to the ancien régime to emerge in eighteenth-century France's public sphere. An alternate discourse did exist, and acknowledging and examining this other utopia helps us better understand the intellectual and cultural transformations in eighteenth-century France, particularly in regard to women.

The memoir-writing courtesan never existed in reality. But for a brief period in the second half of the eighteenth century she could be imagined. From 1739 to 1797, women who rejected a domestic life of marriage, monogamy, and motherhood and who playfully manipulated the men they found at their feet could satisfy and amuse readers. The fact that at least nine different authors took up the genre of the putain memoir and were able to produce at least 123 different editions of their works demonstrates the broad, if short-lived, appeal of the putains. As fiction, the putain memoirs bore no responsibility to depict accurately the lived experiences of real eighteenth-century sex workers or to expose the logical consequences for sexually promiscuous women at that time.

But in the end the fictions of pleasure the putains offered were at odds with the equally elusive but more widely embraced image of virtuous wife and mother. The growing belief in companionate marriage in which a man and a woman married for love and remained faithful until death could no longer accommodate women who disrupted that system. The new republic needed wives and mothers to create good citizens, as did each succeeding regime. By the time of the French Revolution, the idea of an independent, sexually savvy putain was no longer amusing. The gulf between the putain and the virtuous domestic women of the dominant discourses had become too wide, and the putain dropped off the page.

Appendix

Contexts and Summaries of the Putain Memoir Novels

I have listed below all thirteen putain memoirs I have identified. I cross-referenced the titles' publication dates and editions with the holdings of major libraries around the world and, when possible, with the findings of editors of modern editions of the works.[1] Ignoring minor discrepancies in the titles, I assumed that two editions were distinct if a difference in the years or places of publication could be identified, or if the titles were significantly different.[2] Sometimes later editions of a text were identical to previous ones. Sometimes only the title pages and frontispieces changed, and sometimes there were genuinely new editions, with a new preface or introduction added or even with substantive changes made to the text.

For the purposes of this study, a detailed description of all of these variations would prove tedious and add little to the larger conclusions I hope to draw. I will therefore use the terms "edition" and "reprinting" interchangeably, purely for lexical variety. The following summaries of each of the thirteen putain memoirs, along with information about their publication histories and, when possible, their authors, will hopefully clarify what I mean when I refer to the putain memoir genre.

Histoire de Mademoiselle Cronel, dite Frétillon (Gaillard de la Bataille)

As we have seen, the putain memoir genre began as an act of vengeance, when Gaillard de la Bataille published the *Histoire de Mademoiselle Cronel* in 1739, supposedly in an effort to humiliate the rising star of the Comédie française, Mademoiselle Clairon. The significance of this text, as the originator of the genre, warrants a more detailed depiction of the narrative. Frétillon's story begins with the narrator's explanation of her decision to write her memoirs, admitting she cannot resist her desire ("démangeaison") to write, explaining, "The itch to make public my little adventures overcomes even the most sensible reflections. So what can I say? That's enough; I have to satisfy myself" ("La démangeaison de rendre mes petites aventures publiques, l'emporte au-dessus des plus sensées réflexions. Que dirai-je enfin, cela me suffit, il faut que je me contente").[3]

The depiction of Frétillon in this story is far from flattering. She is not very pretty, calling herself "un petit laidron," an ugly little girl. She cannot manage to find a lover without the help of a procurer, and she is completely dominated by her own sexual desires. Frétillon does not know who her father was, because her lascivious mother had several lovers at the time of her conception. Growing up, she quickly comes to understand to what *état* she is destined: not a career on the stage—that only comes later for her in this text—but one as a courtesan or putain, what she later describes as her "profession." After lessons from her mother on the rules of gallantry, how to inspire desire, and how to prey upon the weaknesses of men, Frétillon is ready to enter the family business.

Unfortunately, her first presentation as a young woman available for love, a long stroll through the Tuileries gardens, is a total failure; no one even notices her. She also appears at the theater and the Palais Royal, still without success. Finally her mother turns to an intendant of pleasure (a pimp) to find a rich lover for Frétillon. He arranges for her to meet a young German baron, le Baron de Mélisse, but not before he himself takes Frétillon's virginity. In order to make Frétillon still seem to be a virgin, he gives her a secret pomade to apply to her vagina, and Frétillon is happy to learn this essential trick of her new trade.

Before her first meeting with the German baron, Frétillon's mother, who traveled in her youth and understands the character of different nationalities, advises her not to be coquettish with a German because too much resistance easily puts them off. Her mother must have been right, because the Baron de Mélisse quickly hands over 20 louis d'or to initiate the encounter with Frétillon. But when they try to consummate the deal, she realizes she used too much of the pomade to restore her virginity, and her vagina has shrunk too small for him to enter. Still, the baron is completely charmed by her and willing to provide money and gifts in exchange for the sole enjoyment of her charms.

Frétillon and her mother live happily off the baron's money until he catches her having sex with his friend, the Chevalier de Foliande. Frétillon not only loses her lucrative relationship with the first *entreteneur*, but the baron also publicizes her infidelity, making it impossible for her to find another one. Her mother proposes that she try acting, but after one appearance at the Théâtre Italien, she is advised to go develop her skills in a provincial theater troupe, and so she and her mother depart for Rouen.

In Rouen, she has only mediocre theatrical success, but her skills of seduction and flirtation are much more fruitful in private, as she explains: "In the eyes of these young people, I appeared a thousand times more likeable at the table than at the theater. Their easily inflamed hearts could not resist my provocations" ("Je parus aux yeux de ses jeunes gens mille fois plus amiable à table qu'au théâtre, leurs cœurs faciles à s'enflammer ne purent résister à mes agacements").[4] Soon a handsome young man named Rhidilles steals her heart, but since he himself is not wealthy enough to support a mistress financially—and one man alone could never satisfy Frétillon's lust—she is forced to take on other lovers, but successfully hides those dalliances from him. To show their mutual devotion, the lovers exchange gifts. Rhidilles gives Frétillon an ornate little box; she offers him a tuft of her pubic hair.

All goes well for Frétillon until a young philosophe named Duplessis joins her entourage and exposes shortly thereafter how Frétillon manipulates several lovers at a time so that each one thinks that he alone enjoys her affections. Her promiscuity revealed, Frétillon is publicly humiliated. Even Rhidilles, convinced of her infidelity, ridicules her, making a joke of the intimate gift she gave him and recounting for everyone a night when she performed fellatio on him in a stairwell. When this latter anecdote becomes the subject of one evening's performance at a popular marionette show, Frétillon is humiliated and outraged. But after a while Rhidilles apologizes, and she forgives him. The text ends with their reconciliation and the promise that if the public enjoys this memoir, she will publish the continuation.

The second part of the *Histoire de Mademoiselle Cronel*, added to the 1741 reprint of the original, takes up where the first part left off. At this point the only obstacle the two reconciled lovers face is the disapproval of Rhidilles's older brother, Bagerria. One night, however, Bagerria is seriously wounded in a fight close to Frétillon's apartment. Fortunately, her quick thinking and contacts in the judiciary manage to save Bagerria's life and reputation, earning her the respect of Rhidilles's brother and his family's tacit approval of their relationship. Frétillon then describes a two-week trip to Paris and Versailles she and Rhidilles take so that she may plead the case for her theater troupe, whose production of *Le Tartuffe* offended a prominent Rouenais who saw too great a resemblance to himself in the portrayal of Tartuffe. While in Paris, Frétillon reconnects with the Baron de Mélisse, exposes a plot to overthrow the government of an ally of France, and learns of the death of the intendant from the mercury treatment he was forced to undergo to treat his venereal disease.

Back in Rouen, Frétillon successfully continues her life, hiding the affairs she must maintain for financial reasons from the true object of her affections, Rhidilles. When the theater season closes, Frétillon decides to take a short vacation to Le Havre. During this trip she meets a young libertine who keeps her company, and for the only time in her narrative, Frétillon finds herself pregnant. Fortunately her worries over this unwanted pregnancy are assuaged when the fright from a plank falling just next to her causes her to miscarry. The real tragedy for Frétillon follows shortly thereafter when Rhidilles and Bagerria are called to Spain to visit their dying father. During the voyage, pirates attack their ship and Rhidilles is killed. Frétillon ends this part of her memoir with the life story of an actress and potential rival whom she befriends for their mutual benefit. This woman, Fanchon, narrates the story of her childhood as an orphan and how a priest introduced her into a kind of seraglio, where she learned all about sex and pleasure from the priest and his ecclesiastical colleagues. Frétillon interrupts this story to promise her readers the rest of Fanchon's story, in the next part of her own memoir.

Apparently this edition was a success, as both parts were reprinted the next year. In the following year, 1743, the third part of the same title came out with the astonishing assertion that the second part of her story was completely false. After some speculation as to why someone would try to continue her story—most likely to cash in on the book's success—the third part of the memoir begins back where the first part left off. We find Frétillon and her beloved Rhidilles once again at the moment of their reconciliation. This time Frétillon's mother walks in and, at the sight of the man who so humiliated her daughter, spews forth curses and insults. Rhidilles is able to calm her down by paying for a large dinner at their home. One of the dinner guests, a man named Bertides, arranges a rendezvous with Frétillon's mother for the next morning. When he arrives, he and his friend Carlerio discover Frétillon still in bed. Carlerio is overcome with desire and easily seduces the lubricious putain. At this point in the narration, the names of the two men seem to be reversed, and it is Bertides who has just had sex with Frétillon, while Carlerio was with her mother. In any case, Rhidilles returns to her room and finds her in this compromising position, and his outrage ends their relationship. Before he leaves, he slaps Frétillon's mother, an indignity that sends her into a rage as well. Once the men leave, Frétillon and her mother have a violent argument regarding Frétillon's role in the slap, and Frétillon flees. She goes to stay with her friend the dancer Ton-ton, and after a series of conflicts, including a melee backstage at the theater one night, Frétillon's mother, recognizing her dependence on her daughter's charms, repents and promises to submit to Frétillon's directions.

Sometime later Frétillon runs into Rhidilles at a picnic, where he vehemently refuses to reconcile. This rejection causes Frétillon to rethink her behavior, opting to embrace a life of more restrained libertinage in order to regain some respectability. Frétillon decides to see only Bertides, refusing all other propositions, and thus becomes a model for all her fellow actresses, since, as she observes drily: "An actress is practically a Vestal Virgin when she has only one adorer" ("Une actrice est une demie vestale, quand elle n'a qu'un adorateur").[5] This part of her story ends with her resolution to continue her charade of virtue as her troupe prepares to move to Lille.

That same year, a fourth part of the memoir appeared, continuing the story from part three. Like the first volume, this part begins without a preface, and immediately takes up the story with the move to Lille. Determined to enjoy the respect of her spectators, Frétillon pushes her prudish ruse to an extreme in this new city. Just when her finances and her sex drive are about to make her change course, her mother returns from Paris with the intendant (who died only in the "false" second part, and for this version of events is alive and well). They propose that Frétillon continue the ruse of her virtue in order to attract a potential lover and extract as much money as possible from him. In the meantime, the intendant will pretend to be her uncle so that he can live with her and her mother and keep Frétillon sexually satisfied and able to feign chaste virtue. The narrator promises a fifth part that will explain what happens next, but it never materialized.

Unfortunately we know very little about Gaillard de la Bataille, who was in a sense the father of the putain memoir genre. Although it is very likely that he wrote the original pamphlet *Histoire de la vie et mœurs de mademoiselle Cronel, dite Frétillon*, it is unclear if it was he who reprinted that text and expanded it into the four-part *Histoire de Mademoiselle Cronel*. Literary historians of the nineteenth century had surprisingly little to say about Gaillard. The *Dictionnaire biographique universel et pittoresque* (1834) has a very brief paragraph on him, noting that he was a *trésorier de France* (a financial officer of the French government) who wrote the anonymous works *Mémoires du comte de Kermalec* (1740) and *Mémoires de Mademoiselle Frétillon* (1740).[6] In fact, the *Mémoires ou aventures de Monsieur le comte de Kermalec* saw several editions: in 1740–1741, 1742, and 1749, and Gaillard was also the author of *Jeannette seconde ou la Nouvelle Paysanne parvenue* (1744, reprinted in 1750, 1757, 1758, 1759, and 1771). Despite these attributions, almost every reference to Gaillard states only that he was the author of the famous pamphlet *Frétillon*.

Gaillard's pamphlet, however, laid the foundation for the putain memoir. After Frétillon, all the putains would lack a modest and virtuous mother. Frétillon's public appearances at the theater, not only on stage in Rouen and Lille but also as a spectator in Paris before her career begins, as well as her promenades in the Tuileries Gardens, establish the connection between putains, or *filles publiques* as they were also known, and public spaces. In her relationships with other debauched performers and courtesans—namely, Fanchon and Ton-ton—Frétillon depicts, not the expected jealous rivalry among competitors, but instead genuine friendship and mutual support. And finally, with rare exceptions, the succeeding putains will demonstrate the same fortuitous and remarkable infertility that Frétillon enjoys.

La Tourière des carmélites (Meusnier de Querlon)

The first text to draw upon the same influences as the *Histoire de Mademoiselle Cronel* and to adapt that novel's themes was Anne-Gabriel Meusnier de Querlon's *Histoire galante de la tourière des carmélites*. Its publication in 1743 tellingly coincided with the continuation (allegedly by popular demand) of Frétillon's story.[7] This putain memoir is intended as a female version of the bawdy *Histoire de Dom Bougre, portier des chartreux*—as evinced by a later title describing it as a *pendant* or counterpart to the *P... des C...* (*Portier des Chartreux*)—but this text also borrows important elements from the first putain memoir. The heroine, Agnès, is a former sinner now retired in the convent where she serves as a gatekeeper. Interestingly, though, the published text contains only extracts of what was presumably her full memoir, with italicized explanations by a third-person narrator filling in the gaps. The preface explains that the man who has published the work has read the entire text, but its author only allowed him to publish parts of it. Following this preface is a dedication in which the narrator justifies publishing these memoirs as a means of giving young people an example of behavior to avoid. The text that follows, by contrast, completely lacks any expression of regret or remorse.

Like Frétillon, Agnès explains that she cannot be certain of who her father is because her mother, despite being sent to a convent by her family, had three lovers when she was conceived. Also like Frétillon, she starts having sex out of a desire for physical gratification, regardless of the partner, and only later appreciates how lucrative her relationships can be. But an important change is the heroine's appearance. Because this text was not meant to disparage any one person, Agnès is no "petit laidron," no ugly little thing like Frétillon. Rather, her angelic beauty serves to mask her lascivious ways. The astonishingly and fortunately attractive putain will be a recurring theme of the putain memoirs from here on out.[8]

This *Histoire galante* is a shorter text, and the reader finds Agnès's adventures unfolding in rapid succession. She appears to be the only fertile putain of the genre, with three pregnancies in rapid succession, one from each of her first three lovers, but all three babies disappear immediately from the narration. Like Frétillon, she develops a close friendship with another woman, although for Agnès this friendship develops into a sexual relationship so satisfying that she renounces men for a while. Another remarkable encounter is when one of her clients turns out to be one of her own possible fathers. (Agnès admits with shame that this realization only made her desire him more.)

Unlike Frétillon, who eschews brothels and streetwalking, Agnès explores the full range of the putain's career—punctuated by two stays at the Salpetrière prison and a stint at the Bicêtre hospital to cure a venereal disease. She also works for a time in a brothel, becomes a *fille entretenue*, and eventually opens her own brothel. This final endeavor is a great success until one day when a large group of rowdy men come in and turn violent, smashing the furniture and slicing up Agnès's beautiful face. Now disfigured, she retires to a Carmelite convent where she serves as the gatekeeper. Even though she claims this story is a kind of confession, the only remorse she expresses at the end is regret that her career was cut short, lamenting: "My spring had passed; I admit it. But could I have expected to see my career come to an end so soon?" ("Mon printemps était passé, je l'avoue, mais pouvais-je m'attendre à voir si tôt terminer ma carrière?")[9]

The many editions of this text imply its success. An edition from the publisher Pierre Marteau in La Haye appeared in 1745 and again in 1747, and a version was published in Avignon the following year. Another edition (with the spelling "Tourrière" in the title) claims to have been published in Constantinople "chez l'imprimeur Moufti" in the year 17000 [*sic*] but is generally believed to have been published in 1757.[10] Further editions appeared in 1770, 1774, 1777, 1783, and 1784, and there may have been two editions of the text with the title *Sainte Nitouche* in 1770 and 1784.[11]

We know a great deal more about this author than about Gaillard. Meusnier de Querlon was born in Nantes in 1702 to a ship's captain and his wife. After studying in Nantes, then in Paris, Meusnier became a lawyer in 1723, but abandoned the law in 1727 to work in the Bibliothèque du Roi until 1735, during which time he began publishing articles in the journal *Mercure de France*. Much of his later career was in journalism, editing the *Gazette de France* for a time, collaborating on the *Journal étranger* and the *Journal économique*, and managing the *Affiches de Province*. Meusnier also edited numerous works, including Michel de Montaigne's *Journal de voyage en Italie en 1580 & 1581*, the Abbé Prévost's *Histoire des voyages*, and Jean Racine's *Phèdre*. He died in Paris in 1780.

Psaphion, ou la Courtisane de Smyrne (Meusnier de Querlon)

Another work attributed to Meusnier de Querlon is a putain memoir set in antiquity called *Psaphion, ou la Courtisane de Smyrne* (1748).[12] It is one of several works in a subgenre of the novel that is the story of a prostitute from ancient Greece.[13] In this case Meusnier gives us the full memoir rather than truncated excerpts. This novel is purportedly the transcription of the life story Psaphion is telling at her vanity table one morning. The preface explains how the anonymous publisher had someone write down everything she was saying without her knowledge and then published it.

Psaphion's mother is a slave from Cyprus, a beautiful and successful courtesan who dies in childbirth. Her mother's enslaver and procuress raises Psaphion to be charming and beautiful. When Psaphion is old enough to sell her virginity, her owner must decide whether to market the opportunity to the son of a government official, a very wealthy old man, or the son of a captain in the military. As the procuress is trying to decide, Psaphion sneaks off and gives her virginity to a neighbor's slave, Sunnion, for free.

Psaphion never sees Sunnion again, but she has a brilliant career as a very popular and beloved prostitute. The only times she faces difficulty are the three times she falls in love and refuses to sell her charms. The first time, Psaphion falls in love with the son of a very wealthy man, whom she refuses to leave even when they have spent his fortune, and who ultimately abandons her. Seeking comfort, she meets the young lover of a wealthy older prostitute. The third man is a very handsome musician who comes to Smyrna. Psaphion devotes herself entirely to him until he is called back to his own city.

After these experiences, she learns it is better for her career not to fall in love, and such a realization and finding the self-control this decision requires will be a turning point for many of the putains to follow. As a popular and famous courtesan, Psaphion ironically teaches the men of her town more about honorable behavior than about sexual pleasure. The grateful city erects a statue in her honor that she feels she deserves. At the end of her memoir, she is looking in the mirror and realizes she is getting older and losing her charms. Psaphion is initially upset by this revelation, but she quickly changes her tone, deciding to use all the tricks she can to make the most of what beauty remains. Despite her woes at the physical signs of aging, the ending, like the whole story, is optimistic.

Psaphion's memoir appeared numerous times throughout the eighteenth century under several different titles. In fact, the same year as its original publication in London, another version entitled *La Courtisane philosophe, ou l'Apologie du P****, et Les Hommes de Prométhée* was published in Cologne.[14] Also around that time, *Psaphion* was included in volume 4 (of 6) of the anthology *Bibliothèque choisie et amusante* published in Amsterdam from 1747 to 1750. The London edition reappeared in 1749 with *Les Hommes de Prométhée* added. The publisher Ballinlough, Belser, Wiss., Dienst in London published *La Courtisane de Smyrne* in 1753. In 1761 *Psaphion* appeared again with *Les Hommes de Prométhée* as well as another text, *Le Point de vue de l'Opéra*, under the title *Les Impostures innocents, ou les Opuscules de M**** (published in Magdebourg.) Two more titles—*Serpille et Lilla, ou le Roman d'un jour* and *Cinname, histoire grecque*) were added to this collection in 1763, under the title *Histoire de quelques courtisanes grecques: Précédée du Point de vue de l'Opéra; et suivies de quelques contes. Psaphion* was part of yet another collection: *Manuel des boudoirs ou Essais érotiques sur les demoiselles d'Athènes: Ouvrage plus moral qu'on ne pense, tiré en partie du portefeuille secret du Secrétaire Grec du Scythe Anacharsis* (Cythère, 1240), edited by Claude François Mercier de Compiègne and published in Paris in 1787. The eighteenth century saw one final edition, *La Courtisane de Smyrne, suivie de la Belle Cinname* in 1797. The popularity of *Psaphion* can be seen in these many reprintings as well as in the two translations (into Italian in 1769 and into German in 1776).

Meusnier may well have drawn inspiration for this successful putain memoir from two previous memoirs of courtesans from antiquity. Both *Cythéride, Histoire galante, traduite du grec* (1743) and *Lycoris, ou la Courtisane grecque* (1745) have been attributed to the same author, Antoine Bret. Neither novel seems to have caused much of a stir. *Cythéride* was never republished, and readers would have to wait until 1795 for a second edition of *Lycoris* (although an English translation of it was published in 1779 by M. Hayes).

La Belle Allemande (Bret or Villaret)

The apparently lukewarm reactions to Bret's *Cythéride* and *Lycoris* stand in stark contrast to the greater success this prolific author, critic, and dramaturge would know with *La Belle Allemande, ou Les Galanteries de Thérèse.* Martin, Mylne, and Frautschi believe Bret to be the author, as does Raymond Trousson, while Barbier attributes the novel to either Bret or another writer, Claude Villaret.[15] Whoever wrote it, *La Belle Allemande* was a success. Two editions appeared in 1745, the first one called *Les Galanteries de Thérèse*, and the second one adding *La Belle Allemande* to the title (both published in Amsterdam). Two editions appeared in 1754, as well as one each in 1755, 1764, 1766, and 1774. The story reappeared in 1797 as *Adeline ou la Belle Strasbourgeoise*, reprinted in 1803, and as *La Belle Alsacienne, ou Telle Mère telle fille* in 1801. This novel is the focus of chapter 3, where I summarize the plot and demonstrate how it contributed to the development of the putain memoir genre.

By the midpoint of the eighteenth century the putain memoir novel had become its own genre. There had already been at least four editions of the *Histoire de Mademoiselle Cronel*, four editions of the *Tourière des carmélites*, the same number of printings of *Psaphion*, two editions of *La Belle Allemande*, and one printing each of *Cythéride* and *Lycoris.* These works had created a solid foundation for the genre when Fougeret de Monbron came along with *Margot la ravaudeuse.*[16]

Margot la ravaudeuse (Fougeret de Monbron)

In his in-depth study of Fougeret de Monbron, Emmanuel Boussuge places *Margot la ravaudeuse* in the midst of an evolving literary tradition, based on the anecdotal stories of the dancers at the Opéra from the 1730s and early 1740s. Boussuge argues that with *Margot la ravaudeuse* Fougeret radically transformed that tradition from amusing anecdotes, mocking famous actresses, to a critical mirror held up before the public.[17] In August 1748 Fougeret submitted his manuscript of *Margot* to a publishing pair who were secretly *mouches*, police informants. They passed his name on to the police, and the author was taken to For-l'Évêque prison. In his interrogation he maintained that he had never intended to publish the manuscript, nor the other one in his possession, *Histoire de Mademoiselle* *.[18] Even though the police knew for a fact he was trying to publish *Margot la ravaudeuse*, they could not prove his intent without revealing their informants' identities. Fougeret was released but banished from Paris.

Although this original manuscript has been lost, it is safe to assume that when *Margot* was finally published, there were probably many edits, including the excision of any passages of homosexuality (the manuscript's original title *Margot la ravaudeuse ou la Tribade* hinted at there being at least one homosexual relationship) and some of the more direct critiques of individuals. But the addition of an introduction, with a thinly veiled reference to Nicolas-René Berryer, the lieutenant general of the police, made the published version just as scandalous, if not more so:

> Here at last is that *Margot la ravaudeuse* of which the general of the pigs, at the behest of the harlots and their sidekicks, wanted to make a crime against the state on the part of its author. Because he was accused of no less that having attacked religion, the government, and the sovereign in this work, he has decided to bring it to light, for fear that his silence might speak against him, and that people would believe he was in fact guilty. The public will decide who is right and who is wrong.
>
> (Voici enfin cette *Margot la ravaudeuse*, dont le général de la pousse, sollicité par le corps des catins et de leurs infâmes suppôts, voulut faire un crime d'État à son auteur. Comme on ne l'accusait pas moins que d'avoir attaqué dans cet ouvrage la religion, le gouvernement et le souverain, il s'est déterminé à le mettre au jour, craignant que son silence ne déposât contre lui, et qu'on ne le crût réellement coupable. Le public jugera qui a tort ou raison.)[19]

In this introduction, Fougeret is not only declaring that this work is fiction with an author, referring to the text as an *ouvrage* (a work) with an *auteur* (an author) rather than as an *histoire* or as *mémoires*, he is also openly defying the incredibly powerful head of the Parisian police. His appeal to the reading public, who will serve as the arbiters of the value and the danger of this text, is an important development and manifestation of the authentic public sphere usurping the power of the king and his ministers, a theme I explore in chapter 4.

There is some debate about the date of the first publication of *Margot*. The earliest editions listed "Hambourg, MDCCC" as the place and date of publication.[20] Generally, people believe that the 1800 refers to 1750, because the catalog of the *Bibliothèque du marquis d'Argenson* lists 1750 as the real date of the copy containing the MDCCC reference. But Boussuge persuasively argues that such a note could have been a mistake on the part of this marquis, René Louis Voyer de Paulmy, in preparing the catalog (perhaps mistaking the last L for a C—MDCCC being really MDCCL). Boussuge nevertheless posits that the real first publication was in 1753, based on three facts. First, no one has yet found any reference to the published version of Margot until 1753. Secondly, the text refers to an event that happened in 1739 as "fifteen or sixteen years ago."[21] Mathematically, a 1753 edition (placing that event in 1737 or 1738) makes more sense than 1750 (which would imply that the event took place in 1734 or 1735). A one- to two-year error is more acceptable in Boussuge's view than a four- or five-year error. Finally, Boussuge reminds us that "Hambourg" was listed as the place of publication, and Fougeret did not arrive in Hamburg until 1753. Of course, authors of libertine texts and other works published clandestinely lied about the cities and publishing houses as often as they did about the dates of publication, and certainly Fougeret did not have to be physically present in Hamburg for his manuscript to be printed. However, when we consider, as Boussuge points out, that the artist who engraved the frontispiece of this edition was from Hamburg, the theory that Fougeret had his Margot published while in that city in the spring of 1753 becomes quite plausible.

The first known reference to *Margot la ravaudeuse* is in the *Journal de la librairie 1753* of the police inspector charged with overseeing the clandestine presses, Joseph d'Hémery, who, referring to Fougeret, noted on May 10, 1753, "The author has just published [*Margot la ravaudeuse*]." ("L'auteur vient de . . . faire paraître [*Margot la ravaudeuse*].")[22] (This comment came around a month after Fougeret's arrival in Hamburg.) The next mention of the book is in November 1753, when Friedrich Melchior Grimm's *Correspondance littéraire* mentions it in its literary news.[23] These two simple notes belie the popularity of *Margot*, which was a bestseller of the clandestine book trade. After the false date of 1800, *Margot la ravaudeuse* reappeared in fifteen more editions by 1801, including one edition entitled *Fanchette danseuse de l'Opéra, histoire galante suivie du Quart d'heure d'une jolie femme*, as well as several editions in the collections *Les Aphrodisiaques, recueil de romans libres, rares et singuliers* and *La Bibliothèque des boudoirs, choix d'ouvrages rares et recherchés.*

La Fille de joie (Fougeret de Monbron)

Another putain memoir often associated with Fougeret de Monbron is the French translation of John Cleland's *Memoirs of a Woman of Pleasure*, familiarly known as *Fanny Hill*. The abridged French version, *La Fille de joie, ouvrage quintessencié de l'anglais*, was published in 1751, two years after the original English text. Some scholars attribute the translation to someone named Lambert, based on a note in the *France littéraire* of 1769, although Fougeret is the more likely candidate.[24] We know that Fougeret was in

England at the height of the controversy over Cleland's novel in late 1749 to early 1750 (upon his release from the For-l'Évêque prison).[25] In addition, police inspector d'Hémery attributed the translation to Fougeret: "I have been assured that *La Fille de joie* . . . was by the Sieur de Monbron, author of *Margot la ravaudeuse*, for which he was arrested and exiled." ("On m'a assuré que *La Fille de joie* . . . était du Sieur de Monbron, auteur de *Margot la ravaudeuse* pour laquelle il fut arrêté et exilé.")[26] Also, the marquis d'Argenson included *La Fille de joie* in a collection of Fougeret's works that he claimed led to his exile from Paris in 1749 and his imprisonment in the Bastille in 1755.[27] Furthermore, a close comparative study of *La Fille de joie* and *Margot la ravaudeuse* (such as the careful and detailed work of Dora Bienaimé Rigo) reveals a lexical similarity between the two texts in terms of rhetorical devices and euphemisms, as well as resonances and concordances in the passages cut for the translation, and the brief additions.[28] In any case, *La Fille de joie* was one of the most widely read books in the eighteenth century, according to Robert Darnton's catalog of the "forbidden best-sellers." In fact, this translation ranks number fourteen in his list of most frequently ordered books, according to the records of police and customs confiscations and those of a large Swiss publisher.[29] In fact, *La Fille de joie* saw an astonishing twenty-three editions in the eighteenth century: 1751, 1756, 1758, 1762, 1766, 1770, 1775, 1776 (5), 1780, 1783, 1786, 1787, 1788, 1790, 1793, 1796 (2), 1797, and 1798.

Histoire de Mademoiselle Brion

The next putain memoir to appear after *La Fille de joie* and *Margot la ravaudeuse* was the anonymous *Histoire de Mademoiselle Brion, dite comtesse de Launay*. It was first published in 1754 and saw five or possibly six more editions. Brion's story has one of the most complicated plots of all the putain memoirs. The labyrinth of affairs, customers, *entreteneurs*, and lovers contains many of the typical features of the genre. In the preface, Brion imitates the narrator of Cleland's *Memoirs of a Woman of Pleasure* by addressing a specific "Madame," a friend who has apparently asked her to tell the story of her life and adventures. Like Fanny Hill, Brion claims to be writing only to satisfy her friend's curiosity and hopes the stories of the sins of her youth do not cloud Madame's good opinion of her.

Brion starts her story by refusing to give any more information about her genealogy or family history beyond the fact that her father was named Launay and drove a cab, and her mother was a flower seller. When Brion is around fourteen her mother dies, leaving the young girl alone with a father who begins to show signs of an incestuous desire for his daughter. Thankfully, before his attention develops into an assault, Brion runs to a female friend who introduces her to La Verne, owner of a famous brothel. Here a high-paying customer purchases the right to take Brion's virginity, which is subsequently repeatedly resold to gullible men.

After a while Brion leaves the brothel to work on her own. With the help of a clever and loyal servant, Manon, Brion balances countless intrigues and affairs. Prostitution is Brion's profession as well as a means to satisfy her "libertine temperament." At all times she has at least two lovers: an *entreteneur* and a boyfriend on the side. Balancing these relationships sometimes proves difficult, but the cunning Manon always manages to rescue her lusty mistress from the scrapes in which she finds herself. At one point, one of Brion's lovers, M. L***, jealous that she is cheating on her *entreteneur* with another man in addition to himself, turns Brion in to the police. Before the tribunal, Manon speaks up for her mistress and convinces M. L*** that Brion is pregnant with his child. Brion is in fact conveniently pregnant for the only time in the entire novel, but she knows that M. L*** is not the father. Nevertheless, M. L*** is completely duped, and he drops all charges. To complete the ruse she marries this man, taking delight in how much of a cuckold he is. As soon as the marriage ceremony is over, she goes back to work, with no further mention of her husband or the child.

After recovering from childbirth, Brion is more attractive than ever and makes it known that she is once again available. She finds, among other *entreteneurs*, a wealthy young student at a seminary, where the two lovers enjoy secret trysts. The family of her next young *entreteneur* has her imprisoned until the wayward youth forgets about his expensive passion. Even though she is quickly released, Brion decides to retire to a convent for a time as an excuse for her absence from demimonde society. Obviously, it is not religious devotion that inspires her stay there, but Brion nevertheless relishes her time in the convent—thanks primarily to an understanding nun serving as a gatekeeper who facilitates her latest lover's frequent visits. The irreverence of a sex worker living and loving in a religious house is both an amusing addition to Brion's memoir and a pointed insinuation that other seemingly devout residents of the convent are also engaging in the same illicit behavior. Brion is completely satisfied in the cloister until her gatekeeper dies and is replaced by a less accommodating woman, and Brion must return to society.

At the end of the novel Brion finally settles down to a monogamous relationship with her final *entreteneur*, M. R***. She ends the novel the same way she begins it: on a note of repentance. Throughout the body of the novel, however, the tone is lighthearted with expressions of satisfaction in her independence and pride in her deft handling of so many delicate affairs.

Readers would have to wait twenty years for a new edition of the *Histoire de Mademoiselle Brion.* A version entitled *La Nouvelle académie des dames, ou Histoire de Mlle B***, D. C. D. L.* appeared in 1774 and again in 1776, when another edition, the *Histoire de Mademoiselle Brion, dite comtesse de Launay (honnête putain),* was also published. This title was reprinted in 1783, and the original title—without the "honest putain" qualifier—appeared in 1780. Finally, the Bibliothèque nationale de France has an edition published in "Toulon chez les filles du bon ton" without a date.

Mademoiselle Javotte

In 1757 there appeared another anonymous putain memoir, *Mademoiselle Javotte, Ouvrage moral écrit par elle-même et publié par une de ses amies.* There were at least four more editions of Javotte, including a few reprints appended to the abbé Prévost's *L'Histoire du chevalier des Grieux et de Manon Lescaut.* There is also an interesting relationship between *Mademoiselle Javotte* and *La Tourière des carmélites.* The 1830 edition of *Sainte Nitouche, Tourière des carmélites* claimed to have produced the whole story of Sœur Agnès, reconstructed from Meusnier de Querlon's original manuscript. The Pléiade edition of *La Tourière des carmélites* gives in an appendix one of the missing sections supposedly replaced in the 1830 text, the story of La Duchapt, a character briefly mentioned in Agnès's story as one of the women working for her when she ran a brothel. However, this story is, almost word for word, the same text as *Mademoiselle Javotte.* Could Meusnier, author of *La Tourière,* have written this text as well? The 1967 Tchou edition of *Javotte* asserts the possibility that Paul Barrett wrote the novel but recognizes that it would be pretentious to claim the author with certitude. Another possible explanation is that the editors of the 1830 edition of *La Tourière des carmélites* took up this obscure novel to augment Querlon's text.

The possible author Paul Baret (also spelled Barrett) is just barely less mysterious than an anonymous one. All we know are a few other texts he authored or is believed to have authored. For example, a book entitled *Amours d'Alzidor et de Charisée, ouvrage traduit du grec* that appeared in 1751 is attributed to him. Just a few years before the first edition of *Mademoiselle Javotte,* Baret published other libertine works, hinting at the same irreverent tone as the putain memoirs: *Le Grelot ou les & c, & c, & c, ouvrage dédié à moi* and *Fo-ka ou les métamorphoses, conte chinois dérobé* *à M. de V****. And we know Baret was familiar with the pseudo-memoir genre because he also composed *L'Homme ou le tableau de la vie, histoire des passions, des vertus et des événements de tous les âges trouvés dans les papiers de feu M. l'abbé P****, the purported memoirs of the abbé Prévost in 1777.

In *Mademoiselle Javotte* we find the young, beautiful, but admittedly vain Javotte, who describes how she gets a job working as an apprentice hairdresser with Mademoiselle Villers. The latter sells Javotte's virginity to a wealthy man, who becomes her *entreteneur*. As is often the case, Javotte is far from virginal by the time of her first encounter with this financier. She has already had sex with a member of the king's guard, who has taught her how to manage different men. Plus, she is having an affair with a handsome abbot, and a young lawyer is in love with her, although he is always too emotionally overcome in her presence to make love to her.

There is a long period devoted to Javotte's education. The financier sends her tutors, including a music teacher who gives her more pleasure than lessons. She reads all the libertine literature she can get, thanks to the abbot. After a while her lover, the king's guard, starts expecting her to support him financially, and her lawyer scolds her for selling her charms. Deciding that the guard is too expensive and the lawyer is too serious, she spends most of her free time with the abbot. At one point she visits her old neighborhood to show her family and friends how wealthy she has become. As her old friends admire her coach, her mother expresses shame that Javotte has thrown away her virtue. Javotte drives away and goes to visit her abbot for consolation.

Finally, all her intrigues and relationships collide in a single night. Javotte has the abbot over to spend the night, but when her financier drops in unexpectedly, the abbot must hide. Then the king's guard comes in drunk and challenges the financier, whom he takes to be another rival, to fight for Javotte. The terrified financier tries to get dressed but puts on the abbot's clothes by mistake. As the mayhem builds, the real abbot gets whipped, all Javotte's servants look on in amusement, and the financier leaves her. Humiliated and rejected, Javotte returns to Mademoiselle Villers to seek advice and consolation. Her faithful and loving lawyer continues seeing her, but eventually she is carried off to prison, where—in an unusually tragic twist—she dies shortly after writing down the story of her wayward youth. A friend from prison agrees to publish the memoir for Javotte and hopes her story will warn other young women to avoid a life of vanity and vice. Like Brion, the moralistic tone appears only in the preface and at the end, with the main part of the story full of fun and titillating details.

The 1760s is a quiet decade in the genre of putain memoirs. There are no new novels written in the genre between 1757 and 1770, and even the reprintings of successful memoirs waned during this decade. In 1761 there were four putain memoirs republished (*Psaphion*, *La Fille de joie*, *Margot*, and the abridged/pirated version of *Margot*, *La Brunette ou Aventures d'une demoiselle*), and three in 1762 (*Histoire de Mademoiselle Cronel*, *La Fille de joie*, and *Mademoiselle Javotte*). The next two years saw only one reprinting each (*Psaphion* in 1763 and *La Belle Allemande* in 1764), and the only other putain memoirs to reappear in this decade were in 1766 (another edition of *La Belle Allemande* and one of *La Fille de joie*.) If one compares these eleven reprintings with the fifteen editions (including four new works) of the preceding decade, and the twenty-one new editions (including two new putain memoirs) in the decade following, we can see the 1760s as a relative lull in the development of the genre. One possible explanation is the extraordinary success of Rousseau's *La Nouvelle Héloïse*, which first appeared in 1761 and set the literary tone for several years. Rousseau's sentimental novel made striving for virtue so attractive that one can logically assume no author felt he could sell a novel showing the successes of a life as a sex worker. There is also a shift in the tone of the novels after *La Nouvelle Héloïse*. The characters struggle more, sometimes face public ridicule, and describe the serious and often violent consequences that accompany their illegal activities. Before these harsher, sadder tales begin to appear, however, *Vénus en rut* gives one last example of the pleasures and prosperity a skillful prostitute can procure for herself.

Vénus en rut

The anonymous *Vénus en rut, ou Vie d'une célèbre libertine* came out in 1770, according to Raymond Trousson, although the editors of an 1880 edition of the novel claim their version is based on the first, which appeared in 1771.[30] In the preface the narrator tells her friend Folleville that she is agreeing to her request that she share the story of her adventures, but that she has no intention of publishing the work. This assertion recalls the beginning of Marivaux's *La Vie de Marianne* and its narrator's assertions that she has no authorial talent or ambition. The sincerity of the claims of Rosine—the narrator of *Vénus en rut*—that her memoir is only for one friend is amusingly belied by her references in the body of the work to "the reader" ("le lecteur") and the mention of the name of her publisher.

Rosine's story is divided into six chapters, with titles paralleling her sexual development: "The Narrow" ("L'Étroite"), "The Curious" ("La Curieuse"),

"The Starved" ("L'Affamée"), "The Rabid" ("L'Enragée"), "The Devil in the Flesh" ("Le Diable au corps"), and "The Fuck-Addict" ("La Foutromanèse"). Rosine explains that she grew up in a small village in Provence, where her somewhat wealthy and libertine parents left her to be raised by a wet nurse because they preferred their own schemes and pleasures. Even as a young girl she knows that she will follow in her mother's footsteps and become a courtesan. She is eager to lose her virginity and does so at age fourteen in a cellar on a pile of wood. Bored with her village, she moves to a small town, where she gains a couple of lovers. From there she moves to a larger town and obtains her first *entreteneur.*

Of all the putains, Rosine travels the most. She lives for a while in every major city in Provence—Avignon, Marseille, Aix, and Toulon—as well as Lyon, Paris, Italy, Belgium, and Holland. She acquires a faithful and helpful maid, Fanchette—who resembles Brion's maid Manon in her selfless service but also has a strong sexual appetite of her own—and a handsome young lackey, Honoré, both of whom accompany her during all her moves. Her travels finally bring her to Paris, where she feels she can finally fully explore her sexuality. For instance, on one day she services seven different lovers—a feat that impresses some people but also earns her a bad reputation, even among the libertine society she frequents. Realizing a reputation as a sex fiend might be bad for business, she accepts the proposition of M. Van Bloomdael that she return with him to his estate in Holland. After Bloomdael dies, leaving her a large inheritance, she returns to Paris to enjoy the excitement and pleasures of the city. Her last great exploit is to prepare a young girl for a friend who wants to take her virginity. Rosine must teach the girl to be a skillful lover while maintaining her virginity. She enjoys her role as a mentor and plans to continue to live independently, doing as she pleases.

Mémoires de Suzon

The next putain memoir to appear drew once again upon the success of the *Portier des chartreux,* this time telling the life story of Dom Bougre's sister Suzon. The result, *Mémoires de Suzon, sœur de D . . . B . . . portier des Chartreux, écrits par elle-même, où l'on a joint la perle des plans économiques ou la chimère raisonnable,* first appeared in either 1777 or 1778. Another edition of *Suzon* appeared in 1782 and again in 1783, and there is another early edition lacking a date. Also, a version of the novel appeared as *Mémoires de Suzon, sœur du portier des Chartreux, suivis de l'Histoire de Marguerite, fille de Suzon,* also in 1783.[31] An edition with the same title appeared with the 1784 edition of *La Cauchoise*, and there is another version printed with *La Cauchoise* but without a date.

In the preface to this memoir a friend of Suzon's who was with her in the brothel when she was arrested explains that her dear friend handed her this manuscript before the police took her away to the Bicêtre hospital (for having infected a young nobleman with venereal disease), where she died eight days later. The cries of this sensitive putain, who is distraught at the sight of her close friend being arrested, attract the attention of a young count, who rescues her from the brothel and becomes her *entreteneur*. The two fall genuinely in love. After a while the count catches her reading the manuscript and is curious as to what it is. He begs his lover to read it out loud to him. The preface ends with the words "and I began to read him the following Memoirs." Our access to Suzon, then, is only through a series of narrative replacements: the reader imagines himself to be a count listening to a courtesan pretending to be another courtesan telling the story of her sexual adventures.

Suzon, whose earliest adventures Dom Bougre recounted in his own memoir a quarter century earlier, acknowledges that the reader is surely already familiar with those events, and for this reason she simply glosses over the parts of her own tale the educated reader already knows. Suzon has a lubricious and neglectful mother, Toinette. The local noblewoman Madame d'Inville, Toinette's former employer, offers to pay for Suzon to get a convent education. Upon returning to Madame d'Inville's home, Suzon is seduced by her patroness's confessor the abbé Fillot and becomes pregnant.

The abbot takes Suzon to Paris but abandons her after the birth of their child, and there is no further mention of the baby or its father. Suzon has a series of lovers and wild adventures, until she decides she needs to put her lascivious proclivities to more lucrative use. She finds an aging libertine, whose frustrating impotence and inexplicable passion for astronomy promise to prove worth the patience they require when he dies, because this *entreteneur* has promised to leave his entire estate to Suzon. Alas, he dies the day before his appointment to have her put in his will, leaving Suzon penniless. After a stint as a pantomime in a carnival, she turns to steadier work in a brothel. Her story ends here, although the reader knows that she will soon be arrested and die in the Bicêtre. The tragedy of Suzon's life contrasts sharply with both the happy outcome of another putain's career path, that of the frame narrator, and the amused tone with which Suzon recounts her adventures.

La Cauchoise (Ribié?)

In 1783 the next putain memoir appeared: *La Belle Cauchoise ou mémoires d'une jolie Normande devenue courtisane célèbre, ouvrage pour servir de suite à tous les ouvrages de la philosophie de la nature, par un auteur critico-satirico-dramaturgique*. This novel also appeared in the *Histoire de Marguerite, fille de Suzon* in 1784 and in another edition without a publication date. The 1784 edition of *La Cauchoise* contains a preface that once again destroys the illusion of verisimilitude that most eighteenth-century novels sought so hard to maintain. The editor explains that this is the work of a single author who has also written *Les Héros américains* and is one of the contributors to the *Almanach des spectacles*.[32] This author appears to be César Ribié, but little is known about him beyond the books he wrote and the plays he staged. The author and director named César Ribié lived from around 1755 until around 1830. If Ribié is the author, *La Cauchoise* would have been one of his earliest works, along with a play *La Courtisane vertueuse, comédie en quatre actes, mêlée d'ariettes; le sujet est tiré du roman de Manon & Desgrieux, fait par M. l'abbé Prevôt. Par M.D****. *La Cauchoise* is the subject of chapter 5, where I describe her story in detail.

Anandria, ou Confessions d'une jeune fille (Pidansat de Mairobert)

In 1784 the tenth volume of *L'Espion anglais, ou Correspondance secrète entre milord All-Eye et milord All-Ear* was published in London. Organized as a series of letters, the *Espion anglais* collected articles and observations about all aspects of contemporary French culture, including religion, the arts, commerce, as well as actresses and courtesans. Letters 9, 12, and 14 of that tenth volume tell the story of a young girl, a story entitled *Confessions d'une jeune fille*.[33] Another version, without the epistolary trappings of the *Confessions*, appeared independently in 1789 as *Anandria ou confessions de Mlle Sapho, contenant les détails de sa réception dans la secte anandrine, sous la présence de Mlle Raucourt, et ses diverses aventures*. The same memoir was published two years later under a simplified title, *Histoire de la secte anandryne* as well as one with the title *La Liberté ou Mlle Raucourt à toute la secte anandryne assemblée au foyer de la Comédie française*. In 1793 the *Histoire* received yet another title, *La Nouvelle Sapho ou Histoire de la secte anandryne publiée par la C. R . . .*, and once again in 1797: *La Jolie Tribade ou Confessions d'une jeune fille*.

The man considered the author of this tale is Mathieu François Pidansat de Mairobert. Born in 1727 in Champagne, Mairobert arrived in Paris at a young age and became a part of the influential literary salon of Madame Doublet. Here he met Louis Petit de Bachaumont, whose articles about politics, literature, and the arts he assembled into a successful collection, *Mémoires secrets pour servir à l'histoire de la république des lettres en France depuis 1762 jusqu'à nos jours, ou Journal d'un observateur, par feu M. de Bachaumont* (1777). At the same time, he prepared his own gazette of contemporary issues, *L'Espion anglais.*

Mairobert's ability to uncover important stories and his willingness to publish them drew the attention of the police.[34] He was arrested in 1749 for circulating satirical verses about Louis XV and Madame de Pompadour and spent a year in the Bastille prison. Nevertheless, his later works maintained his satirical eye, such as in his attacks on Chancellor Maupéou. Tragically, Mairobert took his own life on March 30, 1779, just days after the Parlement of Paris publicly denounced him as a creditor of the much-vilified Marquis de Brunoy.[35] His original journal *L'Observateur anglais, Correspondance écrite Milord All'eye, et Milord All'ear* was continued after his death as *L'Espion anglais*, but the *Confession d'une jeune fille* in the 1784 volume 10 is nevertheless, Pierre Saint-Amand assures us, the work of the then-deceased Mairobert. The text, presumed to have been found among Mairobert's papers, was most likely published with only minor editorial changes by his colleagues.

The confession of Mademoiselle Sapho, the "jeune fille" of the title, is encapsulated within the frame of a male narrator who first saw her at the Tuileries where Madame Gourdan was fighting over the girl with her father. This frame narrator is intrigued by the affair, and later at a dinner with Monsieur Clos meets her and hears her story, which she tells to a large group of men. Letter 10 sets up the narrative and begins with her childhood in a village called Villiers-le-bel. She is unhappy there, hating her work, and when at age fifteen her mother scolds her, predicting she will become nothing but a prostitute who dishonors her family, and sarcastically suggesting they should send her to the well-known procuress, Madame Gourdan, the young girl takes her facetious advice seriously. In Paris, Madame Gourdan takes her in and, discovering that she has an unusually large clitoris, suggests that she would make a great companion for a rich *tribade*, Madame Furiel. Indeed, Madame Furiel is thrilled with her, showers her with gifts and has her inducted into the *Secte Anandrine*, for virgins who have never been sullied by men and women who have already performed their procreative duty and have renounced intercourse with men. Then the male narrator provides his correspondent with a discourse that the sect's leader, La Raucourt, gave on the occasion of a young girl's initiation, listing the benefits of same-sex relationships for women.

Letter 12 continues her adventures, including a failed love affair with a young poor man and one with a high official of the Church. The latter sets Sapho up as his secret mistress until she is discovered sleeping with four of his friends. The story ends when this relationship is over, and Sapho returns to Madame Gourdan, awaiting her next *entreteneur.*

Histoire de Juliette (Sade)

The last putain memoir is the *Histoire de Juliette, ou Les Prospérités du vice* by Donatien Alphonse François de Sade. This voluminous memoir first appeared in 1797 accompanying a new edition of his successful novel, *La Nouvelle Justine ou Les Malheurs de la vertu.* First published as *Les Infortunes de la vertu* in 1787, then again as *Justine ou Les Malheurs de la vertu* in 1791, *La Nouvelle Justine* tells the story of an unfortunate virtuous woman who steadfastly remains dedicated to moral ideals despite the unrelenting series of misfortunes she encounters, and crimes she endures. *Juliette* is the story of her sister and complete opposite. Juliette quickly and eagerly adopts a selfish and wicked lifestyle, indulging in her every desire with no consideration for the needs or lives of others. It was this story of the pleasures of vice, this perversion of the putain memoir, that led to Sade's arrest in 1801. Declared insane two years later and sent to the Charenton asylum, Sade would never again be free.

If, as Joan DeJean and Barry Ivker remind us, Sade was the first to identify a libertine tradition while searching for his own literary ancestors, we cannot overlook the putain memoir branch of the libertine family tree.[36] His *Histoire de Juliette* contains the same libertine critiques of conventional morality, materialist philosophy, and narrative structure as a dozen other novels going back to 1739. But if the quest for a narrative of the libertine tradition begins with Sade, the tradition itself, particularly in the form of the putain memoir, ends with Sade's *Juliette.*

Notes

Introduction

1. In fact, this is my dramatization of the bare-bones account given by Clairon in her real memoirs published in 1798.

2. Clairon (Clair-Josèphe-Hippolyte) Leris, *Mémoires d'Hyppolite Clairon, et Réflexions sur l'art dramatique; publiés par elle-même* (Paris: Buisson, An VII de la République [1798]).

3. For instance, actors, including the great Molière, were forbidden to be buried in consecrated ground.

4. [César Ribié?], *La Cauchoise ou Mémoires d'une courtisane célèbre: Roman* (Libidinus, Chez Sensualité, 10308070 [*sic*; probably 1784]), 12. This edition will be cited hereafter. Unless otherwise mentioned, all translations of the putain memoirs are my own.

5. *Le Dictionnaire de l'Académie française*, 4th ed., vol. 2 (Brunet: Paris, 1762). Available at *ARFFL: The Project for American and French Research on the Treasury of the French Language*, https://artflsrv04.uchicago.edu/philologic4.7/publicdicos/navigate/9/8146.

6. *Le Dictionnaire de l'Académie française.*

7. Antoine Alexandre Barbier, *Dictionnaire des anonymes et pseudonymes composés, traduits ou publiés en français et en latin, avec les noms des auteurs, traducteurs et éditeurs*, 4 vols. (Paris: Imprimerie Bibliographique, 1806–1809); Jules Gay and Jules Lemonnyer, *Bibliographie des ouvrages relatifs à l'amour, aux femmes et au mariage et des livres facétieux, pantagruéliques, scatologiques, satyriques, etc.* (Lille: Stéphane Becour, 1900).

8. Jürgen Habermas, *The Structural Transformation of the Public Sphere: An Inquiry into a Category of Bourgeois Society*, trans. Thomas Burger and Frederick Lawrence (Cambridge, MA: MIT Press, 1989). Originally published as *Strukturwandel der Öffentlichkeit: Untersuchungen zu einer Kategorie der bürgerlichen Gesellschaft* (Neuwied: Luchterhand, 1962).

9. Lynn Hunt, *The Family Romance of the French Revolution* (Los Angeles: University of California Press, 1992), xiii.

10. Hunt, *The Family Romance*, xiv.

11. Kathryn Norberg, "The Libertine Whore: Prostitution in French Pornography from Margot to Juliette," in *The Invention of Pornography: Obscenity and the Origins of Modernity, 1500–1800*, ed. Lynn Hunt (New York: Zone Books, 1993), 225–252. Mathilde Cortey also discusses a larger group of courtesan memoir novels, although her definition of a *courtisane* is far broader than what I consider the subversive putain. See Cortey, *L'Invention de la courtisane au XVIII*[e] *siècle dans les romans-mémoires des "filles du monde" de Madame Meheust à Sade, 1732–1797* (Paris: Arguments, 2001).

12. Norberg, "The Libertine Whore," 225–226.

13. Norberg, "The Libertine Whore," 240.

14. For earlier work on Rousseau and women, see Victor G. Wexler, "'Made for Man's Delight': Rousseau as Antifeminist," *American Historical Review* 81 (April 1976): 266–291; Ruth Graham, "Rousseau's Sexism Revolutionized," in *Woman in the 18th Century and Other Essays*, ed. Paul Fritz and Richard Morton (Toronto: Hakkert, 1976); Maïté Albistur and Daniel Armogathe, *Histoire du féminisme français du moyen âge à nos jours* (Paris: Éditions des femmes, 1977); Jean H. Bloch, "Women and the Reform of the Nation," in *Woman and Society in Eighteenth-Century France*, ed. Eva Jacobs (London: Athlone Press, 1979); Zillah Eisenstein, *The Radical Future of Liberal Feminism* (New York: Longman, 1981); Michèle Coquillat, "Nature et sexe chez Rousseau: Au commencement était le phallus," in *La poétique du mâle* (Paris: Gallimard, 1982); Gita May "Rousseau's 'Anti-Feminism' Reconsidered," in *French Women in the Age of Enlightenment*, ed. Samia I. Spencer (Bloomington: Indiana University Press, 1984); Joel Schwartz, *The Sexual Politics of Jean-Jacques Rousseau* (Chicago: University of Chicago Press, 1984); Penny A. Weiss, "Rousseau, Antifeminism, and Woman's Nature," *Political Theory* 15, no. 1 (1987): 81–98; Sarah Kofman, "Rousseau's Phallocratic Ends," *Hypatia: A Journal of Feminist Philosophy* 3, no. 3 (1989): 123–136; Mary Trouille, "The Failings of Rousseau's Ideals of Domesticity and Sensibility," *Eighteenth-Century Studies* 24, no. 4 (1991): 451–483.

15. For more on Rousseau's domestic utopia, see Nicolas Wagner, "Utopie de *La Nouvelle Héloïse*," in *Roman et Lumières au XVIII*[e] *siècle* (Paris: Éditions Sociales, 1970), 189–270; Carol Blum, *Rousseau and the Republic of Virtue: The Language of Politics in the French Revolution* (Ithaca, NY: Cornell University Press, 1989); Guillaume Ansart, *Réflexion utopique et pratique romanesque au Siècle des Lumières: Prévost, Rousseau, Sade* (Paris: Lettres modernes Minard, 1999); Marie-Françoise Bosquet, *Images du féminin dans les utopies françaises classiques* (Oxford: Voltaire Foundation, 2007); Ekaterina R. Alexandrova, "Conjugal Utopia: Marriage and Social Transformation in Rousseau's *Julie, ou La Nouvelle Héloïse* and Leprince de Beaumont's *La Nouvelle Clarice*," *Eighteenth-Century Fiction* 29, no. 4 (2017): 607–634.

1. Subversive Stories

1. [César Ribié?], *La Cauchoise, ou Mémoires d'une courtisane célèbre: Roman* (Libidinus, Chez Sensualité, 10308070 [*sic*; probably 1784]), 120–125.

2. See Sarane Alexandrian, *Histoire de la littérature érotique* (Paris: Éditions Seghers, 1989). Other scholars also trace the history of the broader category of libertine and pornographic writing to this same text. See, for instance, James Steintrager, *The Autonomy of Pleasure: Libertines, License, and Sexual Revolution* (New York: Columbia University Press, 2016), 12.

3. Lynn Hunt, *The Invention of Pornography: Obscenity and the Origins of Modernity, 1500–1800* (New York: Zone Books, 1993).

4. In 1969 Laterza published both the *Ragionamenti* and the *Dialogo* under a single title, *Sei Giornate*, edited by Giovanni Aquilecchia. See the introduction by Rosa Maria

Falvo to Pietro Aretino, *The School of Whoredom*, trans. Rosa Maria Falvo, Alessandro Gallenzi, and Rebecca Skipwith (London: Hesperus Press, 2003).

5. The actual author of *La Puttana errante* is most likely the sixteenth-century Venetian writer Lorenzo Veniero.

6. The pedagogical prostitute dialogue makes an appearance in England in the seventeenth century with *The Whore's Rhetorik* (1683), in which Mother Creswell gives advice to the novice Dorothea.

7. See Hunt, *Invention of Pornography*, 124. On the possible author, Claude Le Petit, see Joan DeJean, "The Heterosexual Turn," in *Reinvention of Obscenity: Sex, Lies and Tabloids in Early Modern France* (Chicago: University of Chicago Press, 2002), chap. 2. A great deal of scholarly work has gone into comparing editions and translations of *L'École des filles* in order to, among other goals, ascertain authorship. See Frédéric Lachèvre, *Les Œuvres libertines de Claude Le Petit, parisien, brûlé le 1er septembre 1662* (Geneva: Slatkine Reprints, 1968); David Foxon, *Libertine Literature in England, 1660–1745* (London: Book Collector, 1964); Pascal Pia, *Les Livres de L'Enfer: Bibliographie critique des ouvrages érotiques dans leurs différentes éditions du XVI*[e] *siècle à nos jours* (Paris: C. Coulet and A. Faure, 1978); James Grantham Turner, "Libertine Literature Forty Years On: I. From Aretino to the School of Venus," *Book Collector* 54, no. 1 (2005): 29–51.

8. The extent to which eighteenth-century readers were aware of the ruses involved in this verisimilitude has been subject to debate. See George May, *Le Dilemme du roman au XVIII*[e] *siècle* (New Haven, CT: Yale University Press, 1963); Vivienne Mylne, *The Eighteenth-Century French Novel: Techniques of Illusion* (Manchester: University of Manchester Press, 1965); Philip Stewart, *Imitation and Illusion in the French Memoir Novel: 1700–1715* (New Haven, CT: Yale University Press, 1969); René Démoris, *Le Roman à la 1e personne: Du classicisme aux Lumières* (Geneva: Librairie Droz, 2001).

9. See Stewart, *Imitation and Illusion*, 19.

10. Michael Danahy has remarked on the relation between the novel as a genre and prostitution. Compared to other, "nobler" genres, early novels were considered to be written by people willing to prostitute "their talent, their art, or their genius" for money, rendering the novel "the epitome of producing on demand to please unknown and indiscriminate customers." Danahy, *The Feminization of the Novel* (Gainesville: University of Florida Press, 1991), 53.

11. On the other hand, La Bois-Laurier, who tells her story within *Thérèse philosophe*, is in fact a prostitute, and the story she tells is not much shorter than some of the putain memoirs. However, aside from enjoying a little amusement from recounting some of her more absurd adventures, La Bois-Laurier takes no pleasure in her profession and leaves it as quickly as possible. In *Situations de Fougeret de Monbron*, Emmanuel Boussuge speculates that Fougeret de Monbron, author of the putain memoir *Margot la ravaudeuse*, may have written this section of *Thérèse philosophe*.

12. Laura Rosenthal, *Infamous Commerce: Prostitution in Eighteenth-Century British Literature and Culture* (Ithaca, NY: Cornell University Press, 2006). In addition to *Infamous Commerce*, a great deal of scholarly attention has been focused on the sex worker in eighteenth-century British literature. See Laura Brown, *Ends of Empire:*

Women and Ideology in Early Eighteenth-Century English Literature (Ithaca, NY: Cornell University Press, 1993); Liz Bellamy, *Commerce, Morality, and the Eighteenth-Century Novel* (Cambridge: Cambridge University Press, 1998); Ruth Perry, *Novel Relations: The Transformation of Kinship in English Literature and Culture, 1748–1818* (Cambridge: Cambridge University Press, 2004); Laura Rosenthal, *Nightwalkers: Prostitute Narratives from the Eighteenth Century* (Peterborough, ON: Broadview Press, 2008).

13. Rosenthal, *Infamous Commerce*, 97.

14. Rosenthal, *Infamous Commerce*, 2. See also Julie Peakman, "Memoirs of Women of Pleasure: The Whore Biography," and Rhoda Zuk, "The Courtesan's Progress in the Late 1790s: Elizabeth Gooch and Margaret Coghlan," both in *Women's Writing* 11, no. 2 (2004); Peakman, *Mighty Lewd Books: The Development of Pornography in Eighteenth-Century England* (New York: Palgrave Macmillan, 2003); and Felicity Nussbaum's work on the scandalous memoir in *The Autobiographical Subject: Gender and Ideology in Eighteenth-Century England* (Baltimore: Johns Hopkins University Press, 1995) and in *The New Eighteenth Century: Theory, Politics, English Literature*, ed. Felicity Nussbaum and Laura Brown (New York: Routledge, 1988).

15. For more on British prostitute narratives, see Ruth Perry's analysis of this literary phenomenon in "Good Girls and Fallen Women: Representations of Prostitutes in Eighteenth-Century English Fiction," in *Narrating Transgression: Representations of the Criminal in Early Modern England*, ed. Rosamaria Loretelli and Roberto De Romanis (Berlin: Peter Lang, 1999).

16. Nina Kushner makes the same point about real Parisian courtesans in *Erotic Exchanges: The World of Elite Prostitution in Eighteenth-Century Paris* (Ithaca, NY: Cornell University Press, 2014).

17. Rosenthal, *Infamous Commerce*, 100.

18. For another comparison of the erotic literature in France and England, and on their reciprocal influences, see, for example, the investigation of the French influences on Cleland's *Memoirs of a Woman of Pleasure* in Sylvie Kleiman-Lafon, "The French Adventures of Fanny Hill," in *Launching "Fanny Hill": Essays on the Novel and Its Influence*, ed. Patsy S. Fowler and Alan Jackson (New York: AMS Press, 2003), 127–151.

19. Rosenthal, *Infamous Commerce*, 121.

20. Voltaire and Émilie du Châtelet are largely responsible for the interest in Newton's theories in eighteenth-century France. Both defended Newton's theories, and Châtelet translated the Englishman's *Principia Mathematica* from Latin into French, with commentary, in 1759.

21. For more on philosophy in libertine literature, see Michel Delon, "De *Thérèse philosophe* à *La Philosophie dans le boudoir*, la place de la philosophie," *Romantische Zeitschrift für Literaturgeschichte / Cahiers d'histoire des littératures romanes* (Winter 1983); Delon, *L'Invention du boudoir* (Paris: Zulma, 1999); Colas Duflo, *Philosophie des pornographes: Les Ambitions philosophiques du roman libertin* (Paris: Éditions du Seuil, 2019).

22. Catherine Cusset, *No Tomorrow: The Ethics of Pleasure in the French Enlightenment* (Charlottesville: University of Virginia Press, 1999), 2.

23. Natania Meeker, "'I Resist It No Longer': Enlightened Philosophy and Feminine Compulsion in *Thérèse philosophe*," *Eighteenth-Century Studies* 39, no. 3 (2006): 363. In this article, Meeker astutely remarks how Thérèse's freedom as a libertine is in her case deliberately limited by the sexual desire her lover arouses. The same contradiction can be observed for any libertine compelled to obey the laws of nature and the sexual desire they ignite. See also Meeker's *Voluptuous Philosophy: Literary Materialism in the French Enlightenment* (New York: Fordham University Press, 2007).

24. Margaret C. Jacob, "The Materialist World of Pornography," in *The Invention of Pornography: Obscenity and the Origins of Modernity, 1500–1800*, ed. Lynn Hunt (New York: Zone Books, 1993), 161.

25. Jacob, "Materialist World of Pornography," 162.

26. For more on the eighteenth-century French lexicon for salacious literature, see Paul Benhamou, "The Diffusion of Forbidden Books: Four Case Studies," *Studies on Voltaire and the Eighteenth Century* 12 (2005): 359–381.

27. Amy S. Wyngaard, *Bad Books: Rétif de la Bretonne, Sexuality, and Pornography* (Newark: University of Delaware Press, 2013). See also Wyngaard, "Defining Obscenity, Inventing Pornography: The Limits of Censorship in Rétif de la Bretonne," *Modern Language Quarterly* 71, no. 1 (2010): 15–49; James A. Steintrager, "What Happened to the Porn in Pornography? Rétif, Regulating Prostitution, and the History of Dirty Books," *Symposium: A Quarterly Journal in Modern Literatures* 60, no. 3 (2006): 189–204.

28. Hunt, *The Invention of Pornography*, 9.

29. In *Situations de Fougeret de Monbron*, Emmanuel Boussuge describes books like *Margot la ravaudeuse*, *La Fille de joie*, and the Bois-Laurier story in *Thérèse philosophe* as "pornobiographique." The combination of "porno," meaning about prostitutes, and "biographique," as the writings about a life, makes the term technically accurate—but the word implies the stories of real lives, and none of those stories, or the putain narratives, is true.

30. See Robert Darnton, *The Forbidden Best-Sellers of Prerevolutionary France* (New York: W. W. Norton, 1996); and see also Darnton, *The Literary Underground of the Old Regime* (Cambridge, MA: Harvard University Press, 1982); Darnton, *Édition et sédition: L'Univers de la littérature clandestine au XVIIIe siècle* (Paris: Gallimard, 1991); Darnton, *The Corpus of Clandestine Literature in France, 1769–1789* (New York: W. W. Norton, 1995); Darnton, *Pirating and Publishing: The Book Trade in the Age of Enlightenment* (Oxford: Oxford University Press, 2021).

31. Darnton, *Forbidden Best-Sellers*, 7.

32. Darnton, *Forbidden Best-Sellers*, 21.

33. Amy S. Wyngaard, "Sade, Réage and Transcending the Obscene," in *The Cambridge Companion to Erotic Literature*, ed. Bradford K. Mudge (Cambridge: Cambridge University Press, 2017), 212; Hunt, *Invention of Pornography*, 305.

34. Hunt, *Invention of Pornography*, 305.

35. Etienne-Gabriel Peignot, *Dictionnaire critique, littéraire et bibliographique des principaux livres condamnés au feu, supprimés ou censurés*, 2 vols. (Paris, 1806), cited in Hunt, *Invention of Pornography*, 303; Wyngaard, "Sade, Réage," 212. Wyngaard also

persuasively argues that Rétif de la Bretonne occupies the same moment of transition as Sade and advanced "the modern form and definition of pornography" with his 1798 *L'Anti-Justine*. Wyngaard, *Bad Books*, 48.

36. Andrea Dworkin, *Pornography: Men Possessing Women* (New York: Dutton, 1989), xxxiii. Wyngaard (*Bad Books*, 66) characterizes Dworkin's description as evoking "the Sadean brand of pornography and its avatars."

37. See, for example, Raymond Trousson' preface to *Romans libertins du XVIII*[e] *siècle* (Paris: R. Laffont, 1993); Lasowski's preface to Patrick Wald Lasowski and Alian Clerval, *Romanciers libertins du XVIII*[e] *siècle*, 2 vols. (Paris: Gallimard, 2000, 2005).

38. René Pintard, *Le Libertinage érudit dans la première moitié du XVII*[e] *siècle* (Paris: Boivin, 1943).

39. Joan DeJean, *Libertine Strategies: Freedom and the Novel in Seventeenth-Century France* (Columbus: Ohio State University Press, 1981), 24.

40. Trousson, *Romans libertins*, xx.

41. Trousson, *Romans libertins*, vii.

42. Steintrager, *The Autonomy of Pleasure*, 10.

43. Steintrager, *The Autonomy of Pleasure*, 19.

44. Steintrager, *The Autonomy of Pleasure*, 20, 22.

45. Steintrager, *The Autonomy of Pleasure*, 22.

46. Peter Nagy, *Libertinage et révolution*, trans. Christiane Gremillon (Paris: Gallimard, 1975), as cited in Trousson, *Romans libertins*, xi.

47. DeJean, *Libertine Strategies*, 23–24.

48. Jean M. Goulemot, *Ces livres qu'on ne lit que d'une main: Lecture et lectures de livres pornographiques au XVIII*[e] *siècle* (Paris: Éditions Alinéa, 1991). In English as *Forbidden Texts: Erotic Literature and Its Readers in Eighteenth-Century France*, trans. James Simpson (Philadelphia: University of Pennsylvania Press, 1994). Importantly, Goulemot does not seek to disparage the significance of erotic texts by distinguishing them from libertine writing. In fact, unlike some critics of the libertine tradition, Goulemot argues that erotic writing is the best example of what all fiction tries to do: take something imaginary and make the reader feel it is true.

49. Goulemot, *Ces livres qu'on ne lit*, 124.

50. Henri Coulet, *Le Roman jusqu'à la révolution*, 9th ed. (Paris: Armand Colin, 2000).

51. For further evidence of the complexity of terms like "erotic," see Bradford K. Mudge, *The Cambridge Companion to Erotic Literature* (Cambridge: Cambridge University Press, 2017), which includes essays on "secular and devotional eros" from the Middle Ages, pornography in early modern England, Sade and the obscene, and Dutch gay novels of the 1950s.

52. Delon, "De *Thérèse philosophe*," 76.

53. Lasowski, preface to *Romanciers libertins du XVIII*[e] *siècle*, xxxvi.

54. Another erotic novel of the late seventeenth century, *Vénus dans la cloître, ou La Religieuse en chemise*, was also a popular reprint in the eighteenth century.

55. Alexandrian (*Histoire de la littérature érotique*, 143) believes the French held the uncontested monopoly on gallant literature ("le monopole incontesté de la littérature

galante") in the eighteenth century, although the international success of Cleland's *Memoirs of a Woman of Pleasure* makes this assertion difficult to support.

2. Fact versus Fiction

1. [Antoine Bret or Claude Villaret], *La Belle Allemande, ou Les Galanteries de Thérèse, deux parties* (1745) (Paris: Aux Dépens de la Compagnie, 1755), 3. I will be citing from this 1755 edition, with updated spelling and punctuation where necessary. All English translations of *La Belle Allemande* are my own.

2. [Bret or Villaret], *La Belle Allemande*, 2–3.

3. [Bret or Villaret], *La Belle Allemande*, 2.

4. [Bret or Villaret], *La Belle Allemande*, 3.

5. [Bret or Villaret], *La Belle Allemande*, xii.

6. [Bret or Villaret], *La Belle Allemande*, xii.

7. See the work of Pamela Cheek, who notes the similarities of these records to erotic novels of the time: "Police and non-police writing also reproduced the same prostitute biography beginning with loss of virginity, or sometimes with a woman's first unruly sexual stirrings, following her through her separation from her family, her sexual tutoring by a more experienced woman, her various alliances, her bouts of disease, and her pregnancies." Cheek, "Prostitutes of 'Political Institution,'" *Eighteenth-Century Studies* 28, no. 2 (1994–1995): 193–219.

8. See Louis-Sébastien Mercier, *Tableau de Paris* (1782), ed. Jean-Claude Bonnet, 2 vols. (Paris: Mercure de France, 1994); Edmond Jean François Barbier, *Chronique de la Régence et du règne du Louis XV (1718–1763) ou Journal Barbier*, 8 vols. (Paris: Charpentier, 1857); Giacamo Casanova, *Histoire de ma vie* (Wiesbaden: Brockhaus, 1960–1963); Alexandre comte de Tilly, *Mémoires du comte Alexandre de Tilly pour server à l'histoire des mœurs de la fin du XVIIIe siècle*, ed. Christian Melchior-Bonnet (Paris: Mercure de France, 1965); Jean-François Marmontel, *Mémoires de Marmontel: Mémoires d'un père pour servir à l'instruction de ses enfants*, ed. Maurice Tourneux, 3 vols. (Paris: Librairie des Bibliophiles, 1891).

9. Erica Marie Benabou, *La Prostitution et la police des mœurs au dix-huitième siècle* (Paris: Perrin, 1987); Nina Kushner, *Erotic Exchanges: The World of Elite Prostitution in Eighteenth-Century Paris* (Ithaca, NY: Cornell University Press, 2014); Clyde Plumauzille, *Prostitution et révolution: Les Femmes publiques dans la cite républicaine (1789–1804)* (Clamency, France: La Nouvelle Imprimerie Laballery, 2016).

10. Most estimates are between twenty thousand and thirty thousand. See Benabou, *La Prostitution*, 327. In the *Tableau de Paris*, Mercier estimates that there were thirty thousand "filles publiques" and ten thousand "entretenues." (1:597).

11. Benabou, *La Prostitution*, 272–273.

12. Benabou, *La Prostitution*, 321.

13. Benabou, *La Prostitution*, 323–324.

14. Benabou, *La Prostitution*, 330.

15. Benabou, *La Prostitution*, 366.

16. Benabou, *La Prostitution*, 343–345.

17. Mercier, *Tableau de Paris*, 1:589.

18. Plumauzille, *Prostitution et révolution*, 63.

19. Plumauzille, *Prostitution et révolution*, 64.

20. Kushner, *Erotic Exchanges*, 3.

21. Kushner, *Erotic Exchanges*, 99.

22. Of course, details about how many copies of each novel were sold, who bought the novels, and who read them are nearly as elusive for many eighteenth-century texts as for the putain memoirs.

23. *Œuvres de théâtre de M. Bret Censeur Royal, & de l'Académie Royale des Sciences & Belles-Lettres de Nancy* (1765), *Œuvres de théâtre* (1766), *Œuvres de M. Bret* (1772), *Théâtre* (1778), and *Œuvres de M. Bret . . .* (1789).

24. Rabelais-d'Aquin, *Almanach littéraire, ou Étrennes d'Apollon pour l'année 1793* (Paris: L'Imprimerie de Clousier, 1793), 78–79.

25. "Le b***" stands for *le bidet*. Bret borrows from Crébillon fils (*Le Sopha*) the trope of an object personified into a voyeur recounting for the reader the adventures it has witnessed.

26. Françoise de Graffigny, *Lettres d'une Péruvienne*, ed. Gianni Nicoletti (Bari: Adriatica, 1967), 27.

27. Bret is named in Agnus Martin, Vivenne Mylne, and Richard Frautschi, eds., *La Bibliographie du genre romanesque* (London: Mansell, 1977; Paris: France Expansion, 1977), and in the introduction to Raymond Trousson, *Romans libertins du XVIIIe siècle* (Paris: R. Laffont, 1993). However, in Antoine Alexandre Barbier, *Dictionnaire des anonymes et pseudonymes composés, traduits ou publiés en français et en latin, avec les noms des auteurs, traducteurs et éditeurs*, 4 vols. (Paris: Imprimerie Bibliographique, 1806–1809), the novel is attributed to either Bret or another unnamed writer.

28. Daunu, "Villaret (Claude)," in *Biographie universelle ancienne et moderne* 48 (Paris: Chez L. G. Michaud, 1827), 512. His other early works include the novels *Histoire du cœur humain, ou Mémoires du marquis de ****(1743) and *Le Coq, ou Mémoire du chevalier V**** (1742).

29. The obvious exception is the Marquis de Sade, about whom numerous biographies have been written. On Fougeret de Monbron, Emmanuel Boussuge has expanded upon the early the findings of Jack Howard Broome to prepare a detailed and thorough biographical study. See Boussuge, *Situations de Fougeret de Monbron (1706–1760)* (Paris: Champion, 2010); Boussuge, "L'Homme au cœur velu: Autour d'une anecdote de la Satire première (Fougeret de Monbron et Diderot)," in *Des sens au sens: Littérature et morale de Molière à Voltaire*, ed. Jacques Wagner (Peeters: Louvain, 2007); Broome, "'L'Homme au cœur velu': The Turbulent Career of Fougeret de Monbron," *Studies in Voltaire and the Eighteenth Century* 23 (1963).

30. See Boussuge's assertions that the similarities between the two texts are proof that Fougeret had at least heard about Crébillon's manuscript, and that he must have had some access to the elite literary circles of the privileged few who knew about Crébillon's text: "To write his parallel text, he must have at least heard about the work."

("Pour écrire son texte parallèle, il fallait bien qu'il ait, au moins entendu parler de l'ouvrage.") Boussuge, *Situations*, 182.

31. The full title is *La Chronique des rois d'Angleterre écrite en anglais selon le style des anciens historiens juifs, par Nathan Ben Saadi, prêtre de la même nation; traduite en français dans le même style.*

32. Boussuge, *Situations*, 205.

33. It must be noted that in the year before he wrote these two odes, Fougeret had inherited enough money at the death of his father that he no longer needed to write for money. Whether his works sold well or not might not have mattered to him. Still, to mock those who praised the king—even if not openly ridiculing the king himself—would have been a risky move.

34. Letter 786, *Correspondance de Madame de Graffigny*, vol. 6, ed. J. A. Dainard, Pierre Bouillagnet, and Judith Curtis (Oxford: Voltaire Foundation, 2000).

35. Letter 786, *Correspondance de Madame de Graffigny*, vol. 6; letter 428, *Correspondance*, vol. 26. Excerpt also cited in vol. 6, as a note to letter 786. Both passages cited in Boussuge, *Situations*, 21–12.

36. Letter 15, *L'Année littéraire*, vol. 1 (Amsterdam and Paris, 1756), 95. Cited in Patrick Wald Lasowski's introduction to *Margot la ravaudeuse* in Patrick Wald Lasowski and Alian Clerval, *Romanciers libertins du XVIII*[e] *siècle*, 2 vols. (Paris: Gallimard, 2000, 2005), 1248.

37. Letter 809, *Correspondance de Madame de Graffigny*, vol. 6.

38. Letter 809, *Correspondance*.

3. *La Belle Allemande*, or The Empire of Beauty

1. [Antoine Bret or Claude Villaret], *La Belle Allemande, ou Les Galanteries de Thérèse, deux parties* (1745) (Paris: Aux Dépens de la compagnie, 1755), 45–46, all cites are to 1755 edition.

2. [Bret or Villaret], *La Belle Allemande*, 46.

3. In another putain memoir, the narrator Margot, pleased with the power of her fame, boasts that she has an ambassador extraordinary at her feet: "I could not hide from myself the joy I felt at having made such an important conquest. What a flattering triumph for my vanity! And how satisfied I was to see at my feet a person who . . . can from his desk change the system of European affairs, and equally contribute to the greater good and the glory of his country!" ("Je ne pus me dissimuler à moi-même la joie que je ressentais alors d'avoir fait une conquête de cette importance. Quel triomphe flatteur pour ma vanité! Et que je m'imaginais de satisfaction de voir à mes pieds une personne, qui . . . peut de son cabinet changer tout le système des affaires de l'Europe, et contribuer également au bien général et à la gloire de sa patrie!") My translation. Louis Charles Fougeret de Monbron, *Margot la ravaudeuse*, 732.

Once again, the putain's elevated position is evoked through the metaphor of feet. An illustrious man places himself before the same body part that walks through dirt and mud and that Margot could use to step on him. This putain is not merely the equal of this preeminent leader—the negotiations for their arrangement having been carried out with all the delicacy and formality of an international treaty—she has the upper hand because of the desire she arouses. Margot imagines herself as a Madame de Pompadour who can use her intimacy with a man in power to affect public policy. Her sexual power easily transforms into financial and political power.

Interestingly, Madame de Pompadour, like the putains, was of non-noble origins and through her charms was able to rise to a position of power and influence. While none of the putains ever entertain the French king, it is quite probable that they are an indirect critique of Louis XV's mistress (and perhaps later Madame Du Barry as well). It is significant that the two decades that saw the largest number of new putain memoirs (the 1740s and 1750s) were also a period of increased criticism of the king and Pompadour, his military failures, and her perceived nefarious influence on his diplomatic policies.

4. According to *Le Trésor*, until 1830 the terms *patriarcat* and *patriarche* were limited to the religious context, referring to the fathers of the Church.

5. [Bret or Villaret], *La Belle Allemande*, 146.

6. [Bret or Villaret], *La Belle Allemande*, 3–4.

7. The narrator of another putain memoir, *La Cauchoise*, recognizes that a true putain should care about pleasure, not family lineage: "I know a lot of my dear and venerable sisters who give themselves a beautiful origin, without really being any nobler because of it. To hear them talk, it would seem that no girl could know how to wiggle her ass without being the daughter of a prelate, niece of a counselor, cousin of a duke and peer of the realm, etc. Such a genealogy is pure folly! A true putain must know only pleasure. She must scorn her birth and her family, and have no other ambition save that of quenching her passion and maintaining useful and agreeable acquaintances." ("Je connais beaucoup de mes chères et vénérables consœurs qui se donnent une belle origine, sans en être plus nobles pour cela. À les entendre, on ne saurait bien remuer le croupion à moins d'être fille d'un prélat, nièce d'un conseiller, cousine d'un duc et pair, etc. Quelle folie qu'une pareille généalogie! Une véritable putain ne doit absolument connaître que le plaisir; elle doit mépriser sa naissance et ses parents, et n'avoir d'autre ambition que celle d'assouvir sa passion et de se ménager des connaissances aussi utiles qu'agréables.") [César Ribié?], *La Cauchoise ou mémoires d'une courtisane célèbre: Roman* (1784) (Libidinus, Chez Sensualité, 10308070 [*sic*; 1784?], 13–14.

8. [Bret or Villaret], *La Belle Allemande*, 62.

9. The subject of Sade's complicated feelings about and depiction of family dynamics, particularly regarding the role of mothers, has received significant scholarly attention and will figure prominently here in chapter 6.

10. In the case of La Dumonci, we find that it is precisely her mother's neglect of her daughter's sexual education that leaves the young woman vulnerable to seduction. As for the narrator of *Margot la ravaudeuse*, it is the sight of her mother's sexual activities that ignites the future putain's curiosity and desires. Further, the physical abuse she receives from her mother drives her out of the family home and into the corrupting clutches of a surrogate mother, Madame Florence.

11. The importance of Juliette's "godmothers" in Sade's *Histoire de Juliette* is highlighted in Jane Gallop, "Sade, Mothers and Other Women," in *Thinking through the Body* (New York: Cornell University Press, 1988); and in Angela Carter, *The Sadeian Woman and the Ideology of Pornography* (New York: Pantheon Books, 1978). Further, the madams who take in Thérèse, Margot, and even Fanny Hill can also be seen as versions of this pseudo-mother or godmother.

12. See, for instance, Jean H. Bloch, "Rousseau's Reputation as an Authority on Childcare and Physical Education in France before the Revolution," *Paedegogica historica* 14, no. 1 (1974): 5–33; Mary Seidman Trouille, *Sexual Politics in the Enlightenment: Women Writers Read Rousseau* (Albany: SUNY Press, 1997); Ruth Perry, "Colonizing the Breast: Sexuality and Maternity in Eighteenth-Century England," *Journal of the History of Sexuality* 2, no. 2 (1991): 204–235. In particular, the increased popularity of breastfeeding one's own babies is cited as evidence of this rising esteem for motherhood.

13. [Bret or Villaret], *La Belle Allemande*, 37.

14. [Bret or Villaret], *La Belle Allemande*, 37.

15. [Bret or Villaret], *La Belle Allemande*, 47–48.

16. [Bret or Villaret], *La Belle Allemande*, 47.

17. "M. de R." is possibly a reference to the duc de Richelieu Louis-François-Armand, notoriously debauched godson of Louis XIV.

18. [Bret or Villaret], *La Belle Allemande*, 60–61.

19. Of course, the trope of the younger, attractive man cuckolding the older, foolish man is not unique to the prostitute narratives. It can be traced back to Molière and the Commedia del Arte, among other sources.

20. [Bret or Villaret], *La Belle Allemande*, 38.

21. [Bret or Villaret], *La Belle Allemande*, 51.

22. See Erica Marie Benabou, *La Prostitution et la police des mœurs au dix-huitième siècle* (Paris: Perrin, 1987), 364.

23. [Bret or Villaret], *La Belle Allemande*, 91–92.

24. Lynn Hunt, ed., *The Invention of Pornography, 1500–1800: Obscenity and the Origins of Modernity* (New York: Zone Books, 1993), 326–327.

25. [Bret or Villaret], *La Belle Allemande*, 9–10.

26. The putain Margot also recognizes the value of interacting with men from a variety of classes and professions, when she asks rhetorically, "Is there any profession whose jargon we do not learn? The soldier, the lawyer, the financier, the philosopher, the clergyman—men from all walks of life seek our company." Fougeret de Monbron, *Margot la ravaudeuse*, trans. Edouard Langille (Cambridge: Modern Humanities Research Association, 2015), 29. ("Est-il quelque profession, quelque métier dans la vie dont nous n'ayons pas incessamment occasion d'entendre discourir? Le guerrier, le robin, le financier, le philosophe, l'homme de l'Église, tous ces êtres divers recherchent également notre commerce.") Fougeret de Monbron, *Margot la ravaudeuse*, 694.

27. [Bret or Villaret], *La Belle Allemande*, 38.

28. [Bret or Villaret], *La Belle Allemande*, 82.

29. In *Margot la ravaudeuse*, we again find a putain speaking to the power of female sexuality when she remarks that because having a mistress is a sign of wealth and

status, it is often the mistress who brings fame and prestige to her benefactor and not the other way around: "In fact, it seems to me that we give life to our lovers. Someone who would have always been lost in the crowd and nonexistent, as soon as he hitches himself to our wagon, it is no longer permitted not to know him. He is a fashionable man. How many despicable publicans would have ever been famous if they had not made us a part of their plunder and misappropriation? We're the ones who pull these people out of obscurity and consecrate their names by the exorbitant expenses we plunge them into." My translation. ("En effet, il me semble que nous donnions l'être à nos amants. Tel qui aurait toujours été confondu et comme anéanti dans la foule, dès qu'il est attaché à notre char, il n'est plus permis de l'ignorer: c'est un homme à la mode. Combien de méprisables publicains qui n'auraient jamais été connus s'ils ne nous avaient point fait part de leurs rapines et de leurs concussions? C'est nous qui tirons ces gens-là de l'obscurité, et consacrons leurs noms par les dépenses exorbitantes où nous les plongeons.") Fougeret de Monbron, *Margot la ravaudeuse*, 720–721.

Margot recognizes the irony that a common woman like herself is more famous and important than the wealthy men who adore her. She mocks the "publicans" who are so insignificant on their own merits that without a famous courtesan at their sides they would never be able to distinguish themselves. While it would be easy to claim that a mistress, even a beautiful and famous one like Margot, is simply the passive accessory that facilitates her lover's rise to fashionable fame, Margot in fact insists on the active role of the putain in that relationship. She gives her *entreteneur* his being, she takes him out of obscurity, and she is the one driving the wagon to which he is hitched. In this way, Margot elevates the putain from the status of a sexual plaything to that of a creator. Finally, Margot irreverently blends religion and capitalism when she claims to "consecrate" the names of her lovers through the frivolous and expensive gifts she demands. This speech inverts the usual hierarchy established with the wealthy and influential *entreteneur* who lifts a beautiful woman out of obscurity. This time it is the fame of the beautiful woman that benefits the man.

30. [Bret or Villaret], *La Belle Allemande*, 130–133.

31. Examples of the putains' generosity toward other women will be further discussed in chapter 4, but two major examples include La Dumonci, who takes in an old friend and fellow putain, and Margot, who seeks out her impoverished mother and takes care of her at the end of her memoir.

32. [Bret or Villaret], *La Belle Allemande*, 146.

33. [Bret or Villaret], *La Belle Allemande*, 146.

34. *La Cauchoise*'s heroine, La Dumonci, also manages to manipulate male desire and her own bout of venereal disease to punish a man she considers deceitful and hypocritical. On her way back to Paris after contracting syphilis in Rouen, La Dumonci encounters in her coach an obnoxious clergyman and an attractive younger man. She proudly recounts how at a rest stop she deliberately has sex with the cleric to infect him but cleverly talks the young man into trying anal sex to avoid harming him.

4. *Margot la ravaudeuse*, or The Libertine Public Sphere

1. Louis Charles Fougeret de Monbron, *Margot la ravaudeuse* (1750), in *Romans libertins du XVIIIe siècle*, ed. Raymond Trousson (Paris: R. Laffont, 1993), 717. My translation. In this chapter, I will occasionally turn to Édouard Langille's 2015 English translation. Unless otherwise indicated, all translations of Margot are my own.

2. Laura Rosenthal, *Infamous Commerce: Prostitution in Eighteenth-Century British Literature and Culture* (Ithaca, NY: Cornell University Press, 2006), 2.

3. Margot's mysterious illness foreshadows Mercier's concept of "urban pathology." See Harvey Chisick, "Urban Pathologies and the Pathology of the Urban in L.-S. Mercier's *Tableau de Paris*," in *Correspondence and Epistolary Fiction: La Fête; Science and Medicine; Voltaire*, ed. Anthony Strugnell (Oxford: Voltaire Foundation, 2002).

4. Most of the police records dealing with madams and prostitutes spend a significant amount of ink listing the women's residences. The practical reasons for such details in the reports of inspectors charged with identifying and monitoring sex workers are obvious. More intriguing is the spillover of these details into fictional autobiographies.

5. For a discussion of how interior spaces represent sex and seduction in libertine novels, see Michel Delon, "L'Espace de la séduction dans le roman français du XVIIIe siècle," in *Littérature et séduction: Mélanges en l'honneur de Laurent Versini*, ed. Roger Marchal and François Moureau (Paris: Klincksieck, 1977), 377–386; Christophe Martin, *Espaces du féminin dans le roman français du dix-huitième siècle* (Oxford: Voltaire Foundation, 2004).

6. Sarane Alexandrian, *Histoire de la littérature érotique* (Paris: Éditions Seghers, 1989), 143.

7. Alexandrian, *Histoire de la littérature érotique*, 166–167.

8. Lynn Hunt, *Eroticism and the Body Politic* (Baltimore: Johns Hopkins University Press, 1991), 5.

9. Walter Kendrick, *The Secret Museum: Pornography in Modern Culture* (Berkeley: University of California Press, 1996), 33.

10. Colin Jones, *Paris: The Biography of a City* (New York: Penguin Books, 2004), 182–183.

11. Benabou describes a famous engraving by Baudouin, *La Soirée des Tuileries*, in which a young man in rumpled clothing gives a handful of coins to a young woman who is putting her glove back on, presumably as payment for the "manualisation" she just gave him. Erica Marie Benabou, *La Prostitution et la police des mœurs au dix-huitième siècle* (Paris: Perrin, 1987), 197.

12. See Susan Conner, "Prostitution and the Jacobin Agenda for Social Control," *Eighteenth-Century Life* 12, no. 1 (1988): 46; Kathryn Norberg, "Prostitutes," in *A History of Women in the West*, vol. 3: *Renaissance and Enlightenment Paradoxes*, ed. Natalie Zemon Davis and Arlette Farge (Cambridge, MA: Belknap Press of Harvard University Press, 1993), 468.

13. See Benabou, *La Prostitution*, 197.

14. Benabou, *La Prostitution*, 205–208.

15. Amy Wyngaard notes that Rétif de la Bretonne links the privacy provided by the anonymous capital with debauched and immoral behavior. Wyngaard, "Libertine Spaces: Anonymous Crowds, Secret Chambers, and Urban Corruption in Rétif de la Bretonne," *Eighteenth-Century Life* 22 (1998): 104–122.

16. Fougeret de Monbron, *Margot la ravaudeuse*, 717.

17. Mercier, cited in Benabou, *La Prostitution*, 935.

18. See the description of the Palais Royal in Johannes Willms, *Paris, Capital of Europe: From the Revolution to the Belle Époque*, trans. Eveline L. Kanes (New York: Holmes and Meier, 1997), 5–10. First published as *Paris: Hauptstadt Europas, 1789–1914* (Munich: C. H. Beck, 1988).

19. Louis Sébastien Mercier, *Tableau de Paris* (1782), ed. Jean-Claude Bonnet, 2 vols. (Paris: Mercure de France, 1994), 2:939.

20. English Showalter Jr., "Symbolic Space and Fictional Forms in the Eighteenth-Century French Novel," *NOVEL: A Forum on Fiction* 8, no. 3 (1975): 214–225.

21. Henri Lagrave, *Le Théâtre et le public à Paris de 1715 à 1750* (Paris: Librairie C. Klincksieck, 1972), 192.

22. See Philippe Ariès, introduction to *History of Private Life*, vol. 3: *Passions of the Renaissance*, ed. Roger Chartier, trans. Arthur Goldhammer (Cambridge, MA: Belknap Press of Harvard University Press, 1993); Dena Goodman, "Public Sphere and Private Life: Toward a Synthesis of Current Historiographical Approaches to the Old Régime," *History and Theory* 31, no. 1 (1992): 1–20; Elizabeth Goldsmith and Dena Goodman, eds., *Going Public: Women and Publishing in Early Modern France* (Ithaca, NY: Cornell University Press, 1995). For work on Habermas's public sphere, see Amy Allen, "The Public Sphere: Ideology and / or Ideal?," *Political Theory* 40, no. 6 (2012): 822–829; Ruth Bloch, "Inside and Outside the Public Sphere," *William and Mary Quarterly*, 3rd ser., 62, no. 1 (2005): 99–106; Pauline Johnson, *Habermas: Rescuing the Public Sphere* (New York: Routledge, 2006); Craig Calhoun, ed., *Habermas and the Public Sphere* (Cambridge, MA: MIT Press, 1992). For studies focusing more specifically on the relationship between the bourgeois public sphere and the French Revolution, see Keith Baker, *Inventing the French Revolution* (Cambridge: Cambridge University Press, 1989); Baker, ed., *The French Revolution and the Creation of Modern Political Culture*, vol. 1: *The Political Culture of the Old Régime* (Oxford: Pergamon Press, 1987); Roger Chartier, *The Cultural Origins of the French Revolution*, trans. Lydia G. Cochrane (Durham, NC: Duke University Press, 1991).

23. As a Marxist, Habermas openly acknowledges that the bourgeois public sphere was in fact not open to all individuals, given that the working classes, who lacked the time and means to access many of the sites, would not be able to participate.

24. Joan B. Landes, *Women and the Public Sphere in the Age of the French Revolution* (Ithaca, NY: Cornell University Press, 1988), 7.

25. See Jean Bethke Elshtain, who traces the association of women with all things private and men with all things public, from antiquity to the present day, in *Public Man, Private Woman: Women in Social and Political Thought* (Princeton, NJ: Princeton University Press, 1981).

26. See Penny Weiss, who, focusing solely on the writings of Rousseau, lists several categories of justifications that were given for excluding women from the public sphere,

including concerns about women's physical strength and mental capacities. Weiss, "Rousseau, Antifeminism, and Woman's Nature," *Political Theory* 15, no. 1 (1987): 81–98.

27. As cited in *La Gazette Nationale ou Le Moniteur Universel*, October 31, 1793, collected in *Réimpression de l'Ancien Moniteur*, 32 vols. (Paris: Plon, 1854), 18:300.

28. *La Gazette Nationale*, October 31, 1793.

29. *La Gazette Nationale*, November 17, 1793, in *Réimpression de l'Ancien Moniteur*, 18:450.

30. Fougeret de Monbron, *Margot la ravaudeuse*, 717.

31. Fougeret de Monbron, *Margot la ravaudeuse*, 697.

32. Fougeret de Monbron, *Margot la ravaudeuse*, 727.

33. Thérèse also refers to the men who come to her home once she is supported by a wealthy *entreteneur*, trading their philosophical talk for the free meals. La Dumonci's financier invites attractive young people to her home for dinners and games as well, and this exposure to others leads her to cheat on him: "I would have surely been faithful, I think, if I had only ever seen my financier. But he often brought me men who were better looking than he." ("Sûrement j'aurais été fidèle, je le sens, si je n'avais vu constamment que mon financier; mais il m'amenait souvent des hommes mieux faits qui lui.") [César Ribié?], *La Cauchoise ou Mémoires d'une courtisane célèbre: Roman* (1784) (Libidinus, Chez Sensualité, 10308070 [*sic*; 1784?], 88.

34. Thérèse also works in and out of brothels throughout her career. At one point she slips out of the home her *entreteneur* provides her to go earn extra money in a brothel. As proof of the high level of traffic passing through this brothel, she coincidentally runs into this very same *entreteneur* there.

35. Robert Darnton, *The Literary Underground of the Old Regime* (Cambridge, MA: Harvard University Press, 1982), 16. Cited in Landes, *Women and the Public Sphere*, 40–41.

36. Landes, *Women and the Public Sphere*, 18–20.

37. Landes, *Women and the Public Sphere*, 39.

38. Fougeret de Monbron, *Margot la ravaudeuse*, 680.

39. La Dumonci makes the same connection at the end of her story. She explains that she has chosen to write her memoirs to pass the time while she recovers from yet another bout of syphilis, and she hopes that the public will give her printed memoirs as warm a welcome as she personally has enjoyed. She is at once openly acknowledging her intention to publish her writing and comparing the potential readers to her former customers. [Ribié?], *La Cauchoise*, 191.

40. [Antoine Bret or Claude Villaret], *La Belle Allemande, ou Les Galanteries de Thérèse, deux parties* (1745) (Paris: Aux Dépens de la compagnie, 1755), 1, 3.

41. For more on the difficulties for women in publishing, see Joan DeJean, *Tender Geographies: Women and the Origins of the Novel in France* (New York: Columbia University Press, 1993).

42. Jean-Jacques Rousseau, *Lettre à M. d'Alembert sur son article Genève* (1758), intro. by Michel Launay (Paris: Garnier-Flammarion, 1967), 173, 197.

43. Fougeret de Monbron, *Margot la ravaudeuse*, 711.

44. Fougeret de Monbron, *Margot la ravaudeuse*, 711.

45. Rosenthal, *Infamous Commerce*, 14.

46. Rosenthal, *Infamous Commerce*, 2.

47. Rosenthal, *Infamous Commerce*, 2.

48. Langille, trans., *Margot la ravaudeuse*, 22; Fougeret de Monbron, *Margot la ravaudeuse*, 686.

49. Langille, trans., *Margot la ravaudeuse*, 39; Fougeret de Monbron, *Margot la ravaudeuse*, 708.

50. Langille, trans., *Margot la ravaudeuse*, 39; Fougeret de Monbron, *Margot la ravaudeuse*, 708–709.

51. Langille, trans., *Margot la ravaudeuse*, 43; Fougeret de Monbron, *Margot la ravaudeuse*, 714.

52. Langille, trans., *Margot la ravaudeuse*, 56; Fougeret de Monbron, *Margot la ravaudeuse*, 730.

53. Langille, trans., *Margot la ravaudeuse*, 56; Fougeret de Monbron, *Margot la ravaudeuse*, 731.

54. Langille, trans., *Margot la ravaudeuse*, 57; Fougeret de Monbron, *Margot la ravaudeuse*, 731.

55. Langille, trans., *Margot la ravaudeuse*, 27; Fougeret de Monbron, *Margot la ravaudeuse*, 691.

56. Rosenthal, *Infamous Commerce*, 7.

57. Rosenthal, *Infamous Commerce*, 127.

58. Rosenthal, *Infamous Commerce*, 2.

59. Rosenthal, *Infamous Commerce*, 2, 9.

5. *La Cauchoise*, or Dear and Venerable Sisters

1. For more on the scholarship of early modern and Enlightenment depictions of lesbianism and female same-sex relationships, see Lillian Faderman, *Surpassing the Love of Men: Romantic Friendship and Love between Women from the Renaissance to the Present* (New York: Morrow, 1981); Emma Donoghue, *Passions between Women: British Lesbian Culture, 1668–1801* (New York: HarperCollins, 1995); Elizabeth Susan Wahl, *Invisible Relations: Representations of Female Intimacy in the Age of Enlightenment* (Stanford, CA: Stanford University Press, 1999); Lisa Moore, *Dangerous Intimacies: Toward a Sapphic History of the British Novel* (Durham, NC: Duke University Press, 1997); Susan Lanser, *The Sexuality of History: Modernity and the Sapphic, 1565–1890* (Chicago: University of Chicago Press, 2014).

2. [César Ribié?], *La Cauchoise ou mémoires d'une courtisane célèbre: Roman* (1784). Libidinus, Chez Sensualité, 10308070 [*sic*; 1784?], 14. All translations from *La Cauchoise* are my own.

3. [Ribié?], *La Cauchoise*, 17–18.

4. [Ribié?], *La Cauchoise*, 27–28.

5. [Ribié?], *La Cauchoise*, 17.

6. [Ribié?], *La Cauchoise*, 25.

7. [Ribié?], *La Cauchoise*, 25.

8. [Ribié?], *La Cauchoise*, 29.

9. [Ribié?], *La Cauchoise*, 37–39.

10. [Ribié?], *La Cauchoise*, 73–74.

11. [Ribié?], *La Cauchoise*, 77.

12. [Ribié?], *La Cauchoise*, 77.

13. La Dumonci employs a variety of insults to describe this financier, including, "le rond financier" ([Ribié?], *La Cauchoise*, 84), "l'imbécile financier" (97), "mon gros amant" (101), "mon brutal financier" (97), and "un maudit homme que je ne pouvais pas souffrir" (137).

14. [Ribié?], *La Cauchoise*, 100.

15. [Ribié?], *La Cauchoise*, 106–107.

16. [Ribié?], *La Cauchoise*, 145.

17. [Ribié?], *La Cauchoise*, 145.

18. [Ribié?], *La Cauchoise*, 147.

19. [Ribié?], *La Cauchoise*, 161–163.

20. [Ribié?], *La Cauchoise*, 160.

21. [Ribié?], *La Cauchoise*, 188–189.

22. [Ribié?], *La Cauchoise*, 89.

23. [Ribié?], *La Cauchoise*, 89.

24. [Ribié?], *La Cauchoise*, 137.

25. [Ribié?], *La Cauchoise*, 40–42.

26. [Ribié?], *La Cauchoise*, 45.

27. [Ribié?], *La Cauchoise*, 156–160.

28. [Ribié?], *La Cauchoise*, 91.

29. [Ribié?], *La Cauchoise*, 102.

30. While sexual tension with another woman is not a common theme in the other putain memoirs, there are examples of other sexually ambiguous friendships. For example, in *La Belle Allemande* the narrator becomes friends with a neighbor and fellow kept mistress. One afternoon she and her friend decide to leave the men they were planning to entertain to attend a wild orgy arranged by a couple of dukes. As with nearly all explicit scenes in this novel, Thérèse refrains from sharing the explicit details; however, one can assume that the desire she felt to attend this orgy came at least in part from the participation of her attractive friend.

31. [Ribié?], *La Cauchoise*, 52.

32. [Ribié?], *La Cauchoise*, 52.

33. [Ribié?], *La Cauchoise*, 53–54.

34. While this fidelity may be seen as the result of a lack of any other willing (male) partners, La Dumonci's description of religious houses and the devotion of their inhabitants to lascivious behavior allows for suspicion that Sister Prudence was not the only debauched nun our narrator could have encountered in her convent.

35. [Ribié?], *La Cauchoise*, 56, 60.

36. [Ribié?], *La Cauchoise*, 61–63.

37. Ula Lukszo Klein, "Dildos and Material Sapphism in the Eighteenth Century," *Eighteenth-Century Fiction* 31, no. 2 (2018): 395–412.

38. In the preface to the *Œuvres érotiques* edition of *La Cauchoise*, Jean-Pierre Dubost also points out the feminine quality of this liquid, but without exploring the cause or ramifications of the lexical choice.

39. Wahl, *Invisible Relations*, 236.

40. Chris Roulston, "Having It Both Ways? The Eighteenth-Century Ménage à Trois," in *Queer People: Negotiations and Expressions of Homosexuality, 1700–1800* (Lewisburg, PA: Bucknell University Press, 2007). For more on this strain of readings of lesbianism in eighteenth-century literature, see Faderman, *Surpassing the Love of Men*; Donoghue, *Passions between Women*; Wahl, *Invisible Relations*. Katherine Binhammer also sees female same-sex desire in English literature as a segment of a continuum that also contains heterosexuality, but it's the extremity that points toward the center. See Binhammer, "The 'Singular Propensity' of Sensibility's Extremities: Female Same-Sex Desire and the Eroticization of Pain in Late Eighteenth-Century British Culture," *GLQ: A Journal of Lesbian and Gay Studies* 9, no. 4 (2003): 471–498.

For an interesting counterpoint, using the primary source for another putain memoir, Fougeret de Monbron's translation/abridgment of Cleland's *Memoirs of a Woman of Pleasure*, see John C. Bunyan, "'Traffic in More Precious Commodities': Sapphic Erotics and Economics in *Memoirs of a Woman of Pleasure*," in *Launching Fanny Hill: Essays on the Novel and Its Influences*, ed. Patsy S. Fowler and Alan Jackson (New York: AMS Press, 2003.) Bunyan effectively takes issue with the interpretation of the female same-sex desire in Cleland's novel as a kind of pleasure that merely serves to whet the woman's appetite for a male sexual partner. He plays upon Eve Sedgwick's notion of the love triangle as a means of homosocial bonding between men to show how Fanny and her fellow prostitutes use their male clients as a means of erotically bonding among themselves. He persuasively analyzes the scene of Fanny's "initiation" into Mrs. Cole's brothel with its female gaze and the caresses of her fellow prostitutes as well as the scene of Fanny's submission to a violent client as a way of pleasing not the man but her madam.

41. [Ribié?], *La Cauchoise*, 58.

42. [Ribié?], *La Cauchoise*, 59. Later in the anecdote, La Dumonci explains that the "dame" broke off with this favorite and chose another woman, L. D. J. de P., most likely La Duchesse Jules de Polignac.

43. David M. Robinson argues that pro-homosexual assertions and passages can and should be taken at face value. Although his work concerns the depictions of male homosexuality in eighteenth-century literature, and his reasoning that such passages can often be read as revealing the author's own closeted homosexual desire does not at all apply to an anonymously published text like *La Cauchoise*, his point is still well taken. See Robinson, *Closeted Writing and Lesbian and Gay Literature: Classical, Early Modern, and Eighteenth-Century* (Burlington, VT: Ashgate, 2006).

44. Lanser, *The Sexuality of History*, 2.

45. Lanser, *The Sexuality of History*, 2.

46. Lanser, *The Sexuality of History*, 10.

47. Moore, *Dangerous Intimacies*, 5.

48. Moore, *Dangerous Intimacies*, 8.

49. Merrick, "Sexual Politics and Public Order in Late Eighteenth-Century France: The *Mémoires secrets* and the *Correspondance secrète*," *Journal of the History of Sexuality* 1, no. 1 (1990): 68–84. The *Correspondance secrète* he examines is a putain memoir that first appeared in 1784, right after the first printing of *La Cauchoise*.

50. Merrick goes on to assert that at the time, intimacy between women was understood as not authentically sexual because without a man and penile penetration, sexual intercourse was considered impossible. Ula Klein rightly questions this interpretation of eighteenth-century attitudes in her analysis of the manifestations of social anxiety and concern about the dildo.

51. Cited in Lanser, *The Sexuality of History*, 6.

52. Wahl, *Invisible Relations*, 14, 177.

53. [Ribié?], *La Cauchoise*, 13.

54. [Ribié?], *La Cauchoise*, 88.

55. [Ribié?], *La Cauchoise*, 88, 13.

56. [Ribié?], *La Cauchoise*, 45.

57. [Ribié?], *La Cauchoise*, 69.

58. [Ribié?], *La Cauchoise*, 144.

59. [Ribié?], *La Cauchoise*, 162.

60. Carole Pateman, *The Sexual Contract* (Stanford, CA: Stanford University Press, 1988), 78.

61. Eve Sedgwick, *Between Men: English Literature and Male Homosocial Desire* (New York: Columbia University Press, 1985).

62. Adrienne Rich, *Of Woman Born: Motherhood as Experience and Institution* (New York: Norton, 1976).

63. Lynn Hunt, *The Family Romance of the French Revolution* (Berkeley: University of California Press, 1992).

6. *Histoire de Juliette*, or The Rejection of Motherhood

1. Hunt, *The Family Romance of the French Revolution* (Berkeley: University of California Press, 1992), 6.

2. Certainly, in the eighteenth century syphilis was a serious disease, with fatal results. In this sense, the putain who deliberately passes along her infection is potentially a killer. The significant difference is that the putains express no homicidal intent and never describe the horrific death of any "victim."

3. The Marquis de Sade, *Juliette*, trans. Austryn Wainhouse (New York: Grove Press, 1968), 299–300; Sade, *Histoire de Juliette, ou Les Prospérités du vice*, vols. 8–9 of *Œuvres complètes du Marquis de Sade: Édition définitive* (Paris: Au Cercle du Livre Précieux, 1967), 8:288–289.

4. Other male writers of libertine literature, such as the author of *Thérèse philosophe*, were more sensitive to the biological realities women faced. Thérèse is very

concerned with not becoming pregnant, and for that reason she chooses masturbation over heterosexual intercourse throughout most of the novel.

5. On the materialist discourse in libertine literature, see Margaret Jacob, "The Materialist World of Pornography," in *The Invention of Pornography: Obscenity and the Origins of Modernity, 1500–1800*, ed. Lynn Hunt (New York: Zone Books, 1993), 157–202.

6. Jane Gallop, "Sade, Mothers, and Other Women," in *Thinking through the Body* (Ithaca, NY: Cornell University Press, 1988), 123.

7. Caroline Weber, "The Sexist Sublime in Sade and Lyotard," *Philosophy and Literature* 26, no. 2 (2002): 399.

8. Marcel Hénaff, *Sade: The Invention of the Libertine Body*, trans. Xavier Callahan (Minneapolis: University of Minnesota Press, 1999), 270.

9. Hénaff, *Sade*, 257.

10. Amy Wyngaard provides a useful comparison of Rétif de la Bretonne and Sade, who, while equally privileging incest in their works, present opposing attitudes toward the family. These observations support her assertion that both Rétif and Sade represent the emergence of modern pornography. See chap. 2, "Inventing Pornography: Sex and Sentimentality in *Le Pornographe* and *l'Anti-Justine*," in Wyngaard, *Bad Books: Rétif de la Bretonne, Sexuality, and Pornography* (Newark: University of Delaware Press, 2013), 47–76.

11. See many of the critics cited in this chapter, including Jane Gallop, Caroline Weber, and Marcel Hénaff, as well as biographies: Pierre Klossowski, *Sade, mon prochain* (Paris: Éditions du Seuil, 1947); Roland Barthes, *Sade, Fourier, Loyola* (Paris: Éditions du Seuil, 1971); Maurice Lever, *Donatien Alphonse François, marquis de Sade* (Paris: Librairie Arthème Fauard, 1991); Laurence L. Bongie, *Sade: A Biographical Essay* (Chicago: University of Chicago Press, 1998); Neil Schaeffer, *The Marquis de Sade: A Life* (Cambridge, MA: Harvard University Press, 2001).

12. One significant exception to this line of biographical interpretation is presented by Laurence Bongie, whose focus on Sade's early years draws on newly found archival evidence—including a letter from Madame de Sade regarding her son the author—and who speculates that the mother–son tension was not, perhaps, as influential as other biographers suggest. Bongie, *Sade*.

13. Lever, *Donatien Alphonse François*, 14.

14. Wainhouse, *Juliette*, 67; Sade, *Histoire de Juliette*, 8:74.

15. Wainhouse, *Juliette*, 79; Sade, *Histoire de Juliette*, 8:86.

16. Wainhouse, *Juliette*, 1152; Sade, *Histoire de Juliette*, 9:547.

17. Weber, "The Sexist Sublime," 399.

18. Angela Carter reminds us that Juliette, unlike Justine, seems never to be alone: "She is never without a faithful entourage." Carter, *The Sadeian Woman and the Ideology of Pornography* (New York: Pantheon Books, 1978), 94.

19. An example of the privileged and powerful position the members of the Sodality enjoy. One of the society's rules states that members of the Sodality may never serve as victims. The by-laws specifically protect Sodality members from any violence greater than "whipping inflicted upon the buttocks only" ("le fouet, donné simplement sur les

fesses"). Wainhouse, *Juliette*, 421; Sade, *Histoire de Juliette*, 8:403. Instead, they—like all the libertines Juliette encounters and endeavors to emulate—sit in a position of power to dole out punishments and torture to others. And along with wealth and pleasure, power is what she seeks throughout her story.

20. Wainhouse, *Juliette*, 423; Sade, *Histoire de Juliette*, 8:406.

21. Wainhouse, *Juliette*, 423; Sade, *Histoire de Juliette*, 8:406.

22. Wainhouse, *Juliette*, 430–431; Sade, *Histoire de Juliette*, 8:413.

23. Wainhouse, *Juliette*, 1152; Sade, *Histoire de Juliette*, 9:548.

24. Wainhouse, *Juliette*, 1152; Sade, *Histoire de Juliette*, 9:548.

25. Wainhouse, *Juliette*, 1153; Sade, *Histoire de Juliette*, 9:549.

26. Gallop, "Sade, Mothers," 128.

27. John Phillips, "'Tout dire'?: Sade and the Female Body," *South Central Review* 19, no. 4 (2002–2003): 36.

28. Phillips, "'Tout dire'?," 39–40. It is troubling that Phillips adopts traditional binaries that oppose female emotion to male reason, but he does link "nature's sovereignty" (as manifested in the maternal power to conceive and give birth) to eighteenth-century anxieties about women's sexual powers over men in a way that raises the important issue of woman's reproductive ability as power.

29. Weber, "The Sexist Sublime," 399.

30. This line of thinking can be seen in Maurice Lever's interpretation of Sade's "negative Oedipus complex" in which the son allies with the father and directs his anger and hostility toward the mother (Lever, *Donatien Alphonse François*, 14). Julia Kristeva agrees with this description of Sade's symbolic family dynamic, noting that Sade "gives up this battle with, or for, the symbolic legislation represented by the father, in order to attack the power represented by a woman, Madame de Montreuil, visible figurehead of a dynasty of matrons toward whom he usurps through writing the role of father and incestuous son." Kristeva, *Desire in Language: A Semiotic Approach to Literature and Art*, ed. Leon S. Roudiez, trans. Thomas Gora, Alice Jardine, and Leon S. Roudiez (New York: Columbia University Press, 1980), 138.

31. On this point, see Gayle Rubin, "The Traffic in Women: Notes on the 'Political Economy' of Sex," in *Feminism and History*, ed. Joan Wallach Scott (Oxford: Oxford University Press, 1996).

32. Juliette brings these two men some sexual pleasure and the satisfaction of watching their protégée wholeheartedly embrace and implement their libertine philosophy, but in return she takes enormous material gain (more than the vast riches they bestow upon her, because she seizes every opportunity to steal from these benefactors) and also a large share of the real power they enjoy. For more on Juliette's autonomy as a sex worker, see Hénaff, *Sade*, 274.

33. Wainhouse, *Juliette*, 1186; Sade, *Histoire de Juliette*, 9:580.

34. Within the story of Juliette's life and adventures, several mother-figures emerge—for instance, the Abbess Delbène, whom Angela Carter refers to as "the first and welcomed fairy godmother in Juliette's history" (Carter, *The Sadeian Woman*, 82). Duvergier, the madam of the brothel where Juliette works after she is expelled from the convent, is another "fairy godmother" (85). Carter sees Durand, the witchlike

poisoner who also takes Juliette under her wing, as the "greatest, most monstrous, most potent of all Sade's cruel godmothers" (93). With her inability to reproduce because of a mysteriously blocked vagina, Durand is instead what Carter calls a "phallic mother": "a virile and nonproductive mother, who chooses her own children and seduces them, too. She is a mother with a phallus; she can rape even nature itself" (115). Jane Gallop also considers Durand the embodiment of such a phallic mother. With her impenetrable vagina, Durand's "lack of phallus is permanently hidden, inaccessible"; as a phallic mother she is omnipotent and serves as "Mother Nature's concealed cause" (Gallop, "Sade, Mothers," 137). Interestingly, these critics never grant the term "phallic mother" (and all the admiration it implies) upon Juliette. In any case, despite these numerous "godmothers," Juliette's own mother remains absent.

35. In French the adjectives are *malheureuse* and *pauvre*.

36. Wainhouse, *Juliette*, 1176; Sade, *Histoire de Juliette*, 9:570.

37. Wainhouse, *Juliette*, 1177; Sade, *Histoire de Juliette*, 9:571.

38. Wainhouse, *Juliette*, 1177–1178; Sade, *Histoire de Juliette*, 9:572.

39. Wainhouse, *Juliette*, 1184; Sade, *Histoire de Juliette*, 9:578.

40. Wainhouse, *Juliette*, 1186; Sade, *Histoire de Juliette*, 9:580.

41. Wainhouse, *Juliette*, 1186; Sade, *Histoire de Juliette*, 9:579.

42. Juliette's success in the male-dominated libertine world is widely recognized. For instance, Phillips ("'Tout dire'?," 31) calls Juliette a "phallic woman" who "masculinizes herself both physically and mentally." Carter (*The Sadeian Woman*, 86) sees Juliette as a woman who has "transcended her gender."

43. Frances Ferguson, *Pornography, the Theory: What Utilitarianism Did to Action* (Chicago: University of Chicago Press, 2004), 75.

44. Ferguson, *Pornography, the Theory*, 75.

45. Ferguson, *Pornography, the Theory*, 78.

46. See, for instance, Charles Bernheimer, *Figures of Ill Repute: Representing Prostitution in Nineteenth-Century France* (Cambridge, MA: Harvard University Press, 1989); Jann Matlock, *Scenes of Seduction: Prostitution, Hysteria, and Reading Difference in Nineteenth-Century France* (New York: Columbia University Press, 1994).

47. Alexandre Dumas fils, *La Dame aux camélias: Roman, théâtre, livret*, ed. Hans-Jörg Neuschäfer and Gilbert Sigaux (Paris: Flammarion, 1981).

48. See Bernadette Fort, "Manon's Suppressed Voice: The Uses of Reported Speech," *Romanic Review* 76, no. 2 (1985): 172–191; Nancy Miller, *The Heroine's Text: Readings in the French and English Novel, 1722–1782* (New York: Columbia University Press, 1980); Miller, "'I's in Drag: The Sex of Recollection," *The Eighteenth Century* 22, no. 1 (Winter 1981): 47–57; Naomi Segal, *The Unintended Reader: Feminism and* Manon Lescaut (Cambridge: Cambridge University Press, 1986).

49. Dumas fils, *La Dame aux camélias*, 96.

50. See, for instance, Charles Bernheimer's study of the grotesque corporeality of the prostitute in nineteenth-century literature in *Figures of Ill Repute*. For a focus on the prostitute's body in *La Dame aux camélias* specifically, see Bernadette Lintz's persuasive article on the preponderance of bodily fluids in the novel. Lintz, "Concocting

La Dame aux camélias: Blood, Tears, and Other Fluids," *Nineteenth-Century French Studies* 33, no. 3–4 (2005): 287–307.

Appendix

1. Particularly useful were the contributors to the two-volume Pléiade edition, *Romanciers libertins du XVIIIe siècle*, ed. Patrick Wald Lasowski (Paris: Gallimard, 2000, 2005), as well as Raymond Trousson's *Romans libertins du XVIIIe siècle* (Paris: Robert Laffont, 1993).

2. Some putain memoirs were published with deliberately fictitious publication dates and publishers, such as the edition of *La Tourière des carmélites* claiming to have been published in the year 17000, or *La Cauchoise* published by "Libidinus" in the year 10,308,070.

3. [Pierre-Alexandre Gaillard de La Bataille], *Histoire de Mademoiselle Cronel dite Frétillon, Actrice de la Comédie de Rouen, écrite par elle-même* (La Haye: Aux Dépens de la Compagnie, 1739), 4. I am citing from the 1741 edition, entitled *Histoire de Mademoiselle Cronel dite Frétillon, actrice de la comédie de Rouen* (with the same publisher as the original edition, Aux Dépens de la Compagnie) and will maintain the punctuation of this edition, while modernizing spelling, as I will for all eighteenth-century editions of the putain memoirs I cite here. The translation into English is my own.

4. [Gaillard de La Bataille], *Mademoiselle Cronel dite Frétillon*, 38.

5. [Gaillard de La Bataille], *Mademoiselle Cronel dite Frétillon*, 72.

6. *Dictionnaire Biographique universel et pittoresque* (Paris: Aimé André, 1834), 465. Note the incomplete titles in this reference.

7. The Pléiade edition of this novel, entitled *La Tourière des carmélites*, lists 1745 as the first publication. Such an edition is not to be found in Martin, Mylne, and Frautschi's *Bibliographie du genre*, which lists the first edition as the 1743 *Histoire galante de la tourière des carmélites. La Bibliographie du genre romanesque*, ed. Angus Martin, Vivenne Mylne, and Richard Frautschi (Paris: France Expansion, 1977). Raymond Trousson also lists this 1743 title in his chronology of libertine literature, *Romans libertins du XVIIIe siècle*. However, I have not been able to locate any existing copies of the 1743 edition, although several libraries hold copies of the 1745 second edition.

8. The only exception to this rule is La Dumonci, narrator of *La Cauchoise*, who admits at the very end of her story that what little beauty she had as a young woman is now fading.

9. Anne-Gabriel Meusnier de Querlon, *Histoire de la tourière des carmélites* (La Haye: Pierre Marteau, 1747), 64.

10. See Martin, Mylne, and Frautschi, *Bibliographie du genre romanesque*, and Patrick Wald Lasowski and Alain Clerval's bibliography of *La Tourière des carmélites* in the notes to the text in *Romanciers libertins du XVIIIe siècle*. Although Lasowski and Clerval claim that the edition they have reproduced, *La Tourrière des carmélites, servant de pendant au "P. des C."* (À Constantinople: Chez l'Imprimeur du Moufti, 17000) was in fact from 1745—as the Bibliothèque nationale de France indicates—they also list

the same title and publication information, but "Augmentée d'une pièce bien corrigée [*L'Origine des cons sauvages et européens*]" as really appearing in 1757. A few libraries mistakenly correct the year of publication from 17000 to 1700, but such a publication date would be impossible because the author was not born until 1702.

11. Martin, Mylne, and Frautschi list both the *Histoire galante de la Tourière des carmélites* and *Sainte-Nitouche* as separate editions both published in 1770, as well as listing *Tourrière des carmélites* and *Sainte-Nitouche* as two 1784 editions. It is possible that these were all published separately, but it is more likely that the sources they consulted simply applied the shorthand title *Sainte-Nitouche* (under which several nineteenth-century versions of the novel appeared) to the 1770 and 1784 editions.

12. Anne-Gabriel Meusnier de Querlon, *Psaphion, ou la Courtisane de Smyrne, Fragment érotique traduit du grec de Mnaseas, sur un manuscrit de la bibliothèque du Lord B . . .* (London: Tomson, 1748). *Psaphion* has also recently been republished by Le Passeur.

13. Other examples that Michel Delon names in his introduction to the 2000 edition of *Psaphion* are Antoine Bret's *Cythéride, histoire galante* (1743) and *Lycoris ou la courtisane grecque* (1746), and Guillard de Beauchamp's *Hipparchia, histoire galante, traduite du grec* (1748).

14. Given that subsequent editions of *Psaphion* are also followed by *Les Hommes de Prométhée*, it is likely that "P****" stands for Psaphion.

15. Information on both authors appears in chapter 2, and a summary of *La Belle Allemande* is in chapter 3.

16. As with *La Belle Allemande*, I will refrain from summarizing the story of *Margot la ravaudeuse* here, since it is the focus of chapter 4.

17. See Emmanuel Boussuge, *Situations de Fougeret de Monbron (1706–1760)* (Paris: Champion, 2010), 276.

18. Patrick Wald Lasowski (*Romanciers libertins*, 1250) speculates that this text may have been *Histoire de Mademoiselle Brion, dite Comtesse de Launay*, which was published anonymously in 1754, but the striking differences in tone and emphasized aspects of these two novels make this assertion difficult to support. On the other hand, Boussuge speculates that this manuscript may have been a draft of the "Histoire de la Bois-Laurier" that appeared in *Thérèse philosophe* (1748), attributing this part—and only this part—of that famous novel to Fougeret.

19. Fougeret de Monbron, *Margot la ravaudeuse*, in *Romans libertins du XVIII*[e] *siècle*, ed. Raymond Trousson (Paris: Éditions Robert Laffont, 1993), 677. The "general of the pigs" is my translation of "le général de la pousse," with "pousse" being a derogatory slang term for the police. Eighteenth-century French readers would easily identify this as a reference to Nicolas René Berryer de Ravenoville, lieutenant of the police.

20. There were no editions of *Margot* without the "Hambourg, MDCCC" publication information until 1772, except for one edition entitled *La brunette ou les aventures d'une demoiselle*, which was an abbreviated version of Margot's tale that appeared in 1761 and is very likely only an imitation published by someone trying to cash in on *Margot*'s success.

21. The event in question is a tragic accident on December 15, 1739, in which a side of the Saint-Thomas-du-Louvre church collapsed, killing six canons. Margot laments that her new *entreteneur* was one of those killed, and a footnote indicates: "This misfortune happened fifteen or sixteen years ago. Several canons met the same fate" ("Il y a quinze ou seize ans que ce malheur est arrivé. Plusieurs chanoines eurent le même sort"). Fougeret de Monbron, *Margot*, 824.

22. BN Fr. 22158, f° 34. Cited in Boussuge, *Situations*, 45n43.

23. Friedrich Melchior Grimm, *Correspondance littéraire*, vol. 1: *1753–1755*, ed. Ulla Kölving (Ferney-Voltaire: Centre international de l'Étude du XVIIIe siècle, 2006). Cited in Boussuge, *Situations*, 45n43.

24. See, for instance, Martin, Mylne and Frautschi, *Bibliographie du genre Romanesque.*

25. Recognizing the similarities between *Memoirs of a Woman of Pleasure* and *Margot la ravaudeuse*, in his introduction to *Margot la ravaudeuse* in *Romans libertins du XVIIe siècle* Raymond Trousson speculates about who influenced whom between Monbron and Cleland.

26. *Le Journal de la librairie 1753*, BN fr. 22158f° 31. Cited in Boussuge, *Situations*, 280.

27. Boussuge (*Situations*, 57) cites this evidence as proof of Fougeret's authorship.

28. Dora Bienaimé Rigo, "La prima versione francese di Fanny Hill," *Rivista di letterature moderne e comparate* 34 (1981): 249–270. In addition, Elsa Grasso and Guillaume Badoual, the editors of a recent printing of *La Fille de joie*, attribute the translation to Fougeret de Monbron. Grasso and Badoual, eds., *Fanny Hill: La Fille de joie, récit quintessencié de l'anglais par Fougeret de Montbron* [*sic*] (Saint-Amand-Montrond: Actes du Sud, 1993).

29. Robert Darnton, *The Forbidden Best-Sellers of Pre-Revolutionary France* (New York: W. W. Norton, 1995), 63–64.

30. See Trousson, *Romans libertins*, lxxxvi, as well as Jean-Pierre Dubost's preface to *Vénus en rut* in *Œuvres anonymes du XVIIIe siècle*, 6:99. The Martin, Mylne, and Frautschi bibliography also recognizes the possibility of the existence of a first edition in 1770, although no copies from that year have been found.

31. The *Histoire de Marguerite* does not qualify as a putain memoir—the narrator is a man who knew Marguerite, and we thus do not have the prostitute telling her own story in her own voice.

32. The text states, "C'est l'ouvrage d'un seul et même auteur." [Ribié?], *La Cauchoise*, 10.

33. Mathieu François Pidansat de Mairobert, *Confessions d'une jeune fille*, in *L'Espion anglais, ou Correspondance secrète entre Milord All'Eye et Milord All'Ear*, 10 vols. (London, 1786), vol. 10, letters 10, 12, 14.

34. Joseph D'Heméry, the police inspector in charge of regulating uncensored publications, once called Mairobert "la plus mauvaise langue de Paris." François Ravaisson, *Archives de la Bastille*, vol. 12 (Paris: A. Durand et Pedone-Lauriel, 1881), 312. Cited in Pierre Saint-Amand's Notice to *Confession d'une jeune fille* in *Romanciers libertins du XVIIIe siècle*, 1573.

35. The *Mémoires secrets* for April 2, 1779, states, "Il est allé chez Poitevin demander un bain, s'est mis dedans, s'est ouvert les veines avec un rasoir, et craignant que cette mort ne fût pas assez sure, s'est achevé avec un pistolet" (14:9). Pierre Saint-Amand recognizes the many ironies of his life: "Mairobert est à la fois frondeur, littérateur clandestin, dénonciateur et censeur royal; complice d'un homosexuel et pourfendeur des lesbiennes; il se trouve au sein de l'administration policière et dans la résistance, blâmé à la fin par le Parlement qu'il a contribué à défendre contre l'absolutisme monarchique. Mais la suprême ironie reste sa mort elle-même: celui qui a passé sa vie à scandaliser les autres est devenu l'objet du scandale, et les *Mémoires secrets*, en commentant la publicité faite autour de son décès, lui reprochent d'avoir mêlé trop de 'bruit' à sa vie" (14:1575). (In this note, Saint-Amand is referring to the reproaches of Mairobert in the *Mémoires secrets* on April 3, 1779, 14:12.)

36. See Barry Ivker, *An Anthology and Analysis of 17th and 18th Century French Libertine Fiction* (Bloomington: Indiana University Institute for Sex Research, 1977); Joan DeJean, *Libertine Strategies: Freedom and the Novel in Seventeenth-Century France* (Columbus: Ohio State University Press, 1981). I borrow the expression "the libertine family tree" from *Libertine Strategies*, 23.

Bibliography

Albistur, Maïté, and Daniel Armogathe. *Histoire du féminisme français du moyen âge à nos jours*. Paris: Éditions des femmes, 1977.

Alexandrian, Sarane. *Histoire de la littérature érotique*. Paris: Éditions Seghers, 1989.

Alexandrova, Ekaterina R. "Conjugal Utopia: Marriage and Social Transformation in Rousseau's *Julie, ou La Nouvelle Héloïse* and Leprince de Beaumont's *La Nouvelle Clarice*." *Eighteenth-Century Fiction* 29, no. 4 (2017): 607–634.

Allen, Amy. "The Public Sphere: Ideology and / or Ideal?" *Political Theory* 40, no. 6 (2012): 822–829.

Ansart, Guillaume. *Réflexion utopique et pratique romanesque au Siècle des Lumières: Prévost, Rousseau, Sade*. Paris: Lettres modernes Minard, 1999.

Aretino, Pietro. *Ragionamento / Dialogo*. Introduction by Giorgio Bàrberi Squarotti. Milan: Biblioteca universale Rizzoli, 1998.

———. *The School of Whoredom*. Translated by Rosa Maria Falvo, Alessandro Gallenzi, and Rebecca Skipwith. Introduction by Rosa Maria Falvo. London: Hesperus Press, 2003.

Ariès, Philippe. Introduction to *History of Private Life*, vol. 3: *Passions of the Renaissance*. Edited by Roger Chartier. Translated by Arthur Goldhammer. Cambridge, MA: Belknap Press of Harvard University Press, 1993.

Baker, Keith, ed. *The French Revolution and the Creation of Modern Political Culture*, vol. 1: *The Political Culture of the Old Régime*. Oxford: Pergamon Press, 1987.

———. *Inventing the French Revolution*. Cambridge: Cambridge University Press, 1989.

Barbier, Antoine Alexandre. *Dictionnaire des anonymes et pseudonymes composés, traduits ou publiés en français et en latin, avec les noms des auteurs, traducteurs et éditeurs*. 4 vols. Paris: Imprimerie Bibliographique, 1806–1809.

Barbier, Edmund Jean François. *Chronique de la Régence et du règne du Louis XV (1718–1763) ou Journal Barbier*. 8 vols. Paris: Charpentier, 1857.

Barthes, Roland. *Sade, Fourier, Loyola*. Paris: Éditions du Seuil, 1971.

Bellamy, Liz. *Commerce, Morality, and the Eighteenth-Century Novel*. Cambridge: Cambridge University Press, 1998.

Benabou, Erica Marie. *La Prostitution et la police des mœurs au dix-huitième siècle*. Paris: Perrin, 1987.

Benhamou, Paul. "The Diffusion of Forbidden Books: Four Case Studies." *Studies on Voltaire and the Eighteenth Century* 12 (2005): 359–381.

Bernheimer, Charles. *Figures of Ill Repute: Representing Prostitution in Nineteenth-Century France*. Cambridge, MA: Harvard University Press, 1989.

Binhammer, Katherine. "The 'Singular Propensity' of Sensibility's Extremities: Female Same-Sex Desire and the Eroticization of Pain in Late Eighteenth-Century British Culture." *GLQ: A Journal of Lesbian and Gay Studies* 9, no. 4 (2003): 471–498.

Bloch, Jean H. "Rousseau's Reputation as an Authority on Childcare and Physical Education in France before the Revolution." *Paedegogica historica* 14, no. 1 (1974): 5–33.

———. "Women and the Reform of the Nation" In *Woman and Society in Eighteenth-Century France*, edited by Eva Jacobs. London: Athlone Press, 1979.

Bloch, Ruth. "Inside and Outside the Public Sphere." *William and Mary Quarterly*, 3rd ser., 62, no. 1 (2005): 99–106.

Blum, Carol. *Rousseau and the Republic of Virtue: The Language of Politics in the French Revolution*. Ithaca, NY: Cornell University Press, 1989.

Bongie, Laurence L. *Sade: A Biographical Essay*. Chicago: University of Chicago Press, 1998.

Bosquet, Marie-Françoise. *Images du féminin dans les utopies françaises classique*. Oxford: Voltaire Foundation, 2007.

Boussuge, Emmanuel. "L'Homme au cœur velu: Autour d'une anecdote de la Satire première (Fougeret de Monbron et Diderot)." In *Des sens au sens: Littérature et morale de Molière à Voltaire*, edited by Jacques Wagner. Peeters: Louvain, 2007.

———. *Situations de Fougeret de Monbron (1706–1760)*. Paris: Champion, 2010.

Boyer d'Argens. *Thérèse philosophe, ou, Mémoires pour server à l'histoire du Père Dirrag et de Mademoiselle Éradice* (1748). Saint-Étienne: Publications de l'Université de Saint-Étienne, 2000.

[Bret, Antoine, or Claude Villaret]. *La Belle Allemande, ou Les Galanteries de Thérèse, deux parties* (1745). Paris: Aux Dépens de la compagnie, 1755.

Broome, Jack Howard. "'L'Homme au cœur velu': The Turbulent Career of Fougeret de Monbron." *Studies in Voltaire and the Eighteenth Century* 23 (1963).

Brown, Laura. *Ends of Empire: Women and Ideology in Early Eighteenth-Century English Literature*. Ithaca, NY: Cornell University Press, 1993.

Bunyan, John C. "'Traffic in More Precious Commodities': Sapphic Erotics and Economics in *Memoirs of a Woman of Pleasure*." In *Launching Fanny Hill: Essays on the Novel and Its Influences*, edited by Patsy S. Fowler and Alan Jackson. New York: AMS Press, 2003.

Calhoun, Craig, ed. *Habermas and the Public Sphere*. Cambridge, MA: MIT Press, 1992.

Carter, Angela. *The Sadeian Woman and the Ideology of Pornography*. New York: Pantheon Books, 1978.

Casanova, Giacamo. *Histoire de ma vie*. Wiesbaden: Brockhaus, 1960–1963.

Chartier, Roger. *The Cultural Origins of the French Revolution*. Translated by Lydia G. Cochrane. Durham, NC: Duke University Press, 1991.

Cheek, Pamela. "Prostitutes of 'Political Institution.'" *Eighteenth-Century Studies* 28, no. 1 (1994–1995): 193–219.

Chisick, Harvey. "Urban Pathologies and the Pathology of the Urban in L.-S. Mercier's *Tableau de Paris*." In *Correspondence and Epistolary Fiction: La Fête; Science and Medicine; Voltaire*, edited by Anthony Strugnell. Oxford: Voltaire Foundation, 2002.

Chorier, Nicolas. *L'Académie des dames, ou la philosophie dans le boudoir du Grand siècle: Dialogues érotiques*. Edited by Jean-Pierre Dubost. Arles: Picquier, 1999.

Cleland, John. *Memoirs of a Woman of Pleasure, or Fanny Hill* (1749). Edited by Peter Sabor. Oxford: Oxford University Press, 2008.

Conner, Susan. "Prostitution and the Jacobin Agenda for Social Control." *Eighteenth-Century Life* 12, no. 1 (1988).

Coquillat, Michèle. "Nature et sexe chez Rousseau: Au commencement était le phallus." In *La poétique du mâle*. Paris: Gallimard, 1982.

Cortey, Mathilde. *L'Invention de la courtisane au XVIIIe siècle dans les romans-mémoires des "filles du monde" de Madame Meheust à Sade: 1732–1797*. Paris: Arguments, 2001.

Coulet, Henri. *Le Roman jusqu'à la revolution*. 9th ed. Paris: Armand Colin, 2000.

Crébillon, Claude-Prosper Jolyot de. *Égarements du Cœur et de l'esprit ou Mémoires de M. de Meilcour* (1738). In *Œuvres complètes*, vol. 2. Edited by Jean Sgard. Paris: Éditions Classiques Garnier, 2010.

———. *Le Sopha: Conte moral* (1740). In *Œuvres complètes*, vol. 2. Edited by Jean Sgard. Paris: Éditions Classiques Garnier, 2010.

Cusset, Catherine. *No Tomorrow: The Ethics of Pleasure in the French Enlightenment*. Charlottesville: University Press of Virginia, 1999.

Danahy, Michael. *The Feminization of the Novel*. Gainesville: University of Florida Press, 1991.

Darnton, Robert. *The Corpus of Clandestine Literature in France, 1769–1789*. New York: W. W. Norton, 1995.

———. *Édition et sédition: L'Univers de la littérature clandestine au XVIIIe siècle*. Paris: Gallimard, 1991.

———. *The Forbidden Best-Sellers of Prerevolutionary France*. New York: W. W. Norton, 1996.

———. *The Literary Underground of the Old Regime*. Cambridge, MA: Harvard University Press, 1982.

———. *Pirating and Publishing: The Book Trade in the Age of Enlightenment*. Oxford: Oxford University Press, 202.

Daunu. "Villaret (Claude)." In *Biographie universelle ancienne et moderne*, vol. 48. Paris: Chez L. G. Michaud, 1827.

Davis, Natalie Zemon, and Arlette Farge, eds. *A History of Women in the West*, vol. 3: *Renaissance and Enlightenment Paradoxes*. Series edited by Georges Duby and Michelle Perrot. Cambridge, MA: Belknap Press of Harvard University Press, 1993.

DeJean, Joan. *Libertine Strategies: Freedom and the Novel in Seventeenth-Century France*. Columbus: Ohio State University Press, 1981.

———. *The Reinvention of Obscenity: Sex, Lies and Tabloids in Early Modern France*. Chicago: University of Chicago Press, 2002.

———. *Tender Geographies: Women and the Origins of the Novel in France*. New York: Columbia University Press, 1993.

Delon, Michel. "De *Thérèse philosophe* à *La Philosophie dans le boudoir*, la place de la philosophie." *Romantische Zeitschrift für Literaturgeschichte / Cahiers d'histoire des littératures romanes* (Winter 1983).

———. "L'Espace de la séduction dans le roman français du XVIIIe siècle." In *Littérature et séduction: Mélanges en l'honneur de Laurent Versini*. Edited by Roger Marchal and François Moureau. Paris: Klincksieck, 1977.

———. *L'Invention du boudoir*. Paris: Zulma, 1999.

Démoris, René. *Le Roman à la 1e personne: Du classicisme aux Lumières*. Geneva: Librairie Droz, 2001.

Dictionnaire biographique universel et pittoresque. Paris: Aimé André, 1834.

Dictionnaire de l'Académie française, 4th ed. (1762). ARTFL: The Project for American and French Research on the Treasury of the French Language. https://artflsrv04.uchicago.edu/philologic4.7/publicdicos/navigate/9/8146.

Diderot, Denis. *Les Bijoux indiscrets* (1748). Edited by Jean Macray. Introduction by Aram Vartanian. Paris: Hermann, 1978.

Donoghue, Emma. *Passions between Women: British Lesbian Culture, 1668–1801*. New York: HarperCollins, 1995.

Duclos, Charles Pinot. *Confessions du comte de* *** (1742). Preface by Béatrice Didier. Paris: Slatkine, 1996.

Duflo, Colas. *Philosophie des pornographes: Les Ambitions philosophiques du roman libertin*. Paris: Éditions du Seuil, 2019.

Dumas, Alexandre, fils. *La Dame aux camélias: Le roman, le drame, la Traviata*. Edited by Hans-Jörg Neuschäfer and Gilbert Sigaux. Paris: Garnier-Flammarion, 1981.

Dworkin, Andrea. *Pornography: Men Possessing Women*. New York: Dutton, 1989.

Eisenstein, Zillah. *The Radical Future of Liberal Feminism*. New York: Longman, 1981.

Elshtain, Joan Bethke. *Public Man, Private Woman: Women in Social and Political Thought*. Princeton, NJ: Princeton University Press, 1981.

Faderman, Lillian. *Surpassing the Love of Men: Romantic Friendship and Love between Women from the Renaissance to the Present*. New York: Morrow, 1981.

Ferguson, Frances. *Pornography, the Theory: What Utilitarianism Did to Action*. Chicago: University of Chicago Press, 2004.

Fort, Bernadette. "Manon's Suppressed Voice: The Uses of Reported Speech." *Romanic Review* 76, no. 2 (1985): 172–191.

Fougeret de Monbron, Louis Charles. *Margot la ravaudeuse* (1750). In *Romans libertins du XVIIIe siècle*, edited by Raymond Trousson. Paris: R. Laffont, 1993.

———. *Margot la ravaudeuse*. Translated by Édouard Langille. Cambridge: Modern Humanities Research Association, 2015.

Fowler, Patsy S., and Alan Jackson, eds. *Launching Fanny Hill: Essays on the Novel and Its Influences*. New York: AMS Press, 2003.

Foxon, David. *Libertine Literature in England, 1660–1745*. London: Book Collector, 1964.

Fréron. Letter 15. In *L'Année littéraire*, vol. 1. Amsterdam and Paris, 1756.

[Gaillard de La Bataille, Alexandre]. *Histoire de Mademoiselle Cronel dite Frétillon, actrice de la comédie de Rouen*. La Haye: Aux Dépens de la Compagnie, 1741. Originally published as *Histoire de la vie et mœurs de Mademoiselle Cronel dite Frétillon, Actrice de la Comédie de Rouen, écrite par elle-même* (1739).

Gallop, Jane. "Sade, Mothers, and Other Women." In *Thinking through the Body*. Ithaca, NY: Cornell University Press, 1988.

Gay, Jules, and Jules Lemonnyer. *Bibliographie des ouvrages relatifs à l'amour, aux femmes et au mariage et des livres facétieux, pantagruéliques, scatologiques, satyriques, etc.* Lille: Stéphane Becour, 1900.

La Gazette Nationale ou Le Moniteur Universel. Collected in *Réimpression de l'Ancien Moniteur.* 32 vols. Paris: Plon, 1854.

Gervaise de Latouche, Jean-Charles. *Le Portier des Chartreux: Histoire de Dom Bougre écrite par lui-même* (1741). Arles: Actes Sud, 1993.

Goldsmith, Elizabeth, and Dena Goodman. *Going Public: Women and Publishing in Early Modern France.* Ithaca, NY: Cornell University Press, 1995.

Goodman, Dena. "Public Sphere and Private Life: Toward a Synthesis of Current Historiographical Approaches to the Old Régime." *History and Theory* 31, no. 1 (1992): 1–20.

Goulemot, Jean M. *Ces livres qu'on ne lit que d'une main: Lecture et lectures de livres pornographiques au XVIIIe siècle.* Paris: Alinea, 1991.

———. *Forbidden Texts: Erotic Literature and Its Readers in Eighteenth-Century France.* Translated by James Simpson. Philadelphia: University of Pennsylvania Press, 1994.

Graffigny, Françoise. *Correspondance de Madame de Graffigny,* vols. 6 and 26. Edited by J. A. Dainard, Pierre Bouillagnet, and Judith Curtis. Oxford: Voltaire Foundation, 2000.

———. *Lettres d'une Péruvienne.* Edited by Gianni Nicoletti. Bari: Adriatica, 1967.

Graham, Ruth. "Rousseau's Sexism Revolutionized." In *Woman in the 18th Century and Other Essays.* Edited by Paul Fritz and Richard Morton. Toronto: Hakkert, 1976.

Grasso, Elsa, and Guillaume Badoual, eds. *Fanny Hill: La Fille de joie, récit quintessencié de l'anglais par Fougeret de Montbron* [*sic*]. Saint-Amand-Montrond: Actes du Sud, 1993.

Grimm, Melchior. *Correspondance littéraire,* vol. 1: *1753–1755.* Edited by Ulla Kölving. Ferney-Voltaire: Centre international de l'Étude du XVIIIe siècle, 2006.

Habermas, Jürgen. *The Structural Transformation of the Public Sphere: An Inquiry into a Category of Bourgeois Society.* Translated by Thomas Burger and Frederick Lawrence. Cambridge, MA: MIT Press, 1989.

———. *Strukturwandel der Öffentlichkeit: Untersuchungen zu einer Kategorie der bürgerlichen Gesellschaft.* Neuwied: Hermann Luchterhand, 1962.

Hénaff, Marcel. *Sade: The Invention of the Libertine Body.* Translated by Xavier Callahan. Minneapolis: University of Minnesota Press, 1999.

Histoire de Mademoiselle Brion dite Comtesse de Launay (1754). Introduction by Guillaume Apollinaire. Paris: Tchou, 1968.

Hugo, Victor. *Les Misérables* (1862). Montréal: Éditions Caractère, 2013.

Hunt, Lynn. *Eroticism and the Body Politic.* Baltimore: Johns Hopkins University Press, 1991.

———. *The Family Romance of the French Revolution.* Berkeley: University of California Press, 1992.

———, ed. *The Invention of Pornography, 1500–1800: Obscenity and the Origins of Modernity.* New York: Zone Books, 1993.

Ivker, Barry. *An Anthology and Analysis of 17th and 18th Century French Libertine Fiction*. Bloomington: Indiana University Institute for Sex Research, 1977.

Jacob, Margaret C. "The Materialist World of Pornography." In *The Invention of Pornography: Obscenity and the Origins of Modernity, 1500–1800*. Edited by Lynn Hunt. New York: Zone Books, 1993.

Johnson, Pauline. *Habermas: Rescuing the Public Sphere*. New York: Routledge, 2006.

Jones, Colin. *Paris: The Biography of a City*. New York: Penguin Books, 2004.

Kendrick, Water. *The Secret Museum: Pornography in Modern Culture*. Berkeley: University of California Press, 1996.

Kleiman-Lafon, Sylvie. "The French Adventures of Fanny Hill." In *Launching "Fanny Hill": Essays on the Novel and Its Influence*. Edited by Patsy S. Fowler and Alan Jackson. New York: AMS Press, 2003.

Klein, Ula Lukszo. "Dildos and Material Sapphism in the Eighteenth Century." *Eighteenth-Century Fiction* 31, no. 2 (2018): 395–412.

Klossowski, Pierre. *Sade, mon prochain*. Paris: Éditions du Seuil, 1947.

Kofman, Sarah. "Rousseau's Phallocratic Ends." *Hypatia: A Journal of Feminist Philosophy* 3, no. 3 (1989): 123–136.

Kristeva, Julia. *Desire in Language: A Semiotic Approach to Literature and Art*. Edited by Leon S. Roudiez. Translated by Thomas Gora, Alice Jardine, and Leon S. Roudiez. New York: Columbia University Press, 1980.

Kushner, Nina. *Erotic Exchanges: The World of Elite Prostitution in Eighteenth-Century Paris*. Ithaca, NY: Cornell University Press, 2014.

Lachèvre, Frédéric. *Les Œuvres libertines de Claude Le Petit, parisien, brûlé le 1er septembre 1662*. Geneva: Slatkine Reprints, 1968.

Laclos, Pierre Choderlos de. *Les Liaisons dangereuses* (1782). Preface by André Malraux. Notes by Joël Papdopoulos. Paris: Gallimard, 2004.

Lagrave, Henri. *Le Théâtre et le public à Paris de 1715 à 1750*. Paris: Librairie C. Klincksieck, 1972.

La Mettrie, Julien Offray de. *L'Homme machine suivi de L'art de jouir*. Edited and introduction by Maurice Solovine. Paris: Bossard, 1921.

Landes, Joan B. *Women and the Public Sphere in the Age of the French Revolution*. Ithaca, NY: Cornell University Press, 1988.

Lanser, Susan. *The Sexuality of History: Modernity and the Sapphic, 1565–1890*. Chicago: University of Chicago Press, 2014.

Lasowski, Patrick Wald, and Alian Clerval. *Romanciers libertins du XVIIIe siècle*. 2 vols. Paris: Gallimard, 2000, 2005.

Léris, Hyppolite Clairon, *Mémoires d'Hyppolite Clairon, et Réflexions sur l'art dramatique; publiés par elle-même*. Paris: Buisson, An VII de la République (1798).

Lever, Maurice. *Donatien Alphonse François, marquis de Sade*. Paris: Librairie Arthème Fauard, 1991.

Linz, Bernadette. "Concocting *La Dame aux camélias*: Blood, Tears, and Other Fluids." *Nineteenth-Century French Studies* 33, no. 3/4 (2005): 287–307.

Lucian. "Dialogues of the Courtesans." In *Selected Dialogues*. Translated and introduction by C.D.N. Costa. Oxford: Oxford University Press, 2009.

Mairobert, Mathieu François Pidansat de. *L'Espion anglais*. In *Les Mœurs secrètes du XVIIIe siècle*. Edited by Octave Uzanne. Paris: A. Quantin, 1883.

Marivaux, Pierre Carlet de Chamblain de. *La Vie de Marianne, ou Les Aventures de Madame la Comtesse de L.* (1731–1745). Edited and introduction by Michel Gilot. Paris: Garnier-Flammarion, 1978.

Marmontel, Jean-François. *Mémoires de Marmontel: Mémoires d'un père pour servir à l'instruction de ses enfants*, 3 vols. Edited by Maurice Tourneux. Paris: Librairie des Bibliophiles, 1891.

Martin, Angus, Vivenne Mylne, and Richard Frautschi, eds. *La Bibliographie du genre romanesque*. London: Mansell, 1977; Paris: France Expansion, 1977.

Martin, Christophe. *Espaces du féminin dans le roman français du dix-huitième siècle*. Oxford: Voltaire Foundation, 2004.

Matlock, Jann. *Scenes of Seduction: Prostitution, Hysteria, and Reading Difference in Nineteenth-Century France*. New York: Columbia University Press, 1994.

May, George. *Le Dilemme du roman au XVIIIe siècle*. New Haven, CT: Yale University Press, 1963.

May, Gita. "Rousseau's 'Anti-Feminism' Reconsidered." In *French Women in the Age of Enlightenment*. Edited by Samia I. Spencer. Bloomington: Indiana University Press, 1984.

Meeker, Natania. "'I Resist It No Longer': Enlightened Philosophy and Feminine Compulsion in *Thérèse philosophe*." *Eighteenth-Century Studies* 39, no. 3 (2006): 363–376.

———. *Voluptuous Philosophy: Literary Materialism in the French Enlightenment*. New York: Fordham University Press, 2007.

Mercier, Louis Sébastien. *Tableau de Paris* (1782), 2 vols. Edited by Jean-Claude Bonnet. Paris: Mercure de France, 1994.

Merrick, Jeffrey. "Sexual Politics and Public Order in Late Eighteenth-Century France: The Mémoires secrets and the Correspondance secrète." *Journal of the History of Sexuality* 1, no. 1 (1990): 68–84.

Meusnier de Querlon, Anne-Gabriel. *Histoire de la tourière des carmélites* (La Haye, 1747). In *Romanciers libertins du XVIIIe siècle*, 2 vols. Paris: Gallimard, 2000 and 2005.

———. *Psaphion, ou la Courtisane de Smyrne: Fragment érotique traduit du grec de Mnaseas, sur un manuscrit de la bibliothèque du Lord B . . .* London: Tomson, 1748.

Millot, Michel, and Jean L'Ange. *L'École des filles ou La Philosophie des dames* (1655). Paris: Éditions Allia, 1997.

Moore, Lisa. *Dangerous Intimacies: Toward a Sapphic History of the British Novel*. Durham, NC: Duke University Press, 1997.

Mudge, Bradford K. *The Cambridge Companion to Erotic Literature*. Cambridge: Cambridge University Press, 2017.

Mylne, Vivienne. *The Eighteenth-Century French Novel: Techniques of Illusion*. Manchester: University of Manchester Press, 1965.

Nagy, Peter. *Libertinage et Révolution*. Translated by Christiane Gremillon. Paris: Gallimard, 1975.

Nerciat, André-Robert Andrea de. *Félicia ou Mes fredaines* (1782). Introduction by Sophie Le Ménahèze-Lefay. Paris: Garnier, 2010.

Norberg, Kathryn. "The Libertine Whore: Prostitution in French Pornography from Margot to Juliette." In *The Invention of Pornography: Obscenity and the Origins of Modernity, 1500–1800*. Edited by Lynn Hunt. New York: Zone Books, 1993.

———. "Prostitutes." In *A History of Women in the West*, vol. 3: *Renaissance and Enlightenment Paradoxes*. Edited by Natalie Zemon Davis and Arlette Farge. Cambridge, MA: Belknap Press of Harvard University Press, 1993.

Nussbaum, Felicity. *The Autobiographical Subject: Gender and Ideology in Eighteenth-Century England*. Baltimore: Johns Hopkins University Press, 1995.

Nussbaum, Felicity, and Laura Brown, eds. *The New Eighteenth Century: Theory, Politics, English Literature*. New York: Routledge, 1988.

Pallavicino, Ferrante. *La rettorica della puttane* (1643). Paese, Treviso: Pagus, 1991.

Pateman, Carole. *The Sexual Contract*. Stanford, CA: Stanford University Press, 1988.

Peakman, Julie. "Memoirs of Women of Pleasure: The Whore Biography." *Women's Writing* 11, no. 2 (2004).

———. *Mighty Lewd Books: The Development of Pornography in Eighteenth-Century England*. New York: Palgrave Macmillan, 2003.

Peignot, Etienne-Gabriel. *Dictionnaire critique, littéraire et bibliographique des principaux livres condamnés au feu, supprimés ou censurés*. 2 vols. Paris, 1806.

Perry, Ruth. "Colonizing the Breast: Sexuality and Maternity in Eighteenth-Century England." *Journal of the History of Sexuality* 2, no. 2 (1991): 204–235.

———. "Good Girls and Fallen Women: Representations of Prostitutes in Eighteenth-Century English Fiction." In *Narrating Transgression: Representations of the Criminal in Early Modern England*. Edited by Rosamaria Loretelli and Roberto De Romanis. Berlin: Peter Lang, 1999.

———. *Novel Relations: The Transformation of Kinship in English Literature and Culture, 1748–1818*. Cambridge: Cambridge University Press, 2004.

Phillips, John. "'Tout dire'?: Sade and the Female Body." *South Central Review* 19, no. 4 (2002–2003): 29–43.

Pia, Pascal. *Les Livres de L'Enfer: Bibliographie critique des ouvrages érotiques dans leurs différentes éditions du XVIe siècle à nos jours*. Paris: C. Coulet and A. Faure, 1978.

Pidansat de Mairobert, Mathieu François. "*Confessions d'une jeune fille*, Lettres X, XII et XIV de vol. X." In *L'Espion anglais, ou Correspondance secrète entre Milord All'Eye et Milord All'Ear*. 10 vols. London, 1786.

Pintard, René. *Le Libertinage érudit dans la première moitié du XVIIe siècle*. Paris: Boivin, 1943.

Plumauzille, Clyde. *Prostitution et révolution: Les Femmes publiques dans la cité républicaine (1789–1804)*. Clamency, France: La Nouvelle Imprimerie Laballery, 2016.

Prévost, Antoine François. *L'Histoire du chevalier des Grieux et de Manon Lescaut* (1731). Edited and introduction by Jean Sgard. Paris: Flammarion, 2012.

Rabelais-d'Aquin. *Almanach littéraire ou Étrennes d'Apollon pour l'année 1793*. Paris: L'Imprimerie de Clousier, 1793.

Ravaisson, François. *Archives de la Bastille*, vol. 12. Paris: A. Durand et Pedone-Lauriel, 1881.

Restif de la Bretonne, Nicolas-Edme. *Le Pornographe* (1769). Preface by Béatrice Didier. Paris: R. Deforges, 1977.

[Ribié, César?]. *La Cauchoise ou Mémoires d'une courtisane célèbre: Roman* (1784). Libidinus, Chez Sensualité, 10308070 [*sic*; 1784?].

———. *Histoire de Marguerite, fille de Suzon, nièce de Dom Bougre suivie de la Cauchoise*. In *Œuvres anonymes du XVIII*[e] *siècle 1: L'Enfer de la Bibliothèque Nationale*, 3 vols. Preface by Jean-Pierre Dubost. Paris: Librairie Arthème Fayard, 1985.

Rich, Adrienne. *Of Woman Born: Motherhood as Experience and Institution*. New York: W. W. Norton, 1976.

Richardson, Samuel. *Clarissa, or, the History of a Young Lady* (1748). Edited by Toni Bowers and John Richette. Peterborough, ON: Broadview Press, 2011.

———. *Pamela: or, Virtue Rewarded* (1740). Edited by Peter Sabor. Introduction by Margaret A. Doody. London: Penguin, 1985.

Richeut (1159). Edited and introduction by Philippe Vernay. Berne: Éditions Francke, 1988.

Rigo, Dora Bienaimé. "La prima versione francese di Fanny Hill." *Rivista di letterature moderne e comparate* 34 (1981): 249–270.

Robinson, David M. *Closeted Writing and Lesbian and Gay Literature: Classical, Early Modern, and Eighteenth-Century*. Burlington, VT: Ashgate, 2006.

Rosenthal, Laura. *Infamous Commerce: Prostitution in Eighteenth-Century British Literature and Culture*. Ithaca, NY: Cornell University Press, 2006.

———, ed. *Nightwalkers: Prostitute Narratives from the Eighteenth Century*. Peterborough, ON: Broadview Press, 2008.

Roulston, Chris. "Having It Both Ways? The Eighteenth-Century Ménage à Trois." In *Queer People: Negotiations and Expressions of Homosexuality, 1700–1800*. Lewisburg, PA: Bucknell University Press, 2007.

Rousseau, Jean Jacques. *Émile, ou De l'éducation* (1762). Edited and introduction by André Charrak. Paris: Flammarion, 2009.

———. *Julie, ou La Nouvelle Héloïse* (1761). Edited by Christophe van Staen. Geneva: Slatkine, 2012.

———. *Lettre à M. d'Alembert sur son article Genève* (1758). Introduction by Michel Launay. Paris: Garnier-Flammarion, 1967.

Rubin, Gayle. "The Traffic in Women: Notes on the 'Political Economy' of Sex." In *Feminism and History*. Edited by Joan Wallach Scott. Oxford: Oxford University Press, 1996.

Sade, Donatien Alphonse François, marquis de. *Histoire de Juliette, ou Les Prospérités du vice*. Volumes 8–9 of *Œuvres complètes du Marquis de Sade: Édition définitive*. Paris: Au Cercle du Livre Précieux, 1967.

———. *Juliette*. Translated by Austryn Wainhouse. New York: Grove Press, 1968.

Schaeffer, Neil. *The Marquis de Sade: A Life*. Cambridge, MA: Harvard University Press, 2001.

Schwartz, Joel. *The Sexual Politics of Jean-Jacques Rousseau*. Chicago: University of Chicago Press, 1984.

Sedgwick, Eve. *Between Men: English Literature and Male Homosocial Desire*. New York: Columbia University Press, 1985.

Segal, Naomi. *The Unintended Reader: Feminism and* Manon Lescaut. Cambridge: Cambridge University Press, 1986.

Showalter, English, Jr. "Symbolic Space and Fictional Forms in the Eighteenth-Century French Novel." *NOVEL: A Forum on Fiction* 8, no. 3 (1975): 214–225.

Steintrager, James. *The Autonomy of Pleasure: Libertines, License, and Sexual Revolution*. New York: Columbia University Press, 2016.

———. "What Happened to the Porn in Pornography? Rétif, Regulating Prostitution, and the History of Dirty Books." *Symposium: A Quarterly Journal in Modern Literatures* 60, no. 3 (2006): 189–204.

Stewart, Philip. *Imitation and Illusion in the French Memoir Novel: 1700–1715*. New Haven, CT: Yale University Press, 1969.

Stretser, Thoman. *A New Description of Merryland*. London: Edmund Curll, 1741.

Tilly, Alexandre comte de. *Mémoires du comte Alexandre de Tilly pour server à l'histoire des mœurs de la fin du XVIII*[e] *siècle*. Edited by Christian Melchior-Bonnet. Paris: Mercure de France, 1965.

Trouille, Mary Seidman. "The Failings of Rousseau's Ideals of Domesticity and Sensibility." *Eighteenth-Century Studies* 24, no. 4 (1991): 451–483.

———. *Sexual Politics in the Enlightenment: Women Writers Read Rousseau*. Albany: SUNY Press, 1997.

Trousson, Raymond, ed. *Romans libertins du XVIII*[e] *siècle*. Paris: R. Laffont, 1993.

Turner, James Grantham. "Libertine Literature Forty Years On: I. From Aretino to The School of Venus." *The Book Collector* 54, no. 1 (2005): 29–51.

Vénus en rut. In *Œuvres anonymes du XVIII*[e] *siècle 1: L'Enfer de la Bibliothèque Nationale*, vol. 6. Preface by Jean-Pierre Dubost. Paris: Librairie Arthème Fayard, 1985.

Wagner, Nicolas. "Utopie de *La Nouvelle Héloïse*." In *Roman et Lumières au XVIII*[e] *siècle*. Paris: Éditions Sociales, 1970.

Wahl, Elizabeth Susan. *Invisible Relations: Representations of Female Intimacy in the Age of Enlightenment*. Stanford, CA: Stanford University Press, 1999.

Weber, Caroline. "The Sexist Sublime in Sade and Lyotard." *Philosophy and Literature* 26, no. 2 (2002): 397–404.

Weiss, Penny. "Rousseau, Antifeminism, and Woman's Nature." *Political Theory* 15, no. 1 (1987): 81–98.

Wexler, Victor G. "'Made for Man's Delight': Rousseau as Antifeminist." *American Historical Review* 81 (April 1976): 266–291.

Willms, Johannes. *Paris, Capital of Europe: From the Revolution to the Belle Époque*. Translated by Eveline L. Kanes. New York: Holmes and Meier, 1997.

Wyngaard, Amy. *Bad Books: Rétif de la Bretonne, Sexuality, and Pornography*. Newark: University of Delaware Press, 2013.

———. "Defining Obscenity, Inventing Pornography: The Limits of Censorship in Rétif de la Bretonne." *Modern Language Quarterly* 71, no. 1 (2010): 15–49.

———. "Libertine Spaces: Anonymous Crowds, Secret Chambers, and Urban Corruption in Rétif de la Bretonne." *Eighteenth-Century Life* 22 (1998): 104–122.

———. "Sade, Réage and Transcending the Obscene." In *The Cambridge Companion to Erotic Literature*, edited by Bradford K. Mudge. Cambridge: Cambridge University Press, 2017.

Zola, Émile. *Nana* (1880). Edited by Alain Pagès. Paris: Éditions du Seuil, 1994.

Zuk, Rhoda. "The Courtesan's Progress in the Late 1790s: Elizabeth Gooch and Margaret Coghlan." *Women's Writing* 11, no. 2 (2004).

Index

About the Author

Alistaire Tallent lives in Colorado Springs, Colorado, where she is an associate professor of French at Colorado College. She has published numerous book chapters and articles in such journals as *Romance Review, French Forum*, and *Theatrum historiae*.